HOW TO STOP BELIEVING IN HELL:

A Schizophrenic's Religious Experience

By Robert Clayton Kimball

Published by

Chipmunkapublishing

PO Box 6872

Brentwood

Essex CM13 1ZT

United Kingdom

http://www.chipmunkapublishing.com

Copyright © Robert Kimball 2012

Edited by Melissa Latchford

ISBN   978-1-84991-817-6

Chipmunkapublishing gratefully acknowledge the support of Arts Council England.

Table of Contents

There are things in this book that are bound to offend many readers. I have no wish to offend anyone, but I need to show my narrator's sin if I am to show his salvation.

Bad Times

And whosoever speaks a word against the Son of man, it shall be forgiven him: but whosoever speaks against the Holy Ghost it will not be forgiven him, neither in this world, neither in the world to come. Matthew 12:32

"Subhuman filth!" I snarl at myself shrilly. A handsome, groomed man passes by and looks away, shaken. I'm on Pennsylvania Avenue near the Hawk 'n' Dove. There are a lot of groomed people around. Few look at me.

"Mary Cunt Slime!" I scream. "Rotting Jesus! I'm in your imagination! You're not in mine! You're the ones who are going to Hell! "

"You should have helped me, you stinking bitch! You screwed all my friends. How could you screw her, you bastard? You were my friend!"

I recognize my reflection in a store window. For a moment I think I'm on television.

"God damn me!" I roar, returning to the sidewalk. I spot my enemy, a black man in a filthy red blazer. He is standing on the opposite side of the street, staring at me. He knows I can't defend myself.

A woman walks by me with a little skip to overtake and pass me quickly. To separate myself from God forever and quit my fear of Him, I howl, "Fuck the Holy Ghost!" and laugh falsely. I'm surmounted by a greater wave of fear. I must have said, "Fuck the Holy Ghost!" incorrectly.

A creature with a resplendent golden face is suddenly standing in front of me. It begins slapping my cheeks hard with its belt. It's trying to drive me out of myself. I can smell the leather and taste the blood. I can't lift my arms or turn away. The slapping continues. It hurts like shame. "It isn't fair," I scream. When it stops I'm crying vocally. The creature leaves, and I fall back into myself.

I'm screaming more and louder now because I'm no longer speaking to people. I'm speaking to people who might not exist and who are, therefore, farther away.

The skipping woman turns around some distance ahead of me and backpedals, staring at me for two seconds. Then she turns again and continues on. She is dressed neatly but unattractively. She is either religious or a Congressional staffer.

My words begin to dissolve. I start to shout nonsense because I'm too exhausted to struggle with meanings. My jaw is in danger of cramping. "Aguar! Janet! Janet! [I know no Janet] Sefuar!!"

Two women, tall as angels, walk towards me. They are conversing. Forty-yards away they see and hear me and are silent. The man in the filthy blazer starts to cross the street. He sees the two tall women and stops. Cars swerve around him, their horns blaring. As the women pass, I want to show them that I'm not ashamed to shout trash, but they look me in the eye, and I'm ashamed. "Quoron! Aworac! Lorus!" I've been doing this for half-an-hour. I'm finally hoarse. Someone hands me a dollar.

A Playing-with-Matches Case

Before the terror, I had a wonderful childhood. I grew up in Tucson when it was a town of thirty-five thousand people. The most beautiful part of the Sonoran Desert reached into it and through it. During summer storms, water flowed down out of the eastern mountains, the Rincon's, and through the arroyo thirty yards from our house. The arroyo always overflowed, turning the whole desert floor into a rushing river three inches deep and fifty yards wide, with isolated stalks of cacti and various other plants poking up out of it,. Our house, adobe in mud-stained white stucco, was always in jeopardy. My father had to wedge paper, bricks and stones under doors to keep the water from entering.

The sirens started about ten minutes after the flood peaked as people throughout the city required rescuing from the various places where arroyos crossed roads and car engines drowned. The city was never prepared. The rains only came three weeks a year, after all.

The moment a rainstorm ended there was a startling peace and an awakening. The birds sang instantly in chorus as though they had never stopped. The flood subsided almost immediately everywhere but in the arroyo itself, where it continued softly slapping and running for about an hour. When we were still too young to be allowed anywhere near the flowing arroyo, we found water to play in at the end of the driveway in the grooves created by the tires of exiting cars. There, where the black gravel had been dispersed and crushed, fine gray silt settled under a perfectly clear puddle. When we stepped in it, the silt swirled through the layer of clear water, but the silt was heavy and would quickly sink, leaving a deepening, transparent layer of clear water again if we left it alone for a few seconds. Stepping into it a second time, the silt squeezed through our toes, thrilling the skin between them with its fine, grainy viscosity.

In summer in Tucson after the rains, the smell of creosote, filled the air. Trying to describe the smell of creosote is like trying to describe the aroma of coffee. As has often been said, the smell of coffee is simple. It can't be divided into parts. It can't be described, only remembered. More than the smell of pines on the mountains around Tucson, more than the smell of jasmine or lime or oleander blossoms in our backyard, the smell of creosote was the smell of life and excited us even more than the rain. It brought some of the passion I felt on seeing Bernini's Apollo and Daphne for the first time, and like that statue, it made vegetable nature a part of us.

Almost as thrilling were the stars. The clear desert sky was a lens. It was possible to point out and trace the constellations with a few words. The Milky Way was milky.

After the rains, the frogs came out of the ground, croaked all night, keeping us awake late, and laid and fertilized their eggs. When they hatched, we'd catch a bowl full of tadpoles. The tadpoles had bellies covered with convoluted lines that looked like fingerprints. They broke into commas and hooks when my brothers and I crushed them with our sticks. The other tadpoles ate the ones we crushed. We'd watch the tadpoles slowly grow arms and legs, lose their tails, change into miniature frogs, and hop away.

Do children ever see tadpoles change these days? I suppose a few have seen it on the nature channels, but movies of frogs and frogs are not the same thing. In a similar way, you can't experience through a screen the feeling of wheeling beneath the Milky Way and almost falling over backwards trying to capture the length and breadth of the thing all at once.

I remember playing on the floor with the jewels in my mother's jewelry box while she put on her makeup. The smell of perfume and scented powders mixed with the bright colors of her stones. The colors included the blue of Neptune and the black, blood red and yellow of sand rubies long before the color of Neptune was seen or I had come across sand rubies. A piece of her nacre showed perfectly with the red and blue striations of a sunset. Her amber was the clear sky at first twilight. My mother's opals were the teeming chaos that was revealed just after God created light and just before He started dividing things. The smallest of her diamonds was a "star pinnacled dim in the intense inane." At the time, I had no way to describe the impression these stones made on me, which made them more mysterious and beautiful. I couldn't keep away from the jewelry box. I loved the colors of glass, stone and metal. I could stare at such things for hours. But I couldn't have named the colors. I couldn't have distinguished them verbally. I remember my sudden enlightenment in first grade when the nun told us that each of five printed groups of letters named the color of the paper on which it was printed. There were five differently colored pieces of paper with letters printed on them taped above the blackboard. I suddenly realized that there were different colors. Before, I had only appreciated them.

One day, when Charlie and I were four and five years old, our parents left us with a maid/babysitter, Jean Ewell, who didn't like her job and didn't like us and probably didn't like white people. Dad, Mom and Sammy, our new brother, headed off somewhere in the Packard. Charlie and I found one of the toilets stopped up. We told Jean Ewell. She told us to pee in the bathtub. My older brother was indignant. He led me on an escape that took us to the edge of our neighborhood where a main thoroughfare headed downtown. We walked almost two miles up to and through an elevated walkway with its pipe and cement balustrade in a dark tunnel under the trains. Below us, the echoing tunnel disgorged cars into the desegregated center of the city. We came up among crowds of people whose colors were slightly askew. This was long before suburban shopping malls. Whites, Mexicans and blacks all shopped downtown.

We went into a large appliance store. Charlie boldly walked up to a salesman and told him we were looking at "ice boxes" that our parents might want to buy and asked him to show us some. The salesman said, "Get out."

We came upon a magic shop filled with fascinating things. There were also disgusting things, a good deal more disgusting than peeing in a bathtub. The proprietor treated us well, even though he must have guessed that we had no money. When Charlie was a teenager, he and the proprietor, Bunny, became close friends.

About half way home, we decided to hitchhike. My brother showed me how to stick out my thumb. I don't know how he knew. A car with three raucous, profane teenagers picked us up and let us off at the edge of our neighborhood. I remember one of the teenagers telling the driver to get his finger out of his asshole so he could drive properly. I accurately guessed what that meant. We were temporarily cured of our sensitivity about excretory parts and functions.

Our parents were standing in the driveway talking to policemen when we got home. My poor mother was so relieved when we arrived that she didn't punish us. She, too, was indignant when Charlie said Jean Ewell told us to pee in the bathtub. Charlie told Mom about the profane teenagers. She explained that strange men would hurt us. She ordered us to stay away from them and to never be caught alone with them. She was visibly frightened and frightened us as well.

Charlie and I were addicted to playing with matches. One of the rooms in our house, the "games room," was paneled in heavily shellacked knotty pine. It was in this room, the most remote in the house that we often chose to light our little fires. Our parents were frantic. They lectured us, threatened us, and even had a policeman come to the house, a perk of my father's political success. The policeman pretended he was investigating a playing-with-matches case in the neighborhood and questioned us. Nothing did any good. After a few more fires we lost interest.

When Sammy was still a toddler, sitting in the front seat of our Packard with Charlie and me, Charlie calmly pushed in the cigarette lighter, withdrew it and, with an attitude of curiosity, burned a red circle on Sammy's leg. This was a leap into the unknown Charlie remained capable of all his life. Sammy didn't cry; he didn't even wince. I was amazed. My mother got into the driver's seat, saw the red circle and asked what happened. I said, "Charlie did it." Charlie said, "Bobby did it." Our parents separated us and questioned us individually. Charlie confessed. I was told he felt bad and that I shouldn't mention the incident to him. I was relieved enough by Charlie's confession to leave him in peace. Nevertheless, for the second time I had felt righteous indignation at being wronged by a "villain," the first time being the episode with Jean Ewell. I began to construct plots whenever anything disagreeable happened to me. I played the victim and assigned the role of villain to anyone who seemed to fit the role, however superficially. I was the object of a kind of counterfeit love. Someone was indebted to me. I imagined them feeling guilty.

At about that time, I had a fantasy involving the reconstruction of my body. I imagined that I was rid of my brain and other messy internal parts and my penis and testicles. Instead of those organs I had two hollow places, a small one in my head and another, larger one in my abdomen. Around these cavities, a uniform, thick, rubbery flesh was all that was left of me. A beautiful, buxom young woman, Artemis, the goddess of Purity in "A Child's Garden of the Gods" (CGG), a picture book with accompanying recording, carried me about in her quiver. I felt snug and safe. The woman was strong and determined to protect me from a deathly pale creature, perhaps not human, that feared her but followed us under cover of a forest. I could think and feel, but I didn't eat or drink or get hungry or thirsty because alimentary functions, like the internal organs they depended on, were nasty. (I'd seen road kill close up.) This fantasy came to me while I was awake but beginning to slide into sleep. The fantasy didn't extend into sleep.

Desert Furniture

The houses in our subdivision, Villa Asoleada, were still few and far between. Wandering in the desert when it was dry, looking at the ground under my feet like Milton's Moloch, I searched for treasure. Treasure for me was any compact, blunt object small enough to fit in my palm and hard. Sparkplugs were fun. When Charlie was still leading me around as though I were retarded, two houses began to be built near us. We liked to steal what looked interesting from the construction sites. We especially liked the nickel-sized metal disks that the workmen pried out of electrical boxes. I learned to value practical-looking artifacts that no longer had any practical use. If they had too much complexity about them, I would mar them, peeling that complexity away if I could. They stimulated my imagination, especially if I didn't know what they were. When my father explained the sparkplug in my hand to me, sparkplugs stopped being interesting. I often gave the pieces that I kept an identity. One might be a frozen wave, another, a conjurer's crystal. I imagined that they held a secret power – a charm. Sometimes I named them, as Davy Crocket named his rifle "Betsy." By that means one could take more intimate possession of whatever one had; one adopted it.

We stole things from the building sites sometimes that were valuable. I remember, it must have been on a Sunday, when Charlie and I each took an end of a long two-by-four we could scarcely lift and carried it to our side patio. Charlie explained to me that it was all right to take it because "they have extras." We called each other José and Carlos, the names of workmen we'd run into at the sites. We briefly fought over who would get to be called Carlos and who would have to be called José. The names didn't mean anything, of course, but we both sensed that one was more dignified than the other. We employed lots of hammers, saws, nails and other tools from the utility closet off the kitchen. As we worked, we pretended to speak Spanish. We had some of the accent and could insert interrogatory and exclamatory intonations after chunks of nonsense. We made a mess of the clean two-by-four, took it back to the worksite, and got another.

About the time my youngest brother, Jimmy, was born, Grandpa took Charlie and me to a theater, which was later refurbished. The balcony became the Hotel Arizona. The movie Grandpa took us to was "King Solomon's Mines" starring Stewart Granger. In one scene, Maasai, hopping up and down as though they were on pogo sticks, chanted what sounded like a single word over and over. They shouted "heladotin." It was the best scene in the movie, of which my brother and I understood little. As we left the theater Charlie and I began chanting "heladotin" and hopping up and down. Grandpa asked us what we were doing. We explained. He told us the Maasai in the picture were not saying "heladotin." We insisted that they were. There was such freedom in the chanting of the word. Thirty years later I watched King Solomon's Mines on television. No one said "heladotin" or anything close to it. But Charlie and I still say it.

I remember being fascinated by a Tarzan comic book I found in the neighbor's trash. I begged my mother to read it to me. There was a beast in it, hostile and solitary. Overlapping folds of red and maroon skin hung from it on all sides. All other creatures avoided it. It had no eyes. It killed by its odor. The comic book had in it an enormously fat villain who couldn't walk; he had to travel by rolling. He was hunting Tarzan to kill him. There was a picture of him rolling down a lonely mountain road. He had no speed; he only had persistence and tough skin. He was called Rotoro. He was white. The Africa of Tarzan was full of sinister white freaks.

Apes named and raised Tarzan, of course. They spoke their own language, rendered in the comic books as a mixture of nonsense and Pidgin. The ape-enemy of Tarzan was Bungdolo, who liked to say, "Bungdolo kill!" Tarzan's foster mother liked to say, no doubt cooingly, "mogololulu."

My brothers and I rarely fought physically. But we had a private, inane language of insults. One of us might scream at the other, "Sis babe girl of the Amazons!" or "Fairy farmer butt!" I don't know how these phrases originated. They were just verbal weapons. They didn't mean much to us. The term "fairy" referred to a tiny, flying storybook creature that lived outdoors. We no doubt got the word "sis" from Ernie's older brother who called Ernie, our sometimes playmate, by that name. I didn't know that it was short for "sister." We were developing a real prejudice against rural persons, though we didn't know yet what the slurs "Redneck" and "Cracker" meant. The word "farmer" struck us as descriptive of an ignorant, stupid, dirty person. We had no real opinions about girls, with whom we were largely unfamiliar. When my mother heard us shout "Sis babe girl!" she would, with a puzzled look, sometimes say, "I'm a girl." We knew that, of course, but we also knew that boys shouldn't act like girls and, therefore, it was an insult to refer to a boy as a girl. I have no idea why we used the word "Amazons" in our insults, unless the name appeared in some derogatory fashion among the other accessory details of Greek mythology in CGG.

Cactus makes a walk through the desert an adventure every time. We called cholla "jumping cactus." We gave it a wide birth. The segments of cactus didn't jump, of course, but they were easily broken off the plant and the thorns were especially long and sharp so that, if you brushed a segment, however lightly, it came off on you. We were amazed that doves, with their smooth soft bodies, made their nests in cholla.

Sammy, who cried at strange times when he was little, began sobbing in the front drive while we waited to get in the car to go somewhere. With tear-blinded eyes and heartrending gasps, he wobbled, despite our warning shouts, right into a prickly pear, the purple kind with tiny orange thorns. My mother undressed him and spent about half an hour plucking the hair-like thorns from his thin white body. When he was old enough to ride a tricycle, blinded again by tears, he fell onto a barrel cactus full of coarse, sharp hooks. We couldn't extricate him. Mom cut the thorns off near where they entered his hand and took him to the doctor, who pulled the remnants out with pincers. Sammy's whole body shook while the doctor worked on him. We were horrified and more wary of cactus than ever after that, but our wariness rarely inhibited our explorations.

My three brothers and I stalked doves, sparrows, cactus wrens, thrashers, roadrunners, gophers, chipmunks, jackrabbits, cottontails, an enormous variety of reptiles and much more.

Most of the animals knew to hide in cactus. As I said, the cacti made us especially wary, so we were likely to notice half-hidden animal colors and movements among the thorns but were often unable to take advantage of our observations. Charlie, would sometimes reach into the cactus, despite the things that had happened to Sammy. Sometimes he would catch a lizard.

There were a great many in Tucson when I was growing up. The gradations of their colors and sizes, like the gradations of Darwin's finches, shaded into each other so subtly that it was sometimes hard to know whether we had seen any one species before. But, over the whole range of their various species, the lizards' differences were much greater than the difference between Darwin's finches. We very often had an opportunity to chase and capture wholly unfamiliar types. I'm sure Charlie caught many that aren't on the list of the Arizona-Sonora Desert Museum. We saw the lizards with greater clarity and detail than any zoologist ever could. Of course, we didn't use Latin terms to describe them; we didn't use terms; we didn't describe them. We remembered them.

Horny toads were the type of lizard we saw most frequently. Our folklore held them to be good, probably because they ate ants, which bit. Horny toads were "lucky."

Other animals, like the thrasher, a bird, were bad. Thrashers had long curved beaks they used to pierce and consume the contents of other birds' eggs. That was wrong, and we were shocked by it. For a while we hunted only thrashers with our BB guns, ridding nature of evil.

We hunted other things. I shot and killed a mourning dove. Its warm, limp, soft body in my hand and the embedded BB in its eye were piteous. I vowed never to shoot another bird. The pity went away, but within a few weeks of getting them, we stowed our BB guns. They had quickly become boring.

The front yard of the old house was as fruitful a hunting ground as any when we were children. It was especially so because there were faucets, put there to water the desert in the vicinity of the house. The desert could be lush if it got enough water. Even the brief rains were enough for about two months of greenery. But we didn't use the spigots to water anything. We attached a hose from the back patio to the front yard spigots to force water down the holes of gophers and ground squirrels. It was hard to guess which of the many other holes would be the escape route. Only once do I remember catching a gopher. That isn't to say we didn't drown a lot. The gopher we caught passed out as soon as it exited the hole. It was panting terribly. I immediately felt guilty and felt sorry for the gopher. Charlie picked up the gopher and laid it on its back in the palm of his hand the better to study it. I waited for its two long, dirty teeth to sink into his fingers. I advised him to let it go. He wouldn't. After a while he grew bored and laid it on the ground. It sprang to its feet immediately and ran away.

Gophers were the same color as the dirt they lived in. Our own skins were tanned that color by the sun. "Dust thou art and unto dust thou shalt return," we heard each Ash Wednesday. The cloud of dust blown heavenward in front of the silver storm turned much of the sky brown, but lightning might still be seen slashing through the streaks of approaching rain and heavy-laden air. We would have believed Empedocles; earth, air, fire and water constituted everything.

Our explorations often led us farther afield. About a quarter mile from our house, the stalky, pale-brown desert from time to time sprouted a stuccoed adobe sofa, a part of a wall enclosing nothing, a whole portico leading from desert to desert, a few steps climbing nowhere or a dry fountain with basin, all popping up, like mushrooms out of the ground within a mile of each other, the same color as the dirt and made out of it, just like our house. These things were inexplicable and beautiful. They made the desert familiar and mysterious at the same time. When we came upon a new piece of this surprising furniture, we spent a lot of time lolling around and over it. Years later, I discovered that these constructions were WPA projects. They and the desert they were in, a forest of creosote, have been replaced by a huge park of green grass, baseball diamonds and shady, alien species of trees. Where the dry fountain stood, there is a large artificial pond, built to attract migrating ducks and stocked with fish, neither native to dry desert. Desert owls, the larger species, swoop in and behead and eat the ducks.

There is one spectacular remnant of the desert furniture that survived, a huge tower with a black weathervane atop a red-tiled, peaked roof over four huge multi-paned windows with corresponding decorative balconies sculpted with festoons divided by blank heraldic shields. The tower was about five stories tall. There were no decorations or interruptions of any kind the whole smooth length of the tower except at the very top. There was no way to see anything through the high, black, multi-paned windows. To be seen, someone would have had to appear out of the black darkness holding his face almost pressed to the glass. The huge stucco walls showed the plasterer's swaths, like relief maps, at the base and, presumably, all the way up to where the walls met the windows. The great wooden double doors were always chained. Though we could pull them apart a couple of inches, we couldn't see between them into the dark interior and didn't know what purpose the structure served. It was the same color as the dry desert dirt at its base. It looked like it might contain Dr. Frankenstein's lab.

We later learned that, inside the building, there were no floors, only a common steel water tower of the sort had by practically every small town along the highways of America.

A Pretty White Dress

I sometimes managed to avoid the humiliations that are so very hard for children. In first grade, during Lenten Benediction among the nuns and the rest of the gathered students, I remember turning to the boy kneeling next to me and whispering: "I wet my pants." He looked down, saw the puddle and started giggling. Then I started giggling. That made it all right. Of course, before I wet my pants, I could have asked the nearest nun for permission to go to the bathroom, but standing up, walking down the wide aisle alone, interrupting a praying nun, speaking to her of "the bathroom," then leaving Benediction would have caused me more anguish than the possible blasphemy of peeing on the church floor. The memory of this incident has never bothered me, but the thought of many things of which I was proud as a child, have me cringing, that is, trying to hide from myself, to this day.

My peculiar and humiliating attitude towards sex began to develop very early. I recall an occasion, long ago, when my mother and Charlie and I were having a bath together. I pointed at her nipples and asked what they were. She said they were nipples just like mine and pointed back, but I knew this wasn't true; her nipples were prominent and ugly; they had to be something else. They were like the nipples on a baby bottle, only there was no bottle. There were no breasts. She was flat as a blackboard, which made her nipples more prominent. We never took a communal bath after that. She must have seen the distaste on my face. Things were different back then. Marilyn Monroe and the other cows of Hollywood hadn't happened yet. I didn't ask my mother about the hair between her legs. I knew what that was — ugly, kinky hair.

Probably the worst physical experiences I had as a toddler were the enemas. It had been the fashion to give young children periodic enemas in accordance with some doctor's widely broadcast, idiosyncratic advice. I remember lying with my abdomen and groin in my mother's lap and, after a painful initial poke, feeling the water build inside of me until it hurt. I asked my mother why she was doing this. She didn't answer. The enemas continued every few days for about a month and then tapered off and stopped. These things weren't sexual, but they probably influenced my attitude toward sex.

Kathy, a girl my age, pulled her pants down in the arroyo and asked me to touch her. Her labia looked peculiar to me, a deformity. I refused. Some weeks later, she wanted me to go into the arroyo with her and take down my pants. I said no. She invited me to climb a tree in her front yard and take down my pants there. The tree had sparse foliage and wouldn't have hidden much. I refused again. When I was told about sex by a neighbor boy I was shocked by the ugliness of his description. I didn't believe him.

A year later, a delicate blond girl, the prettiest in second grade, asked to go to the bathroom during class, and left. She didn't come back. The nun left to see what had happened and returned without her. I asked to go to the bathroom. I passed the girl outside where she was sitting on one of the school's green wooden benches. She was crying and trying to hide behind her forearm. The lap of her white dress was wet. The stain had no ting of yellow. She had obviously accidentally splashed water on herself while using one of the sinks or drinking fountains. She wouldn't come back into class. Her mother had to come to school to take her home. Her mother arrived just as I was walking back to class. I remember the little girl's heart-rending humiliation and the appalled and frightened look of her mother. Our sensitivity about excretory functions is probably brought about by confusion over nascent sexual urges.

One day Ernie told me that, before a man and woman could get married, they had to see each other naked. I thought how impossibly embarrassing that would be. I told Ernie it was the dumbest thing I'd ever heard. Ernie insisted that it was true. I was obdurate. More, in Utopia, has prospective newlyweds brought into each other's presence naked to make sure neither of them irremediably disgusts the other, but, of course, we hadn't read Utopia, and no child's illustrated version, if one existed, would have dared to include that passage. Ernie was obsessed with sex and not at all shy about it.

As I said, Ernie's older brother always called him "Sis," to their parents' dismay, and couldn't be cured of the habit. It shamed poor Ernie. Ernie later married, and still later he

20

"came out." We know from prison behavior that sexual orientation can change permanently, usually without trauma. I suspect that Ernie's older brother changed Ernie.

Ernie's younger brother, Al, who committed suicide when he was quite young, was Sammy's friend for a while. Later Al paired off with Butch, another neighbor their age, and made a game out of ditching Sammy, who would come home crying again and again. I hated Butch and Al, and they knew it, so they stayed clear of me. A couple of years later Butch assumed most of the care of a baby sister who was born after Butch's father deserted the home. The father had demanded that Butch's mother abort the baby when she announced she was pregnant. She wouldn't. The father left and almost immediately got himself a very public girlfriend. Butch was protective of the unborn child and extremely angry at his father. He took his father's place and followed through. He and his mother, who was sick, raised the child, a phenomenal thing for a small boy to do. He gave up play altogether. Now that he's grown, he has a wife and four children and is a church-going, believing Catholic, most especially as regards sexual morality and abortion.

The House

The house on the corner of Via Piedad and Via Riachuelo was full of homey smells. A blind man could have found his way through it sniffing. There were distinct sounds in most of the rooms, too, depending on whether you were walking on wood, linoleum, carpet, concrete or tile. Strange noises sometimes issued from the sealed attic. Sometimes the air made a noise like a seashell as it slowly wafted through the house.

When we were children, the roofs of our house were a great attraction. The largest paloverde tree I've ever seen shaded one kitchen window and abutted the outer wall, allowing us to climb to the top of the house. The paloverde's huge trunk was green, like the rest of the tree, but laced with thin grey wrinkles, unlike younger, smooth-skinned palo verdes . Outside the house, there were unaccountable adobe ledges and buttresses, which also gave access to the roof. There was a window above the stairs that opened onto the first floor roof.

I always climbed to the first floor roof by the safest rout. I walked up the heavily carpeted stairs under an inaccessibly high window, which was, in the eyes of childhood, a dusty mystery, and went out through the low window at the stairs' end. On the roof we could look down to the stairs through the now-accessible, high window. The roof's red tiles crunched under our feet. We broke so many there were leaks during storms.

Mom heard some unusual overhead noises one day, came out of the house and discovered three of her children and a neighbor boy hobbling about on the roof. She forbade us to walk on the fragile tiles. But Charlie ventured out one more time. None of us had had the courage or ability to ascend to the roof of the second story. You had to hang there from the tiles, which could slide and fall if any weight were put on them. Then you had to pull yourself up over the edge, and kids our age normally didn't have that kind of upper body strength. But Charlie somehow ascended and, while we watched from the grass of the larger patio, walked along the crest of the second story roof far above us like a pirate on the mainmast—an apotheosis. He walked until he got to the eucalyptus branches hanging over the opposite side of the roof where there were vents in which a family of desert owls, the smaller species, roosted. He contemplated descending through the eucalyptus but the limbs at the top were thin and eucalyptus breaks easily. There was nothing else to do; he dropped from the roof of the second story where he'd gone up, broke another tile and came down by the window at the head of the stairs.

In our house there were fourteen rooms, two staircases and a hallway. The games room, the room in pine, was entirely out of character with the rest of the house. It was marvelously vulgar. It held a pine bar with bright copper trimming and life-size, golden copies of the comedy and tragedy masks on the wall behind. The floor was red cement, which harmonized with the golden color of the shining pine and copper. The only windows were two large glass block constructions, which shone golden in the declining sun but through which nothing could be seen. Of course, they didn't open. Their orange light at sunset melted into the colors of the room. The effect was so sad that, in the late afternoon, we usually avoided the games room until the sun had gone down. At other hours we would play with the bar toys: bar tools, plastic ice cubes with flies imbedded in them, a miniature ventriloquist's dummy that spouted booze when its lever was pulled, *etc.* The pine walls of the room held numerous mementos and souvenirs that could be easily fixed to the pine-paneled walls.

We would pretend to play poker or Mah Jong at the pine poker-table in front of a long, curved, pine booth. The booth was hollow beneath the seat. The hollow part was about 15 inches square and enclosed by slightly smaller doors on either end. It was, perhaps, four yards long. We stored our unwanted toys on the floor inside the booth. That was where we stowed our BB guns. Many long, straight nails pointed downward into the hollow from the booth's seat. Charlie dared me to crawl through the hollow, and when I was inside, closed the doors. I could hear him laughing.

My father held his political celebrations in that room. Sometimes, when we were very young, my mother brought Charlie and me, in our pajamas, into those parties to be petted and cooed over by the guests before we were put to bed. The first time this happened I think I was three. I remember the clinking of glasses and the iced, amber liquid in them the same color as the glistening room. My first impression of liquor was that it was beautiful.

Oddly placed, clear, wood-framed windows on every side of the house let in the freshness of the days, the cactus, the smells of creosote or various flowers, bird song and the mountains. My bedroom projected into the desert, as did my parents' bedroom. From inside the house, on an overcast day, the desert was an inviting, peaceful, dusty gray-green and brown, the colors in the background of Goya's portrait of the Marquesa de Pontejos (on the internet) and several other Goya paintings. Waking, I once saw a family of quail walking by, near enough to touch. They were two adults, the first larger than the other, followed by four perfect miniatures, all in a line, in order of dominance, all with the small single black plume, like a backwards question mark, bobbing from their foreheads. They were all the color of the desert. It amazed me that such beautiful, delicate animals could survive in wilderness.

The upstairs bedroom was usually forbidden. It was the brightest and most richly furnished room in the house with six windows and the leaves of the eucalyptus and tamarisks mottling the light. I dreamed of finding a secret door behind the headboard of the enormous upstairs bed. The door led to an unending succession of other rooms. Some of the dream rooms were filled with bright treasures, but most were empty, varying only in their architecture, like the succession of drab apartments in which I would spend the rest of my life. When Mom sold the old house many years later, she bought a much smaller house, one of three repeated models in a subdivision of tight little lots. It wasn't home. It wasn't really a house. It was a small set of those drab apartments.

The crawl space under our old house began beneath a panel in the linen closet below the stairs at one end, reached under the wood floors and over the dirt, and ended at the exit just below the ceiling of the basement at the other end of the house. Amazing us when he emerged, Charlie crawled through this space the whole dark length of the house. The house now belongs to Sammy. Recently, Charlie's grandson, Michael, crawled the length of the house through the same crawl space. His parents were furious when he emerged covered with dust. God knows what animals had dens down there. Badgers can be aggressive and quite vicious. Michael is just like Charlie. When he enters grade school, a time when most children are quite malleable, he will enter the domain of Neo-feminists who will try to break his marvelous confidence because he is a boy. I don't think they will be able to do it. They may turn him into a criminal, but they won't be able to destroy his courage.

What we called the "sunroom" opened onto the large patio through three curved double doors, "French doors" my mother called them, with numerous glass panes. The living room included a large fireplace and mantel. The living room windows were set in deep alcoves where we could sit or lie down. The living room led to the vestibule that held a writing table and two chairs. Above the table there was a hanging set of mahogany shelves with beautiful, shining, white art-deco sculptures of antelopes in various postures. The vestibule held the massive wooden front door that was always unlocked.

There was an oil burning heater in the basement feeding steam into an old-fashioned system of radiators. They were in every room. The basement was warm in winter, and its depth made it cool in summer. Because of the thick adobe, as thick as the walls of the mission church on the largest Yaqui settlement, this was only slightly less true of the whole house. It was like a deep, bright cave.

The fourth bedroom we called the "maid's room." It was used to house a maid only twice that I know of. On one wall there was a frayed European tapestry, naked, plump Artemis, the goddess, in the style of Rubens, in a wood with her bow and a quiver of arrows surrounded by deer. Normally we used the maid's room as a second playroom. When Charlie was in second grade, I wasn't yet in school. He had received his first Communion and volunteered to show me how it went. He put on a green blanket for a chasuble. We used an old trunk for an altar. In front of and under the maid's room tapestry, which served as our reredos, I knelt at Charlie's feet my hands folded in prayer. With great seriousness, he placed on my tongue a "Host" that he had made out of Rainbow Bread. It had a dill pickle slice in it. I didn't know about the pickle until I tasted it. Charlie thought that was enormously funny. My mother heard what we were doing from the kitchen and admonished us.

There was a kitchen and a breakfast room and a formal dining room with a buzzer on the floor under the rug at the head of the table to call a maid from the kitchen. The buzzer was never put to its intended use that I know of. The dining room held a huge chandelier and two matching candelabras. At dawn, when the sun shone through the windows into the glass of the chandelier and candelabras, there was a spectacular array of scintillating spectra on every wall.

There was a laundry room and an ironing room adjoining the maid's room. These opened onto the smaller of two patios. The larger patio was enclosed by a high, thick adobe wall where I sat after all-night reading binges when I was older to watch the sunrise over the Rincons. Yellow wasps nested in the larger patio under the upper story eaves above blossoming jasmine. When we were little we sprayed them with the hose, ruining their nests, and cried when they stung us. We did the same again the next golden summer.

There were two chimneys. Something died and fell into the kitchen chimney. The kitchen smelled of decay for about two months. We never were able to reach the corpse to get it out; it just slowly stopped smelling. There's probably a small feathered skeleton still wedged in that chimney.

Oleanders divided the smaller patio from a half-acre desert lot where we played. The lot was full of sticker patches and loose, dead, painful stickers that taught us to wear shoes. We dug up the ground and built rickety constructions mimicking various things. When I was twelve, I built a pit and lean-to to hide behind when I experimented with explosives and electricity. There were sand pools on this lot, which was one flood path leading across Via Riachuelo into the arroyo. Over our lot flowed most of the near neighbors' share of the water that fell during summer storms.

Around the house, in addition to the paloverde, eucalyptus, two short rows of oleander, and the long row of tamarisks, there were Aleppo pine, Mexican Broom, creosote, ocotillo, mesquite, saguaro, yucca, three varieties of prickly pear, staghorn cholla, silver cholla, a row of jasmine with a smell as strong as church incense, a plum tree, a lime tree and a couple of palm trees.

The trek home from school, which we walked a thousand or more times, showed us how special our neighborhood was. The adobe houses on large lots and the close presence of luxuriant desert contrasted enormously with the long stretch of tiny tract housing and dry, pale-green imported lawns that we walked past on our way home. As soon as we crossed Country Club Road, the world changed. Our neighborhood was almost always silent, except for bird sounds. There was never heavy traffic, rarely more than a single car driving slowly by. The winding streets in our neighborhood formed no grate or other regular pattern. They meandered so as to prevent drivers from speeding. Drivers couldn't tell what was around the bends. The streets had no sidewalks but sprang out of the dirt or grass. They cracked in the heat of summer and, when the cracks were filled, formed webs of the newer street matter everywhere. The streets added much to the fairy tale charm of the complex adobe houses they skirted.

There was a network of ponds with canals between them over which huge white swans glided year round in an elderly neighbor's excavated back yard. We could see the swans sometimes from the street. The elderly neighbor had a small rowboat and rowed us through this green swamp. The swans, imprisoned by a seven-foot, vine-covered wire fence and too little space to gain the speed to lift over it, sometimes rested their heads on their chests, as though they were ashamed. The old man told us that one of the swans sat on a dead egg for most of a year until the old man smashed the egg with a long pole. The swan attacked the pole savagely. The old man said the swans were surprisingly strong and could often be quite mean. The swans and the pond are gone now, which is fine with me; I never did feel quite right about them. Newcomers to Tucson were always trying to bring in foreign species, normally plants. The old man's swans were the most extravagant import.

Once, while I was walking home from school, a huge, sick, gagging, vomiting vulture landed upon the bare earth to one side of our lot and stared warily at me where I had halted, paralyzed and astonished ten feet away. "Being so caught up, so mastered by the brute blood of the air," I couldn't have been more surprised if it had been an airplane or something from a horror movie. It was black and filthy. It had no majesty. We had watched in wonder as the great birds rode the updrafts far above the desert floor. Here was one I could have touched.

Sammy was an inordinately sensitive homebody. He cried easily, but I don't ever recall him laughing as a child. He cried for weeks when he was separated from the house to be put in school. During recess, I'd find him stumbling aimlessly around the schoolyard, blinded by his tears. There was nothing you could say to console him. It made me angry. I was ashamed for him. Sammy was frightened, even though both his older brothers were at the same school and home was less than a mile away. Sammy was withdrawn from St. Ambrose, but St. Ambrose really wasn't the problem.

At the front of our house, below the entrance, there was an unenclosed platform of red cement. We called it the "porch," but it looked more like the memorial slab over a grave. It didn't seem to be part of the house, though it was flush with the house at the front door. Sammy got home from grade school one day and found no one in the house. He couldn't abide being in the empty house. He got a knife, as he told me many years later, and sat on the red platform mulling over the idea of plunging the knife into his chest. Of course, he wouldn't have been physically able to do that, but he believed otherwise. When that huge house was empty, it could be terrifying. You felt the emptiness of every empty room. It was as though all other members of the family had died. It was as though the house had ghosts that were only placated when two or more people were at home. I remember driving up with Mom and finding Jimmy, home from grade school, on the red platform crying. I remember being on that red platform myself, rigid with fear. I don't know about Charlie, but I suspect he felt similar fear finding the house empty at one time or another. He probably just shrugged it off. The rest of us didn't know how to do things like that. Nowadays, I understand it's usual for no one to be at home when a child returns from school.

My mother was almost always at home to receive us when we returned from school; unless she had one of her rare out of town convention engagements my mother didn't have to work. She sometimes did. She tried to develop a career as a comedienne. She had made many comic presentations at conventions and meetings of various service clubs in Tucson. She practiced her routines on her children. We never laughed. We were too young. Besides, her skits were clever rather than funny.

My mother usually made her comic presentations gratis at charity events. Like my father, she was locally famous. For one of these events, Bob Hope had been persuaded to come to Tucson and appear on stage. He saw her warm-up act and invited her to Hollywood for a screen test. She was hesitant. My father tried to persuade her to take the offer. In the end she declined because she thought her children were too little to be separated from her for very long. Before her alcoholism kicked in, my mother was a real country girl. Most modern American women sacrifice their children's interests rather than their own. They call women like my mother "co-dependent." Those who can't understand conventional women being willing to make the sacrifices they make are, like me, simply too selfish to be parents. They should avoid becoming parents by avoiding sex. I did.

The Broadway Village, the nearest mercantile building, was half a mile away. It served our neighborhood and looked like the houses in our neighborhood. It was two story adobe and stucco with red clay tile roofs. It was full of nooks and ledges. It wasn't built in a line but in an irregular curve with irregular additions piled on top of one another like an Anasazi pueblo. It had a slow, mossy fountain over perfectly clear, black water and black, dead leaves in a black basin with black catfish sliding over and disappearing under the darkness. A series of businesses rented space in the Broadway Village. They came and went, but the drugstore, the enormously successful magnet store, stayed. So the collection of stores slowly changed most of its membership and remained forever interesting.

Land and Seascape

The outside walls of our house were covered over with grainy stucco. On the inside, the plasterer's swaths were not grainy and made maps in relief. There were lakes and continents and oceans and peninsulas and islands. As a child, I could sit and stare at them until I lost all sense of time. Even now the idea of an endless, flat earth always full of fresh undiscovered lands with strange people and animals and oceans appeals to me. The idea of an infinite earth stretching out forever seems more in tune with the detailed, perspective illustrations in the British storybooks our parents supplied us with in abundance. The two-dimensional cartoons that illustrate American children's books deaden the imagination. There are no trees in the distance that one wants to climb, no mountains one wants to ascend. I often had a dream of effortlessly climbing a smooth path up ever higher mountains where hidden plateaus with small sapphire lakes and bright meadows appeared out of the forest.

Least resembling the mountains in my dream, the small desert peaks, the Tucson Mountains to the west of Tucson, are like the pyramids. Little grows on them. You can see the dirt and stone they are made of. They stick up out of the flat desert, belonging to it and made of it. From downtown you can see the brown desert earth, cacti and desiccated weeds extending up the mountainsides to the top. On the other side of these mountains, opposite Tucson, there are hundreds of giant saguaros and steep, red-rock cliffs. During summer, wildflowers blossom on that side of the mountains, changing the mountains' appearance utterly for about five days. Yellow poppies and purple lupine are the most common of the flowers. The rest of the year, the peaks have a dry deathly majesty, like the Moon. They are low, old mountains, worn down by hundreds of millions of years of erosion. On the southern end they have peculiar, precarious shapes. At the northern end, at its base, the land looks like small islands, isolated circles of primeval, green shrubbery popping up out of a flat sea of barren dirt.

The place reminds me of the scattering of nameless small islets in the bay in Miami below Jimmy's glass-walled condominium. Manatees, stingrays, dolphins and other dramatic sea life swim just below the gasoline-streaked surface of the water in the marina under one of Jimmy's balconies. The desert animals in the Tucson Mountains are faster, smaller and harder to spot when you come upon them. There are savage, abandoned dogs that have been known to kill children.

The Santa Catalinas, to the north of Tucson rise steeply out of the low desert floor. They skirt the city limits of Tucson, looming over it in a blue vastness that seems part of the sky. It was thrilling and frightening to drive up the road to the tiny community on Mt. Lemon, the largest and highest summit of the Catalinas. The road hugged cliffs over precipices that fell a thousand feet. The vegetation for a while remained cactus, largely saguaro, and desert scrub increasing in profusion as we ascended. Then, the desert suddenly became meadows with grass and large-leaved trees, cottonwoods, oak and, still, an occasional saguaro in the middle of thick, golden grass, a contrasting, succulent army green. Finally, before we could see them, we smelled the pines. In the climb to the top of the mountains we were apotheosized. We were gods as we looked from the heights back down on the city, a small gray stain far below.

At the top, on Mt. Lemon, hidden in those huge pines, there was a community, Summerhaven, and much later a ski resort. Our parents rented a cabin in Summerhaven, to get us out of the desert heat. We wandered through the folding terrain and streams at our pleasure, a dangerous thing we should not have been allowed to do. People often got lost up there. A terrified, lost woman started a forest fire so that the forest service would find her. They did and, pitiless, billed her for the forest fire.

Nevertheless, we bounded, like young Wordsworths, except we were preschoolers, "over the rocks and cataracts," collecting the little ingots left over from horseshoeing and gathering clumps of glittering mica.

We collected huge mushrooms from which our mother told us she would make mushroom soup. When we had collected all we wanted she drove us to "the mushroom man" who knew which ones were poisonous. He lived in a little trailer at the end of the road. He never said any were inedible. My mother then proceeded to serve us Campbell's mushroom soup in which, she alleged, there were pieces of the mushrooms we had collected. It didn't look or taste any different than plain Campbell's mushroom soup, but we believed her, disappointed though we were in the absence of great chunks of mushroom we could bite into and chew.

Some years after our mountain vacations had ceased, a woman was rushed from Mt. Lemon to a hospital in Tucson because she had eaten mushrooms that the mushroom man had approved. It seems he only knew one kind of poisonous mushroom, a dry, fleshless, brown bag that puffed out yellow spoors when you poked it. We had always known those were poisonous, and they were obviously inedible.

There were lots of animals in the Santa Catalinas that we didn't see in the desert: porcupines, gray squirrels, skunks, eagles, puma, trout, and bear. In fact, the Papagos, the most populous tribe in the county, called Mt. Lemon "Bear Mountain." The people on Mt. Lemon were sometimes strange, too. We had unusual neighbors living in a nearby cabin. They were permanent residents of Summerhaven, living there through the cold, snowy winters. They were a woman and her boy. He was our age, but he had a 22 rifle and could make the bullets for it. He had neat tools that allowed him to melt and pour lead into a mold that formed six slugs. We were fascinated. I suppose he reused his spent shells, but I don't know how he fitted them with new caps or where he bought gunpowder.

Our fascination over these things wasn't enough to make us see him as a friend. He and his mother were too foreign. They were mountain people, a different kind of being. They had found a home in the middle of the desert. The boy was lonely. I don't know of any other children who lived up there year round. Perhaps the boy and his mother had thick accents. I don't remember how they talked. I don't know where they were from. The mother looked at us with suspicion. Their home was, literally, a log cabin. The only manmade elements in it were the cement in the chinks between the logs and two small glass windows. Glass windows and concrete are both Roman inventions from the time of Jesus. The cabin was dark inside. I'm sure there was no electricity.

The biggest difference between the desert and high mountains is the sky. Among the tall pines you only see the sky near zenith. Direct sunlight reaches you for, perhaps, two hours a day. "In the pines, in the pines where the sun never shines" it's as though you were an insect in a bucket. The sky is the most prominent feature of the desert. It raises you above the earth, and it comes down to you. You are at home.

Forts

The largest and most common trees in our neighborhood were the eucalyptuses. An entrepreneur had brought them from Australia, where a certain variety could be used as lumber. They grew quickly, so the entrepreneur thought he could make his fortune in the lumber business. He brought over and planted in the more humid parts of the desert the wrong variety. The variety he planted was too easily splintered to serve as lumber. For us, that was wonderful. During most of the summer storms, at least one huge branch from the top of one of the eucalyptuses in the neighborhood broke off and came crashing down. The morning after the storm we would be confronted with a lush forest of fragrant leaves, a piece fallen out of the sky. It would immediately become a "fort." We would climb through it and hide under it until it became dry and gray. That would take a couple of days. Before it was hauled away, we played to our heart's content in the magical sky forest.

Paper sacks and cardboard boxes carried up by the dust-devils to great heights had something of the effect of the brittle, eucalyptus limbs, only the sacks and boxes were exalted as they rose. The swirling funnels often raised them high enough to disappear entirely.

We paid as much attention to the earth beneath our feet. Mixed in the arroyo sands, were tiny "sand rubies" that we would patiently separate from the sand with tweezers and store in cleaned, glass medicine bottles. Filled, the bottles showed like blood, black, red and yellow, dark and translucent, when held against the sunlight.

We dug pits for "forts," too. Excavating one fort we uncovered the white skull of a large, unidentifiable animal.

Another thing we ran across in the creosote forest was a series of five mounds, like graves, all the same size. A plank of rotting wood protruded from one of the mounds. Charlie pulled at it, thinking it might be part of a coffin. The plank spilled its dirt and swung wide, revealing a deep black hole with wooden stairs leading down into the darkness. Charlie went down all five mounds. There were a few small, unidentifiable, rusty items at the bottom. We never went back. We decided the mounds were probably full of scorpions.

I wonder what's hidden beneath the sands of the Sahara. I wonder how deep the sands are.

One afternoon, in a remote section of the arroyo, when Charlie was in school, I found a bullet lying by itself on the sand. There it was, an object that really had a secret power, and it was mine! I took it to the nearest house, Kathy's house, to show it. Kathy's mother took it away. I cried. A few minutes later she gave it back. She told me that her husband, a general in the Air Force, had opened the bullet, poured the powder out, struck the cap and put the bullet back together again. Kathy's mother phoned and told my mother about the bullet. When I got home, my mother took it away a second time. I didn't care very much. The hidden power was gone. I went to my bed and sat staring at the curtains.

Later it occurred to me that I could go back to the arroyo to see if there were any other bullets. I sneaked out the front door while my mother was in the kitchen. I found the approximate place in the arroyo where I'd made my earlier discovery and pored over the sand, flicking and stirring it with a twig. Suddenly, very large, strong fingers closed around my ankle, tripping me so that I fell to the ground. When I fell, I was dragged back a couple of inches, and sand spilt into my shorts. There was a second of insufferable terror. Then I had no will and ceased to exist. Possibly the fingers were only an exposed, twisted root of mesquite in the eroded bank of the arroyo, but, when I awoke, I felt that something very unlucky had happened to me.

Despite Mom's rules, I preferred not to wear underwear, and, when I hiked up my shorts, I felt them sticking to my chaffing buttocks. It was very difficult to walk because of the chaffing and because of what I supposed was more sharp sand in my anus. It was very painful. I arrived home, went into my room and found underwear and a clean pair of pants. In the bathroom, just before I thrust my dirty shorts under the other dirty clothes in the hamper, I noticed there was both blood and shit on the back. I washed my behind, and tried to extract the grains from my sore anus. I conducted a brief, painful search and found a single grain. Then I put on the underwear and the clean pants and went to my room. I was too disturbed to play and just stared at the curtains again until my mother called us for dinner.

When she next did the washing my mother held out to me my soiled shorts with their now uniformly brown, dry stain. With a disgusted look, she asked me what happened. I answered, truthfully, that I didn't know. She said, "I told you to wear underwear." She handed me the dirty shorts and told me to throw them in the garbage.

I wish my mother had let me keep my powderless bullet. I should never have shown it to anyone. It was the perfect hard little metal object to own. If she'd let me keep it I wouldn't have gone back to the arroyo that day. I might have had a healthier childhood. I blame my mother for nothing.

Boys' fascination with weapons is strong. Ernie's teenage brother, who had just purchased a new switchblade knife, gave Charlie his old one. Mom confiscated that, too; Charlie was six years old. She put it in the secretary. It was decided that Charlie could play with the switchblade under my mother's supervision for exactly one minute each day. She would take it out and give it to Charlie for a minute of flicking once a day while she scowled. Then she would put it back until the next day. Charlie soon got tired of asking for it.

In the summer, when the desert had dried up, the heat once reached 118.° Charlie and I liked to run about outside until we were close to sunstroke then race into our parents room where the best and most fragrant swamp cooler in the house was located, stand in front of it until we were shivering, jump into the bed that caught the cooler's wind most directly and pull the heavy satin quilt over us, so that we grew slowly and deliciously warmer. Then we got up and stood in front of the cooler again. Then we ran outside for another round of extreme heat. Under their exterior boxes the dripping coolers watered Lilliputian gardens of bright green moss in the otherwise barren desert.

Even dry, as it was almost all the time, and even as an occasion of fear for me after my "mishap," the arroyo was green and beautiful. Every inch of it, wet or dry, held a curiosity. And the whole was some of the time a refuge against the desert's scorching heat because unusually large, unusually green mesquite trees met and canopied over it. The sand, stones and caliche that constituted it changed form with every flood. Once, the rushing water dug out a hundred smooth caves just big enough for a child to hide in; after another rain, there were little mesas of mud, after another, a smooth, fragile pavement of dry, congealed sand.

After we moved out of the old house, the Tucson City Planner sent men on bulldozers to turn the arroyo into a uniform, barren ditch. A neighbor spotted the bulldozers just as they began to uproot mesquite. He managed to stop them with the help of a rifle. This was before the fashion called environmentalism; so the neighbor had no cause other than his own. I believe a warning shot was fired.

In summer in Tucson after the rains, the smell of creosote, filled the air. Trying to describe the smell of creosote is like trying to describe the aroma of coffee. As has often been said, the smell of coffee is simple. It can't be divided into parts. It can't be described, only remembered. More than the smell of pines on the mountains around Tucson, more than the smell of jasmine or lime or oleander blossoms in our backyard, the smell of creosote was the smell of life and excited us even more than the rain. It brought some of the passion I felt on seeing Bernini's Apollo and Daphne for the first time, and like that statue, it made vegetable nature a part of us.

Almost as thrilling were the stars. The clear desert sky was a lens. It was possible to point out and trace the constellations with a few words. The Milky Way was milky.

After the rains, the frogs came out of the ground, croaked all night, keeping us awake late, and laid and fertilized their eggs. When they hatched, we'd catch a bowl full of tadpoles. The tadpoles had bellies covered with convoluted lines that looked like fingerprints. They broke into commas and hooks when my brothers and I crushed them with our sticks. The other tadpoles ate the ones we crushed. We'd watch the tadpoles slowly grow arms and legs, lose their tails, change into miniature frogs, and hop away.

Do children ever see tadpoles change into frogs these days? I suppose a few have seen the transformation on the nature channels, but movies of frogs and frogs are not the same thing. In a similar way, you can't experience through a screen the feeling of wheeling beneath the Milky Way and almost falling over backwards trying to capture the length and breadth of the thing all at once.

Rory was my best friend in the first few years of grade school. He was good at baseball. He always nominated me to be the umpire because, if one of my calls worked to his disadvantage, he would loudly complain and then I would change the call. Then he would laugh while the opposite team was screaming. Sometimes if the screaming was loud enough I would change the call a second time. Rory's family was German-American like my immigrant grandmother's, but my German grandmother didn't like the Nazi's. Rory once said to me, "You know, Hitler had the right idea. He just went about it the wrong way." I didn't know who Hitler was, but I agreed.

Near the end of spring, when the hot school day had concluded, Wayne and I used to accompany Rory to his house across the street, having had no water other than the warm stuff in the school's drinking fountains for six hours. We hoped for a drink from the pitcher of water in Rory's refrigerator. Rory would take a mouthful directly from the pitcher and spit it back leaving many particles suspended in the cold water. He offered us the pitcher, smiling. We no longer wanted a drink. Rory drank it all. Rory did this several times at the end of several other increasingly hot school days. One day Wayne grabbed the pitcher from him and drank all of the particle-laden water, responding to my amazement, "It's still got cold water in it."

In fourth grade, during my free drawing time, I always drew pictures that incorporated the bullet that my mother had taken away from me, war pictures. My war pictures included lots of corpses and exploded body parts. There were always many sleek, bullet-shaped rockets and projectiles and me. I drew myself as a round, fat hero with stunted limbs and a small head, like a full tick. I wanted to look like fat Rory. I ate a lot of donuts to build myself up.

In our backyard, one of the huge eucalyptuses that were dispersed around the neighborhood invited ascent. Charlie liked to climb this tree with Ernie. I was afraid to climb it; the bark looked slippery. Ernie fell and broke his arm. I felt rewarded for my fear.

My spirit of adventure was further stunted when I became afraid of being adrift on the open sea. This fear developed during one of our summer vacations in California. Feeling brave, I swam far beyond the breakers on a very small rubber raft. I was fifty yards from the nearest swimmer and even farther from the beach. Suddenly, a green, webbed fin poked up out of the murky water about a foot from my paddling hand. It was very large. I could see under the murky water a few flashing scales above a huge shadowy shape. My limbs contracted onto the tiny raft. I tried to pray, but, in my fear, I couldn't remember even the simplest, most common prayers, so I started rapidly repeating "heladotin." It took twenty minutes for me to find the courage to drop my arms and legs and start paddling back to shore. On the way, in the surf, with a gulp of seawater, I swallowed a small fish. Back on the beach, the allergic reaction almost stopped my breathing. The pain of asphyxiation is made entirely of fear.

Wild things in the desert are mostly small. A coyote was the biggest animal we ever saw, although once, a mountain lion was discovered in the next subdivision. A policeman shot the lion before it hurt anyone. Another patrolling policeman, who often stopped to talk to us, claimed he'd seen a lone, lost javelina near the arroyo. The owl's roosts in the vents of our attic were just above the tamarisks with their seasonal load of insects. The vents were red clay pipes about seven inches in diameter just below the peak of the second story roof. I never saw anything the owls killed. There were no indigestible clumps of hairy feces or vomit. The owls probably ate the insects. Once, a fledgling fell, something inaccessible in the sky brought magically to earth. We found it in the dirt, still alive. Our attempts to keep it so failed. We left it where we found it, and the next day it was gone.

Mourning doves were the most common birds around Tucson. When Tucson was riddled with tuberculosis asylums there was a campaign to wipe out the doves. Hunters with their shotguns set out to kill them all. This was because their call, two short timid notes, was deemed to sound like the words "no hope." There was no cure for tuberculosis at that time, and it was feared the tuberculosis patients would become depressed hearing the call of the doves, which sounds nothing like "no hope" nor any other English words. We have abundant mourning doves here in Ixtec, the Mexican village where I enjoy my retirement.

On summer evenings, I liked to stand on the arroyo side of the house at night, alone, feeling the desert breeze through the tamarisks and smelling the clean desert smells in the warm darkness. The long row of tamarisks, with its tens of thousands of insects of a thousand species, hummed like the telephone network in The Castle, a beautiful, accidental music. Under the tamarisks nothing grew. We raked up huge piles of soft needles when they fell. The barren, smooth, hard clay surface we exposed was the purest patch of dirt we would ever see. We could have played tennis on it.

We hunted insects for our collections. The insects favored the eucalyptuses and tamarisks. Collectively they made so much noise that an elderly neighbor of ours cut down our best hunting ground, an enormous eucalyptus behind his house, solely because the insects' noise made it impossible for him and his wife to sleep. He apologized to us for cutting down the tree.

There were lots of butterflies. They made no noise and took nourishment among flowering cactus and weeds, not trees. Charlie started picking up dead butterflies, a habit he later built into a studious hobby of butterfly collecting.

There were also small scorpions. The small Arizona scorpions are extremely dangerous. Our parents made sure we were afraid of them. Charlie found a dead one behind a couch. Dad sat down on the floor and started to give us a scorpion lesson over the corpse. Mom sat down to listen with Sammy, my baby brother, in her lap. Sammy reached out one hand, grabbed the dead scorpion and put it in his mouth. Dad coaxed him into opening his mouth and pulled out the corpse. Sammy was unhurt.

A few people here in Ixtec, eat scorpions. A woman I know here, a Gringa, gave her gardener a scorpion she had just killed. The gardener greedily ate it on the spot. Most of the

Gringos here have been stung once or twice. A scorpion fell from the ceiling onto my stomach a few nights ago. I backhanded it off and crushed it on the floor next to my bed. I failed to capture the stinger under my slipper. The stinger extended itself fully in a straight line an inch long and patted an arc of floor back and forth feeling for something to sting. It had stung me when I brushed it off my chest. It was less painful than a wasp sting. The Ixtec scorpions are not deadly, but sometimes they do hurt a lot, depending on the scorpion and the person stung. Ixtec children play at catching them by grabbing the stinger from two sides with their fingers.

A fellow retiree here was a member of the Hitler Youth when he was a boy. He is still loyal to the ideals of that organization and does very mean but legal things to people. The Mexicans call him "El Alacrán."

Religion Practice

The menace of eternal pain cripples some Catholics. The responsibility is greater than they can bear. "Religion is a crutch," people say, but it doesn't pretend otherwise. Once crippled by religion I was willing to take up the crutches of religion, but first I had to practice.

At St. Ambrose, in second grade, we had to be made ready to make our first Confession and take our first Communion. Sister St. Thomas prepared us. She taught us that everything had an essence, which was real, and an appearance, which was not real. She said the essence of the Host we would receive was the body and blood of Jesus and the appearance of the Host was bread. The Host was sacred. We were to receive it with the utmost reverence, not biting into it but allowing it to dissolve in our mouths. We were in awe.

I remember asking my little nephew if Porky Pig was real. He pondered, said "No," then pondered and said "No" again, more confidently. The idea that we would eat and digest God was staggering. But if Sister St. Thomas had taught us, with the same emphasis, that Porky Pig was real, we would have believed her. The induced gullibility of Catholic-school children sometimes leads to mental illness. We learned the Eucharistic doctrine and ceremony and, one by one, approached Sister St. Thomas's desk to be quizzed to make sure we understood and were qualified to receive Jesus. All but one of us passed the quiz.

When we passed, we made our first Confession. Confession required an examination of conscience and remorse. These ideas were carefully defined. The bottom line was that you couldn't make up sins just to have something to say in the confessional. I confessed having committed adultery, by which I meant that I'd looked at a girl named Kathy with her pants down two years earlier. The Sixth Commandment says only, "Thou shalt not commit adultery." In the eyes of the Church, in the person of Sister St. Thomas, adultery included all sins of lust. I don't remember how Sister explained that to us. The priest hearing my Confession didn't skip a beat, which was a relief because I didn't want to get more specific.

Once, after a rain, when the smell of creosote made it difficult for us to settle into our desks, Sister St. Thomas called us, "little demons" and then had to explain that demons were "disobedient angels fallen from Heaven to Earth and Hell where they tempt or torment souls." Sister also taught us, that we all had an immortal soul and that, if we were good, our souls would go to heaven when we died, and, if we were bad, they would go to Hell to be among the demons. Her description of the soul left me with an image of a black, irregular lump inside my chest like the potatoes they bake at barbecues by burying them in the coals. I was indifferent to the fact that, if I was bad, my soul would go to Hell. Who cares what happens to a black potato?

Two years and many Confessions and Communions later a schoolmate explained to me that *I* was my soul and that *I* was immortal. That was the beginning of my religious fear. I asked God to turn me into an angel because angels, those who didn't rebel, can't sin; they no longer have free will. Angels don't have to worry about Hell. I also asked God to take away my immortality like the Centaur, Chiron, who suffered an incurable wound and asked Zeus to take away his immortality so that his pain might end. For good measure, I also asked God to keep me from having children.

One day, after school, wandering the desert alone, thinking stygian Catholic thoughts, I saw a turbulent face, golden like the comedy mask in the games room. The face was smiling as it stared down at me from one of the stucco tower's black multi-paned windows. Until I came to the conclusion that the face was only an inanimate object, a mask, I was afraid. When my fear of the mask left me, my fear of Hell, left, too, making a long noise like a punctured tire. The face was charmed. In the only way I could, I took possession of it as though it were an interesting stone or scrap of metal in my hand. Remembering Davy Crockett and Betsy, I named it "Lorus," after our nearest neighbor's yellow cat.

The next school year, another teacher, also a nun, reawakened my fear. She explained to the class that sin was "in the will," and that it was not a sinful act but *wanting* to commit a sin, "consenting to temptation," that made something sinful. The next day, at home, sitting on the swing in the larger patio, it occurred to me that I might have thought a bad thought, and I wondered if I had "consented" to it. Was I in mortal sin and in danger of eternal Hell? I raced off to the St. Ambrose rectory on my bike and asked one of the priests who lived there to hear my Confession.

From that time on, for about a year, blasphemous thoughts assailed me, and unsure of whether or not I had consented to them, I headed to the rectory, sometimes twice in the same day. If it was Saturday I went to the regularly scheduled Confessions for the parish at large in the church proper and once fainted and fell off the kneeler in the middle of an hour long Confession that forced all the other parishioners to join the two lines waiting for the alternate priest. I woke from my faint and continued with my Confession. When I finally emerged I saw the grinning golden mask I had seen in the tower window. Lorus stood full bodied with an ear against a confessional door. There was a red light over the door indicating that a confession was underway. The people standing in the lines stared appalled at Lorus, who approached me and told me that I shouldn't go to Confession if I felt shame or remorse. Lorus told me that guilt turned a person inside-out, that "remorse" almost always meant guilt, that "shame" meant guilt sometimes, but "embarrassment" and "humiliation" never meant guilt at all. Lorus said if I wanted to go to Confession to embarrass and humiliate myself, that was ok.

Lorus was with two other creatures. I use the word "creatures" in the sense that the word is used in sci-fi movies and comic books or by my mother when referring to one of my friends of whom she disapproved. Lorus told me the creatures were sexless and could have no offspring, that they had no digestive systems, and that they spat and threw up a lot. Lorus introduced me to the other creatures without giving any names. With ritual formality, it touched a shoulder of each in succession while pointing at me with its free hand. I named the other two creatures Aworac and Quoron after our nearest neighbor's two black German Shepherds. Like Lorus, its two companions had turbulent, golden faces. Quoron simply stared at me, measuring me. Aworac told me that I had no will, and so I wasn't responsible for my thoughts. It occurred to me that Aworac might have eavesdropped on my Confession, which was composed entirely of

44

sinful ideas. I asked myself if the creatures were demons. I listened carefully to their arguments, possibly "entertaining a near occasion of sin," which sent me back to the Confessional as soon as I escorted the creatures to their car and watched them drive away.

In between Confessions, I buzzed with rapidly repeated prayers to push blasphemous thoughts out of my mind. Charlie refused to be around me in public. My parents were deeply worried and my mother took to making me do various chores whenever she saw me muttering to myself.

One of the priests, Father Towner took special notice of me. He became my regular Confessor. The summer of that year, when I told him that our family was going to Long Beach for our annual two week family vacation, he told me not to go to Confession in California, since a strange priest wouldn't know what to make of my problem. Father Towner's command was law. Not to obey would be a sin in itself, and after two weeks without Confession and a pile of possibly deliberate blasphemies, I stopped trying to stifle my thoughts and the fear left me.

Sammy had transferred to public school. He and other Catholic children who didn't go to St. Ambrose proper received religious instruction at night in one of the St. Ambrose classrooms from a lay volunteer. The instructor told the children that a man who was thought to be dead was buried and woke up inside his coffin. He realized where he was and, horrified, drove his fingers through his skull, killing himself. The instructor said that the man was in Hell because he had committed suicide, a mortal sin. Sammy came home terrified. He couldn't sleep until he pinned a note to his blanket: "Don't bury me. I'm not dead." Wisely, my mother, already saddled with my fears, no longer required Sammy to go to the religion classes.

Nevertheless, Sammy and the rest of us got a thorough religious education from Bishop Fulton J. Sheen on his weekly network television show, Life Is Worth Living. Sheen declared and explained Catholic doctrine. Each show served an audience of about thirty million. The program survived from 1951 to 1957, opposite Milton Berle. Sheen won an Emmy.

Primitive Politics

My father was majority leader of the State Senate. He worked and campaigned in in very primitive terrain. When the Senate was in session one of my father's fellow Senators always looked to his wife in the gallery to see how he should vote. He and she were there for every day of the session. She signaled him, none too subtly, by lifting her left or right arm.

At Democratic rallies one local politician held up a small black notebook that, he said, contained the truth about his opponent. "In the interest of clean elections," he had decided never to reveal the notebook's contents.

In an election for sheriff, one of the candidates, a pink, chubby policeman, campaigned by carrying out his motorcycle patrols on the crowded, integrated downtown streets with a kind of halter over the top of his uniform bearing his name and the word "sheriff" fore and aft. He moved slowly, weaving through the creeping traffic, waving alternately to the indifferent shoppers on each sidewalk as though he were in a parade. The other candidate for sheriff, a tall, swarthy Mexican with a Zapata mustache referred to his opponent at every rally as "Porky-Pig-on-a-Motorcycle," as though it were a proper name.

Another politician said that his opponent had "not completed high school." Based on his high school record and the recommendations of his teachers, his opponent had been admitted to college a year early. Another politician, apparently familiar with the Claude Pepper hoax, said at rallies that his opponent's sister had been a "thespian" in New York. There were always some gasps. This all occurred at a time when a few politicians at the state and local level could exercise more power than most politicians at the Federal level. My father exercised that kind of power. He lost it all in a bid for governor. He ran for county supervisor sometime after that and lost again. Then he was given an appointment as City Magistrate. By then, he was quite sick.

He had always been sickly. His mother had brought him from Springfield, Massachusetts to Tucson as a boy because he had asthma and Tucson's air was good then. After he left the legislature, he spent a lot of time in the hospital. He wasn't billed. As majority leader, he had championed the causes of the medical profession and this was payback. Payback was much more common then and not entirely unjustified. A contractor offered to pave our long, curving front drive as a gift. But, for some reason, the driveway gift went beyond the limits of what was acceptable, and the threat of scandal brought the project to a halt. On the other hand, we had 24 cases of expensive Scotch in the upstairs closet.

Charlie and I were glad the driveway-paving gift fell through. We didn't care at all, of course, that it was graft. We were pleased because we were periodically assigned the task of raking to the center the gravel that was scattered to either side of the drive path by churning tires. The extremely fine dust of crushed gravel mingled with the still whole stones a centimeter in diameter. When Charlie and I began raking the stones we ran, moving the rakes like wrongly slanted snowplows, shoving the gravel into the driveway rather than out of it. We ran from opposite ends of the drive screaming until we met in the middle. We raised a tremendous dust cloud that seemed to change the weather and almost blot out the sun. The very heavy dust quickly settled. But we felt powerful. During the rainy season it was that dust that had made the silt we liked to squeeze through our toes when we were little.

My father had been involved in two scandals at least. He had spent some of the money belonging to the local chapter of Kiwanis when he was its treasurer. He managed to pay it back before it became a question for the prosecutor, but the news of the pilfering was passed around town, and my mother got a few dirty looks. She was puzzled and asked us if we knew the reason. When she asked my father why people were snubbing her, he only said, "It's taken care of."

The other scandal was less serious but appeared in the newspapers. The publishers of the Arizona Daily Star hated my father for failing to follow their instructions in the legislature. News media commanded politicians then, as now. They accused him of acquiring some slot machines that were found in the Old Pueblo Club, my parents' hangout where adults drank and had swank parties at night and children celebrated fancy birthdays during the day. The slot machine story died without consequence simply because it wasn't true.

Shortly after I learned to talk, Dad was driving us through the UA campus to see the various tableaux created by the different fraternities in some kind of homecoming competition. He pointed out buildings he and his Senate colleagues had appropriated the money for. We wouldn't have understood an explanation of "appropriated." So he told us that he "owned" the buildings he was pointing out. He "owned" most of them. In the Senate, my father had worked especially hard for many years for the UA. He chose to forgo what would certainly have been a lucrative career as a lawyer to serve in the Senate, for which the state paid him less than $1,500 a year plus a *per diem* plus a few expenses. That the UA would wave his children's tuition (about $150/semester) was not unjust. Without the wavers we could not have afforded to attend the UA. We would not have been among the burgeoning University of Arizona (UA) student population that my father had made possible. We were white males and had a big house. Today's political idealists would have kept us from college. Classifications of people are more complicated than classification by race, sex and religion. But I suppose this must be added to the list of potential scandals that could have destroyed my father's reputation had he lived.

When he was Magistrate, until he got too sick to work, my father drove to the Tucson City Hall each weekday morning. Sometimes he took me with him. While he was disposing of the vagrants and prostitutes, I cleaned his law office next door. He gave me $2.00 for my effort. The office had been the scene of many deals and favors. Adlai Stevenson had visited it seeking support and election advice in 1951. I despise Adlai Stevenson. Few do more damage to the world than holy men who get involved in politics but are interested principally in promoting their own holiness. It took little time to clean my father's office since it was no longer used. He kept it for sentimental reasons.

I found out my father was sometimes a weak judge. Once, a woman was arrested for trying to stab a policeman in a hotel room. I had finished my cleaning and was sitting at the back of the courtroom when she was brought in for a hearing. My father saw me, and, to make things interesting, he asked the woman if she had her clothes on when the policeman entered. The woman became irate and loudmouthed my father, which scared him because he knew he had overstepped his bounds. He let her go with some kind of probation. Afterwards, in the Magistrate's office, he asked me what I thought. I said I thought trying to stab a policeman warranted more severe punishment. The prosecutor agreed with me.

My father wasn't always lenient. A priest had tipped over a golf cart while trying to get back on at the "Nineteenth Hole." The manager of the golf course and the bartender got angry when the priest swore at them as they picked him up and set the cart to rights. The manager called the police. The priest was arrested for public drunkenness. My father's close, old friend, Monsignor Hughes, came to our house that night, to try to convince my father to set the priest free to avoid scandal to the Church. My father refused. He had allowed me to remain in the room during Monsignor Hughes' plea.

After he lost his political power my father often became inexplicably angry. He sat Charlie and me down one evening to formally teach us that "Reporters are stupid." I don't remember any of the explanations that he gave, but I remember, "Reporters are stupid."

Not long after that, he and my mother began quarrelling. I've always suspected she caught him with another woman, but I don't have any evidence for that conclusion. Eventually, my mother asked my father for a divorce, which would have undermined any political ambitions my father might still have had. They were sitting in the living room one afternoon. Charlie and I and Sammy had just come in and didn't know the seriousness of what was going on. My father turned to us and asked, "If your mother and I split up, which of us would you like to live with. Charlie and I said, "Dad!" Sammy, showing insight and compassion far beyond his six years, went over to our mother and, sitting close to her, said, "I'd live with Mom," with a look of sad remonstrance toward my father. My mother put aside her request for a divorce because she thought my father could take her children from her. He, being a lawyer, knew that that would be nearly impossible. When we were adults, Sammy was the most successful of all of us. I was the least. I think Sammy's discernment and my lack of it made the difference.

The biggest adventure in my father's judicial career occurred when Judge Howsair, my father's co-Magistrate, left a man who was an avowed Communist in jail for ninety days without charges or a hearing. My father didn't know about it until two of the man's friends, also known Communists, drove into our driveway and rang the doorbell. My mother was pleasant to them and let them in the house. My father recognized them and told them to wait in their truck. He got something from his room and went out to talk to them. They told him about their jailed friend. My father said he would investigate. If their story was true, he said he would have their friend released immediately. Then he told them to leave. He made a phone call, and the prisoner was released that day. My father sat us down and explained to us what had happened. He said the man in jail had constitutional rights even though he was a Communist, but he noted, "You don't invite such people into your home." He thought Communists were usually murderously self-righteous egoists/idealists, a verdict that has been powerfully verified since. I wondered if what my father got from his room was a gun, though I'd never seen one in our house.

The grade school nuns were less strict than the Sisters of St. Elizabeth Seton who later taught us in high school. The grade school nuns were the nuns you see portrayed in old Bing Crosby movies, the Sisters of St. Joseph of Carondelet. I think now that their habits were sexy. Certainly the nuns in the Bing Crosby movies were sexy.

The Sisters of Saint Joseph of Carondelet were, I see in retrospect, peculiarly knowledgeable. Just a few years ago, after the fall of Communism, the Washington Post reported as its headline story that its investigative journalists, in conjunction with officers of the Chinese government, had the opportunity to research newly opened Chinese archives. The journalists discovered that, in the late fifties, 50,000,000 to 80,000,000 Chinese starved to death as the direct result of Communist policies instituted with the knowledge that they would kill masses of people. Among other astonishing government actions, cadres entered the villages and farms in states where the famine was to take place and seized *all* the food that was stored to keep the peasants alive during winter. The peasants were reduced to cannibalism. Starving peasants approached full government grain warehouses to beg for food. Armed guards turned them away. As a gesture of solidarity with the starving peasants, Chairman Mao gave up meat for six months.

The Sisters of Saint Joseph of Carondelet knew about the imposed "famine" while it was still going on. I don't know how. Perhaps the Church had contacts with clandestine Catholics in China.

For political idealists, society is like clay with lumps in it. The lumps have to be crushed so that the clay can be reduced to a perfect plasticity and made to conform to the shape the idealists wish it to take. The shape is their ideology. The lumps are people.

The Black Book of Communism: Crimes, Terror, Repression, an 800-page study by European scholars concludes that, taken together, all the Communist countries in the last century killed approximately 100,000,000 of their own citizens. None of this toll died in war.

Solzhenitsyn in his The Gulag Archipelago. states that gulags come into existence when the natural criteria for truth are replaced by adherence to an ideology. Many people nowadays want to destroy the concept of truth to promote equality. It apparently seems unfair to them that some statements are admired above others by virtue of being true.

When I was fifty years old I re-embraced much of Catholicism after having fought hard and successfully to escape it. One reason was the Churches' stand against Communism. The other was the Churches' proselytizing for the idea of truth, which needs defending in the world of Postmodernism and Deconstructionism. I no longer believe most of the Church's other doctrines, although they are an indelible part of me.

Nature

Apart from the arroyo and the summer storms, my relationship with nature was not always pleasant. When my parents forced me to go to camp for the first time, I was five years old. I was sent to a place called The Little Outfit in beautiful green woodlands under the Santa Rita Mountains. The mountains are the highest and most distant of the four ranges that surround Tucson. There is a large observatory near the top. One year, in a blizzard at the top of the highest peak, a troop of thirteen boy scouts froze to death. There is a bent, crudely painted tin plaque at the top commemorating their fate. The Little Outfit was in a lowland area called Patagonia, a famous bird sanctuary.

I was to remain in camp for a week. My father drove me down. I was just in time for dinner. For dessert, they served Jell-O squares with shredded carrots in them. They might as well have fed me headcheese. I tried to eat it and threw up profusely. I spent the rest of my week at camp in the infirmary and was glad of it. I was afraid of the other, older kids.

Three years later, back in Tucson Wayne got in the habit of riding his high, wide-wheeled bicycle all over the stretches of desert in the city. He found an abandoned garden next to the El Conquistador Hotel. It had been given back to nature years before as a money-saving measure, but water still trickled through it from leaky irrigation pipes. The place was overgrown with green and golden tall grass; the trees were green and bright and thickly leaved. There were unfamiliar birds and mice. It looked like the sides of the road half way up the Catalinas, but it was in the middle of dry, deep desert. It was a paradise. I was amazed when Wayne showed it to me. We were alone there; no one else knew about it. From that time until they tore down the stately old adobe hotel and graded and cleared the land to build Tucson's first mall, the El Con Mall, we told no one.

When we were ten, Wayne and I collected some food, sleeping bags and other camping gear and got Wayne's parents to drive us to Sabino Canyon in the Catalinas. This was in the middle of summer. The creek was dry with the exception of an occasional, shaded puddle in the small hollow of a rock. We hiked well beyond the road, deep into the heart of the canyon. We walked for, perhaps, two hours and came to a beautiful, deep pool, large enough to swim in and absolutely clear. It was cut into a rock over which the stream had flowed. There were already small water plants growing in it, and there was a small, green, swimming snake. We spent the night camped by the pool. I had difficulty spotting constellations. Some were camouflaged by nests of other stars that couldn't be seen in the city. We awoke with the sun. We hadn't gotten much sleep. We decided to walk back to the drop off point. We refilled our canteens from the clear pool and walked until we got to the edge of the raw desert where there were no trees other than a few black, leafless mesquites. A woman stopped her car. She had her two children with her. She asked for water. Our canteens were empty by that time, but we pointed out an amber puddle by the side of the road. She looked at it, thanked us and drove away. We refilled our canteens with the amber water. Then we entered the desert. We surprised a large group of deer, mule deer probably. Neither of us had ever seen deer before in the wild. They didn't hang out in the arroyo. Naked Artemis could have been standing in the middle of them for the effect it had on us.

In Sabino Canyon, waiting for his parents to pick us up, Wayne and I continued wandering aimlessly in the growing heat. We periodically ran out of water and continued drinking from stained puddles. Wayne's parents showed up early, anticipating our boredom. I didn't much like nature for a couple of years after that.

When I was eleven, I was forced to go to camp again. This time I went to the Triangle Y Summer Ranch Camp north of the Catalinas. I hated the Triangle Y even more than the earlier camp. For me, camp wasn't about nature; it was about scary kids and their ways. I remember a boy, Emile, at Y-camp who lived in Tucson by our arroyo but far downstream in a neighborhood near the railroad tracks. He asserted that there were bums living in the arroyo who, if they captured you, "would make you suck their cocks or fuck you in the ass." I reacted as I had reacted to Ernie's story five years earlier about engaged couples having to see each other naked. I told Emile I didn't believe him. I was ten years old and didn't understand why anyone would even want to have someone suck his cock or fuck someone in the ass. I still don't understand. I had never seen bums hanging out in our stretch of the arroyo. (Where did that bullet come from?) I was mostly upset because Emile's statements suggested that something awful might have happened to me when I passed out in the sand six years earlier. I began to feel a great shame. I didn't tell Emile about those events. He got angry at my naïveté and started shouting at me. I called him a dirty liar. He shoved me and I surprised myself by shoving back. We continued until a counselor came into the tent.

I remember another kid at camp whose face was unique and repulsive. He seemed to be missing some essential feature, not his eyes, not his nose, not his lips, not his ears, but something. His name fit his face. It was Malcolm Shmerl. What struck me as curious and unfair was my reaction. He had done nothing wrong. He hadn't had time to do anything wrong. But my revulsion was strong the instant I was introduced to him. It bothered me that my emotions could be so unjust.

There were juvenile delinquents in camp who were being given a reward for good behavior before being sent back to Fort Grant, a brutal reformatory. One of the delinquents at camp boasted that he and his friends, armed with a 22 rifle, came upon a couple fucking in a car at night in the desert. He thrust the point of the rifle into the open window and said, "If you hump one more time, I'm going to blow your brains out." He forced the couple out of the car. He recognized the girl and took her aside. She was a neighbor. She asked him not to tell. He said he wouldn't if she didn't. The delinquent interrupted his story to ask those of us within earshot shot not to repeat what he was about to say. We promised. He said he would hurt us if we broke our promise. He then finished his story. As the girl and boy were putting their clothes back on, he shot the boy in the buttocks and told the girl she'd better drive.

This same, gratuitously violent kid beat up a fat Jewish boy who arrived at our tent with his prodigious belongings stacked in a wheelbarrow the counselors had lent him. "You fucking Jew," the delinquent said as he pummeled the Jewish boy. The delinquent kid was a racist, obviously. That statement is not like the prissy, false accusations of racism we make today. I would have been hesitant to say, "I hate Jewish food" around the students I studied with at UVA. I did nothing to help the Jewish boy, and, like me, he did nothing to help himself.

I worked in the camp kitchen earning my camp costs. My mother believed she needed to teach her children to work. The kitchen job gave me a certain status. The delinquent kid, for that reason, hated me as well as the Jew. He was on the point of hitting me one day, but, again, a counselor walked in.

One night after supper, out among the trees, one of the delinquent kids took a Flashlight and starting hypnotizing other kids. Supposedly hypnotized kids were wandering about swaying and stumbling like drunks. I asked to be hypnotized. The hypnotist failed in my case. He informed me that you couldn't be hypnotized unless you believed in hypnotism. Faith required before evidence was something I was familiar with. I didn't believe. Still, there were all those kids stumbling around.

One delinquent kid at Y camp, the toughest of them all, Don, became my friend even though he was much older than me. I saw him smoking and promised not to rat on him. After I became his friend, no one messed with me. When he breached some camp prohibition, his sentence was to be thrown with all his clothes on into the horse trough. Before the other kids came to get him, he hid a bucket in the trough. When the kids threw him in, he grabbed the bucket and tossed buckets of water back on them. He was the son of the most prominent Tucson TV newscaster. It took special influence to get him into camp in lieu of spending his full sentence in Fort Grant. He'd been arrested in a gang fight using a bullwhip with razor blades attached to the end.

Each tent had a counselor and a junior counselor overseeing the kids in it. One of the counselors was drafted into the army half way through the summer. The camp administrator decided to have one tent under the charge of two junior counselors. Wayne, who had been sent to camp with me, had always been drawn to nature, and the place held some natural beauty. Wayne was large and content. He was made a junior counselor. He was paired with LeCave. LeCave was rich. His father owned the biggest donut factory in Tucson. "LeCave" had become a term of derision in camp. It was used to describe a foolish mistake. "That's a LeCave!" both kids and counselors would say. On the day of the arrival of the new shift of kids, the youngest were assigned to Wayne's tent. LeCave decided to give them a lecture. He told them, among other, similar, things, that they were not in camp to have fun; they were there to learn to be men. Wayne had to quietly and privately tell each kid that everybody knew LeCave was a silly person and that they should not pay any attention to what he said.

On my last day in camp I did a generous thing. It was the custom of the kids, when it was time to go horseback riding, to race at a signal to the stables and mount the best riderless horse they could find. I was always the slowest. During one race I passed by a new kid, a replacement in our tent, who had stopped and was leaning over a fence. He seemed on the verge of passing out. At first I was glad because that meant I would get the next-to-last horse. The last horse was a mean, lazy swayback that couldn't keep up and would bite you any chance it got. It was a misery to ride. I felt sorry for the gasping boy and went back to see if I could help. He explained to me that he had asthma and couldn't run more than thirty yards without stopping to catch his breath. When he ran, he said, the air built up inside his lungs and he couldn't fully exhale. I told him my father had asthma. We made a fast connection with that comment. We walked together slowly to the waiting riders. I offered, sincerely, I think, to ride the mean swayback. He insisted that he would ride it. I wish my life were filled with events like this, but it's not.

Sucked into Existence by Nothingness

A recurrent dream I had when I was a child seemed to be about Hell. I'm not entirely sure because memories of dreams mix with thoughts we have waking up or even thoughts we have days later. Often, when falling asleep prior to the dream, I had a vision of the world before the world came to be, a vision of infinite lines, ugly twisting shapes and endless, dark, churning geographies of chaos. Everything touching me, including my own body, felt impossibly coarse. There was a loss of tactile orientation. I couldn't identify any of the bedclothes. They all felt impossibly heavy and as thick as a mattress. Suddenly, I didn't know where the bedclothes ended and my body began. I was swallowed by matter and unable to move. In this state, if I didn't pull myself out of the drift toward sleep, I fell through the earth and had the Hell dream, which forced me out of bed altogether in uncontrollable panic the moment it came upon me.

In the dream, I was eternally alone without a body in an endless black void forever. I wasn't alone because there were no other people present; I was alone because there was no such thing as another person, real or imagined. In contrast to the dream's wakeful prelude, the universe and I were entirely immaterial. There was no reality outside the overwhelming horror of my solitude. The dream and its prelude were at opposite poles of being. But there was no difference between them, and that seemed to explain something. I remember my father catching me tumbling from my bed in my gasping despair and walking me around the house to wake me up entirely. As it came to me that he was with me, I awakened fully. What was especially terrifying was that the moment of the dream was timeless; I knew, awake, that it was still going on. Dying in one's sleep has always sounded like a terrible death to me. "For in that sleep of death what dreams may come," a phrase I heard years later, in a crowded theater, brought the first attack of incontinence I'd had since 1st grade. Long after the dreams stopped, I wondered if they were Hell itself. The dreams were waiting. Of course, I couldn't have articulated my nothingness Hell dream very well at the time, but the images stayed.

I wonder now if the bedclothes impeded my breathing. I wonder if being infinitely small, bodiless and alone in a black void eternally is what suffocating feels like. I could almost wish to have the Hell dream again to see if suffocation would explain it. At least in some circumstances, suffocation is painless. George, the ex-WWII submariner in AA, tells me he had occasion to help rescue several drowning sailors. Their breathing had stopped and their lungs were full of seawater. When their lungs were cleared and they began to breathe, all of them told George that the pain of asphyxiation had ended when their resistance broke down and they took a full breath of water. After that they claimed they were perfectly calm until they passed out. The description made me think of babies breathing the amniotic fluid in and out, as they must do to be born with healthy lungs. Does seawater bring back the comfort and security of the amniotic fluid? How easily babies move in that fluid.

The Church dogmas may have caused my nightmares, but they also soothed them. During the dreams, for an instant, I was eternally damned. But after and outside of them, the Church's sacraments, ceremonies and doctrines were salvation when I was awake in daylight and could have recourse to them.

I got stuck in a bathtub some years ago. I tried to get out of the tub for half-an-hour, but for some reason my muscles were impossibly weak. I couldn't stand. I couldn't sit up fully and certainly not step over the rim. I screamed fruitlessly for help many times. Instant by instant the fear increased. Something like the nothingness Hell dream seemed to be coming true. But I was only in a bathtub! I made myself laugh at the absurdity of my fear and was finally able to pull and push half of my slippery body outside the tub, shifting myself and my center of gravity enough to tip like a teeter-totter and slide over the rim.

The Hell dreams were the beginning of my solipsism. When I was five, before the dreams started, no philosopher could have explained "consciousness" to me, much less that I was trapped in it. My vision was pure; I knew I wasn't alone. Over the next few years, primed by the Eucharistic teachings of Sister St. Thomas and my dreams, I slowly came to see myself as the whole of existence. In the end I knew that being eternally alone and Hell were the same.

After I had managed to disregard my blasphemous thoughts, I discovered that my father wanted a genius child, and he thought it might be me. He kept taking note of things like my frequent headaches and my religious obsession as signs that I was especially imaginative and intelligent. At the time there was a repeated TV advertisement for aspirin with the line: "Do you know that intelligent people have more headaches than other people?" To my father, I was the child genius. To my priest, I was the child saint.

There was an astronomy text in our house in which I discovered a table showing the distance of each planet from the sun. I memorized those distances and several other basic facts about the planets and, during show- and-tell time at school, I displayed balls of hardened clay showing the relative sizes of the planets and told everyone how big and far away from the sun each planet was.

When I had established myself as the class intellectual, to the great delight of my father, I expanded my repertoire a little bit and my presentation became a ceremony repeated each year for the remaining years of grade school. It was important to me that everyone know I was smart.

My father had been awarded a large cup engraved with his name and the words, "Arizona Oratory Champion" when he was in Tucson High School (THS). The cup stood with other family trophies in the games room. It was an inspiration to me. In grade school, I volunteered to take part in a debate. The issue was whether the persecutions under the Communists were worse than the persecutions of Christians in Roman times. I took the side that said the Roman persecutions were worse. I remember my opponents claiming that the Communist persecutions victimized a far greater number of people. (As I indicated, the teacher had told us of massive deaths in Communist China). I retorted: "So what? It's not just the number of dead; it's how you die. Lions don't just shoot you; they chew you like gum." The class surprised me; they burst into laughter. I never knew if that was a good sign or a bad sign.

My interest in astronomy had a more ingenuous aspect. I was interested in how the universe came to be. I decided it was sucked into existence by nothingness. I explained this theory to a brighter friend who explained to me that suction was gas pressure and not a property of a vacuum. Still I held to the theory. My brighter friend is now a Vincentian priest and Bible scholar. Decades later, Ed tried to convince me that, in accordance with the speculations of some cosmologists, I was right all along; some sort of Ur-suction having nothing to do with gas pressure might have drawn the universe into being. I doubt it, even though it's no crazier than other cosmological theories which are being taken seriously by the performing scientists on television.

My interest in astronomy persisted. I got a telescope and saw the redness of Mars, the four largest moons of Jupiter, the rings of Saturn, the Horse Head Nebula, the Andromeda Galaxy and the Orion Nebula. Single stars were a relatively dull sight; they remain pinpoints of light even through the largest telescopes. The first time I trained my telescope on one, however, I saw a large opalescent mass, and, for a moment that took my breath away, I thought I was seeing the body of a star. Then I realized that the telescope was out of focus.

One night Charlie and I were out on the back lot. We looked up and saw a huge, gray, oblong shape with a string of lights like windows along its side. It was clearly neither an airplane nor a zeppelin. We gazed at it for a minute or more. Then it disappeared. When we returned to the house, we found Mom and Dad sitting in the living room. Charlie excitedly told them what we'd seen. Dad, who'd just come home, said he'd seen it, too, as he drove along Via Riachuelo. I don't remember any of this. Charlie swears it's all true.

After the nothingness-suction theory of how the universe came to be, I thought for a while and came up with another theory, developed in partnership with Byron, my best friend at the time. This we called the "Eternal Cone Theory." According to this theory, the universe consisted of planets and stars that were the atoms of greater planets and stars in a greater universe, and those greater planets and stars were the atoms of still greater planets and stars in a still greater universe, and so on. This worked in both directions such that the atoms of our universe were stars in a smaller universe, etc. "And other fleas have other fleas to bite 'em. And so *ad infinitum.*" I'd guess that five percent of the kids in the U.S. in my generation have dreamed of the Eternal Cone in one way or another at one time or another. I once saw it in a comic book. Having these theories was enormously satisfying. They were intellectual possessions that made me feel fulfilled without the material artifacts of my childhood. I decided I wanted to become indifferent to material reality and live an entirely mental and spiritual life. By way of accomplishing this goal and making myself smarter, I read books that were over my head. One of these was Alan Watts' deeply confusing The Way of Zen. But his statement "Reality is only an inkblot" made sense to me and seemed to verify my solipsism.

There were other books that affected me in a different but equally noxious way. My ambitious reading habits brought me Thais, by Anatole France, and The Kreutzer Sonata, by Leo Tolstoy. Both books were probably on the Index. Surprisingly, I understood t much of what they said.

In Thais, an anchorite is corrupted by his lust for the courtesan he has converted. His pride in his spirituality and in his conversion of the famous courtesan makes him vulnerable to corruption. He turns into a vampire. She becomes a saint. In fact, the anchorite was canonized as well as the prostitute.

In The Kreutzer Sonata, a man who has no sexual morality killed his wife for her unfaithfulness because it offends him. He tries to convince the man to whom he tells the story that he should have been executed. He was not punished because the homicide was thought to have been justifiable. He was supposed to have been driven mad by his wife's unfaithfulness, but he says he wasn't insane at all. He was just angry to have lost face. He didn't love his wife and wasn't jealous. Tolstoy urges the reader to "stop believing that carnal love is high and noble."

About that time I heard in a television western the statement, "When a man has lost his wife's honor no posse on earth can get it back for him!" The theme of both the novels and the television western was the mix of pride and chastity. I read them as injunctions against any sexual involvement. In Tolstoy's case I was correct. He thought sex was always illicit, even in marriage, and said so in his epilogue. I revered him. I swore "under pain of sin" to remain forever celibate. I hoped for chastity, but mostly I wanted to avoid creating another immortal life and to "cease thinking that carnal love is something …exalted." My desire to rise above carnality wasn't great enough to make me see that my childish spiritual pride resembled the anchorite's, nor was my rejection of materiality sufficient to make me recognize in it the elements of my nothingness Hell dreams. However, after my vow, I asked God to take away the dreams.

Naked, slender Artemis, in the style of Praxiteles, was standing in front of and close to me when I finished taking my vow and concluded my prayer. She congratulated me in her trembling siren voice, smiling warmly, tempting me to violate my oath. I believed that she was willing. Then I wondered if she was a demon. She was at least a false god, and fucking her would be the gravest sin I'd ever committed. (Some Bible-illiterate Catholics think concourse with demons is the unforgivable sin.) On the other hand Artemis was the goddess of chastity, and I was thirteen years old. I wouldn't have been sure how to go about fucking her. Before my hands reached her breasts I shouted "No!" snapping back my arms tightly across my chest and closing my eyes. Thereafter I cultivated a general distrust of women to help me keep my vow.

About that time, a neighbor gave me a substantial amount of rather sophisticated chemistry equipment. I was delighted. I forgot my wish to reject the material world and live entirely in the intellect and spirit. I set up the equipment with an artist's eye until it looked like Frankenstein's lab. I didn't do anything with it to speak of, except rearrange it every so often to look like some other version of Frankenstein's lab. Sometimes I was able to reproduce some exciting reaction I'd accidentally happened upon -- the generation of a rancid gas or an explosion or the fermentation of various sugary juices.

I took up smoking. I began with the dead, dry stalks of rag weed that grew on the arroyo's banks. The soft, crisp wood burned evenly and had a small passage in its pith that allowed for the easy flow of smoke. If you inhaled too quickly, your throat would be burned. When I began fooling around with my chemistry equipment, I started a pipe collection. I smoked my pipes. You didn't have to learn anything to do that. I became a dedicated smoker of expensive foreign cigarettes as well. My career as a pipe and cigarette connoisseur lasted far beyond my school years. I enjoyed smoking. At first, I smoked in the basement of our house, which I had appropriated for my "lab." The chemical smells camouflaged the smell of tobacco.

School Days I

When my friends and I were in eighth grade, there was a donut shop around the corner from St. Ambrose. The donut shop had a special that never changed. For sixty cents you could get a soft drink and all the donuts you could eat. That was cheap even for those days. In eighth grade, it became our custom to go to the donut shop after school and eat as many donuts as we wanted. Then we started to compete. Ed, the smartest student in our class, ate 14 donuts. A week later, Nick ate 15. Nick was the tallest and fattest boy in our class. He was Lebanese and Mexican. His Mexican mother made enormous Mexican and Lebanese meals for the nine members of the family. The day he first set the record, Nick went home and ate twelve tacos for dinner.

Nick's record didn't last long. He had serious competition, Paul, a bright student about two-thirds Nick's size. Paul took the record at 17. Nick set a new record at 18 donuts. The next day, Paul ate 20 donuts, sitting on the floor of the donut shop while cramming the last one down. The record built until Paul won again at 24 donuts. Nick gave up. Through all this the counter lady stared at us with a mix of disapproval and amazement, but she never cut us off.

I won the junior high science fair at the UA in eighth grade. I made a chamber that I heated and filled with carbon dioxide. This supposedly recreated the probable conditions on the surface of Venus. I put a cactus in it to see if life could exist on Venus. I stole the whole idea from an episode of Science Fiction Theatre, but I was able to ignore that. I accepted the trophy as confirmation of my superior intelligence.

With the same project, I had previously failed to place in the Catholic grade school science fair. The bishop's niece won first prize. Her project was baking bread. When she graduated from high school, she became a nun who, after some years, was asked to leave the convent because it was felt she was using her supposed vocation to escape the world; later still, she became a drug addict; and, finally, she committed suicide. When she won the Catholic school science fair and I didn't, my father, touring the displays, made a loud ugly crack about her relationship to the bishop.

The last year of grade school I was allowed to have a graduation party. I was set to invite a select group of friends from my graduating eighth grade class. I was afraid to invite the whole class because I was a snob and because one of the students in class was a dedicated bully. He would help his uninvited bully friends from other schools to crash my party and then pick fights. The group I planned to invite included Byron. Byron, as I said, was my best friend. My parents, probably at the behest of the school, told me that I couldn't invite Byron unless I invited my whole class because parents would be incensed if a black child were preferred over their children. I decided not to invite Byron. This created the most severe conscience problem of my life. My betrayal of Byron made me feel awful when I finally faced up to what I'd done. After the party, when Byron asked me why he hadn't been invited. I immediately recognized how hurt he was. I told a half lie and said my parents had forbidden me to invite him. I apologized. That seemed to satisfy him somewhat, and we remained friends through most of high school.

One Saturday, standardized IQ tests were given to the entering freshmen at Salpointe, the Catholic high school we would attend. A month later I found out I wasn't to be in the "honors class." I was just regular – no genius. My father was so upset he couldn't speak to me. Instead of average, I felt positively inferior. I had been an extravagant extrovert in grade school. Now I was a mumbling, droop-headed thirteen year old introvert. Is it self-pity to feel sorry for yourself as you were when you were a child if you don't feel sorry for yourself as you are? Byron was to be in the honors class. I became a more fervent Catholic as a way of filling the void of my mediocrity.

Ed began stealing cars that year. The first time he did it he drove up to my house in a convertible and stopped where Byron and I were standing out of view of the house discussing the Eternal Cone and smoking imported cigarettes. The sight of our friend driving a car amazed us. He told us he'd stolen the car and invited us aboard. We immediately got in. We were sure, if we were caught, it would all be Ed's fault. He said he had grown tired of walking when he saw the convertible with the keys in the ignition. So he got in and drove away. We set off on an adventure that lasted about ten minutes. Ed let us off and went to ditch the car. He stole nine cars before being chased by a cop into a tree and ended in a high-class reformatory. Lots of people in Tucson left their keys in the ignition at that time. Car theft was something that happened in Sal Mineo movies.

Catholic Instincts

That same year, Byron, told me that a priest he knew had said self-abuse was not a sin. I clung fiercely to Confession again to cover my lapses when I found out that my new habit was, in fact, a mortal sin. Artemis was always my fantasy. I would bind myself, "under pain of sin," to say a certain number of rosaries if I fell. Each time I fell, I said the required rosaries. Then I renewed the vow, adding another rosary to the number I had to complete when I fell again. There are a minimum of 65 prayers in a rosary. It takes about 15 minutes to say them all if you pray at top speed. I ended up having to say 35 rosaries at one time and, at the urging of Quoron, stopped making the pledge. My never-satisfied lust for Artemis became a constant struggle.

Once, I fell two days after going to Confession. At that time, two Redemptorist Fathers were giving a retreat at St. Ambrose. During the retreat one of them shouted at us that "boys shouldn't wear jeans that looked like they were painted on." Some of the girls giggled. Some of the boys might have divined that this was a dangerous priest if they hadn't been forbidden to imagine such a thing. The priests heard Confessions in the course of the retreat. When I confessed having fallen two days after my last Confession, the Confessor refused me absolution. I knew Redemptorists were strict, but I was in shock. I'm the only Catholic I've ever known who has been refused absolution. I didn't know how long I had to wait to go to Confession again and I forgot to ask. I assumed I couldn't immediately walk over to the alternate confessional and make the same Confession to the other Redemptorist. The refusal of absolution had something of the same effect as Father Towner's command that I not go to Confession for the two weeks my family was in California. Initially, both events left me clawing at air to regain the support of my religion.

My vow of celibacy was made for life, unlike my vow to say rosaries, which only applied if I renewed the rosary vow. I had to confess self-abuse not only as a sin in itself but also as a violation of my oath to remain perpetually celibate. (I never confessed to the priest that my imaginary sexual object was the Greek goddess Artemis). Perhaps my vow of celibacy was what angered the priest; he'd taken the same vow. I was devastated. I was mediocre and my religion had failed me.

Mexican attitudes toward sex are ambiguous. They are everywhere both puritanical and licentious. There was a woman in Hermosillo, where I once taught, who wandered through the town every day, all day with her retarded, deformed adult son behind her. The son was the result of an adulterous tryst. The woman spoke of him as the punishment for her sin and warned those she passed of the consequences of lust. On the other hand the red light district in Hermosillo is directly behind the police station and prostitution is illegal.

Once one of my fellow teachers and I visited Copper Canyon, taking the train up from Los Mochis, Sonora, into Chihuahua and returning to Hermosilla by bus through Agua Prieta, Sonora, about 50 miles from Fort Huachuca, Arizona. We got off the bus in Agua Prieta to get some sleep, which we sorely needed and which can't be gotten on a stuffed Mexican bus. Exhausted, we checked into the first hotel we found, got a room for about three times the going rate in Hermosillo and went to sleep. We woke up around 1:00 p.m. We didn't realize, until we got to the lobby and saw some of the pornographic paintings we hadn't noticed when we checked in, that the hotel was a bordello and that a large part of the city was dedicated to servicing the soldiers from Fort Huachuca. We had been rented a room for sex.

When I was teaching in Hermosillo, I directed a movie written by the kids. Their script was about a heroic girl who, after becoming pregnant by her absconding boyfriend, refuses to get an abortion. The background music they chose for every scene was Madonna singing, "I made up my mind. I'm keeping my baby." The Mexican kids didn't know that Madonna was a whore.

American sexual attitudes were less sophisticated. At St. Ambrose, Father Towner was in charge of school discipline. He would come over from the rectory to take care of behavior problems. Before he broke with the Church, he asked a kid in Charlie's sixth grade class, Benito Lopez, to explain to him what "fuck" meant. There was some hemming and hawing, but

Benito eventually explained it to him. It was a big thing to say, "fuck" at St. Ambrose. Most of us thought it was a mortal sin that required yet another embarrassing trip to the confessional. After Father Towner's interview with Benito some kid probably got a paddling. Paddlings are surprisingly painful.

In my eighth grade class, a boy named Gontron, followed two girls home, repeating to them that he was going to "fuck" them. They arrived home in tears. That Gontron wasn't expelled was amazing. I suspect he convinced everybody that he didn't know what "fuck" meant. He probably didn't.

That same year, a short freckle-faced kid named William Schaeffer was known to be fucking his sister who was in the seventh grade, too. It was said that he used the severed fingers of a rubber glove as condoms. Somehow the story came to Father Towner's attention. That was the last we ever saw of William Schaeffer. His sister got away with it by claiming she was forced. She was much bigger than he was. She was sexually active in high school. She would make out with one or another boy on the bus. Their activity disgusted me because she had freckles and I couldn't forget that she had fucked her brother.

The nuns at St. Ambrose, who were somewhat aware of the scandal, started a prayer promotion program. Each week one kid in each class was given a plastic statue of the Blessed Virgin Mary. The bottom unscrewed and, inside, there was a huge rosary, the kind the Sisters of Saint Joseph carried on their belts. The kid was supposed to take the contraption home and convince his family to say the rosary together every night that week and then return the statue and rosary for the next kid. My mother took it seriously. She was a sincere Catholic, as was I. Sex was almost never discussed in our family.

Sex instruction from a nun in school was unthinkable. When it came time for Charlie then me to be told about sex my father was too embarrassed to do it. He seemed to think anything having to do with love and girls was icky. I remember my mother, in her slip, waking me then sliding under the covers next to me late one night to explain sex. I was so shocked to hear my mother speak about sex while lying in my bed in her slip that I was cringing all the time she talked. For a moment I thought she was going to touch me. It was a repugnant experience, complementing my developing attitude towards sex.

The reputation of Monsignor Hughes for running a tight ship might have been damaged by the Schaeffer scandal since the consequent gossip couldn't be contained, but he ran our parish so well there was a huge surplus of donations for the bishop to dispose of as he wished. During the Second Vatican Council, Monsignor Hughes was invited to Rome to speak to interested bishops on how to raise money. He boasted to the congregation that he had been invited to speak to the bishops in Rome on "the theology of giving." Monsignor Hughes, in retrospect, was a corpulent eunuch. No hint of sexuality ever escaped him.

When we were younger and he somewhat thinner, Monsignor Hughes was often invited to the house on Thanksgiving and Christmas. He always brought a new magic trick he had purchased, presumably from the scatological enterprise we had happened into several years before when we ran away, Bunny's store. The tricks amazed us. Happily Monsignor Hughes showed us how they were done after the performance.

As a trim young man, shown in a photo in the rectory, and a recently ordained priest, Monsignor Hughes smuggled Mass accessories into Mexico to say illegal masses for the persecuted Catholic population during the presidency of Plutarco Calles. He smuggled the accessories in a golf bag. If he had been caught, he would have been shot. I assume he feared dying in mortal sin and avoided the fleshpots of Mexico, if he had any inclinations as a youth in that direction.

Graciela, my godmother, came from Mexico as a child before Plutarco Calles and the Cristeros. Her Catholicism was the overarching fact of her life. I can't imagine her having sex with her very passive husband. She well might not have; they had no children. She was the granddaughter of Tucson's first American mayor, the first mayor after the Gadsden Purchase, Esteban Ochoa. I don't know if Esteban considered himself Mexican, Spanish or American. He most likely considered himself a Spanish-American, given the prejudices of upper class

Latinos. To do him credit, that was probably true. I doubt that anyone in Esteban's family had Indian blood.

Surprisingly, there are many Catholics who actually believe that bread and wine become the body and blood of Jesus during Mass, and Graciela was probably one of these. I was, too. She liked me, and, with some foreboding, I liked her back.

Graciela's dark old house, full of mahogany and religious artifacts, was scary. Dark was best in the era before dependable cooling systems. Graciela herself was gray rather than brown. She had black hair. She was somber. Both she and her husband were teachers at a time when teachers had authority. She was frighteningly strict. Graciela owned land in various places in steadily expanding Tucson. She was land-rich. My mother thought she might leave me something, but she didn't. She would have taught me Spanish, but I didn't ask, despite my mother's urgings. I didn't want to spend time in that dark, scary house. Graciela and her mother used to make green corn tamales as gifts each year on their back porch. For me, to this day, the smell of fresh masa is deeply redolent of my early childhood. There was a patio with trees, flowers and a clean, bright-blue pond beside a statue of the blue-veiled Virgin Mary that I loved. When Graciela and her mother and daughter-in-law came to visit us, they always settled in the games room, the room for parties and play. Graciela smiled there, not in her house. Graciela's visits were fun. Mexicans like children. A godmother or godfather is an important person in the life of a child among Mexicans. "Compadre," that warm Mexican word for an intimate friend, more formally means "godfather to my son" or "father to my godson."

Graciela died when I was still young. On her deathbed, she was in severe pain. She kept repeating that she must have offended God in some way to be suffering so. There is no difference between the Mexican Catholic version, the AA version, and the psychotherapists' version of deserved pain. We hurt because of our decisions, so we deserve the pain, whether we will to sin and reap promised punishment or simply decide to feel awful. Whatever her most secret desires, Graciela was an unfulfilled woman.

Later, when I discovered that I didn't believe in God anymore, the world turned gray. There were no objects of wonder. The Moon was a drab rock. Life was chemicals. But I believed more fervently in Hell. Lorus taught me that the probability that God exists is inversely proportional to the probability that Hell exists. Until I took God's side again, I lived in terror that I was dead and that I already was in Hell. The philosophical and theological passages in these reminiscences are intended to disprove the existence of Hell. Many of the arguments may not be compelling. Perhaps I don't believe them, but if they seem more likely to me than Hell, they help.

Belief

In contrast to the Papagos, who are often fat with bad complexions, the Yaquis are usually handsome. When I was a child, three small Yaqui villages were within the city limits of Tucson and contiguous South Tucson. The Yaquis aren't under the authority of the BIA. They had come to Tucson requesting that the city officials, not the Federal Government, grant them asylum. They were fleeing Mexico and the Mexican troops who were intent on wiping them out. The city officials granted the Yaquis' request illegally.

During the Easter season, the Yaquis held colorful ceremonies. Anglos often watched. Memo, a schoolmate of mine, was allowed to strum his father's twelve-string guitar on the bench where the coarse Yaqui band drummed and fluted accompaniments to some of the ceremonies. Anselmo, the Yaqui chief, had taken a liking to Memo.

During Easter week, the most pagan ceremony, at which photos and Memo's twelve-string were not allowed, was the deer dance. Three dancers and a singer were brought up from the principal Yaqui tribal reserve in Mexico. They pantomimed the pursuit of a deer either by hunters or coyotes. The singer sang songs in Yaqui. Anselmo translated a snatch for us. It went like this:

> The deer coming from the sunrise
> outside the house of the hunter
> is about to play in the water.
> See the dancing flowers in the water.
> See a deer with flowers.

I don't think Anselmo was supposed to translate the song for Anglos. The "flowers" were blood, of course.

When the hunter dancers presented masks on one side of their faces they represented coyotes and danced part of the time on all fours. The deer dancer wore strings of dry deer hooves wound around his waist and dried cocoons around his ankles. These served as rattles. The deer dancer, shirtless, hairless and lean, covered with the dust he raised, carried gourd rattles in both hands. He had the stuffed head of a deer, with polished obsidian eyes, bound to the top of his head. Red ribbons and sometimes other objects that were said to capture souls were tied to the deer's antlers. While keeping the jaw line of the deer level the deer dancer stamped out the increasingly frenetic beat of the deer's hooves. Another participant beat out the accelerating heartbeat of the deer on a water drum. A violinist and harpist were sometimes present. During pauses, the beardless deer dancer turned the deer's head to listen for the approaching hunter or coyotes. The deer dancer's eyes were closed, and underneath the deer's head he wore a tight white scarf that hid his scalp and eyebrows. The effect was that of a death mask. The deer dancer wore a knee-length skirt, wound from a rebozo. He was barefoot. His legs were naked but for the strings of rattles on his ankles. An old, somewhat crazy Indian said to me that, near the moment of the kill, Yaqui members of the audience, focusing on the obsidian eyes, believed the deer and not the dancer. The shuddering exhausted spasms and kill (and evisceration when the hunters were coyotes) were piteous. But, rarely, the deer mocked its pursuers and escaped; then the deer dance represented the survival of a hunted people, Memo said. The deer dancer I knew is no longer around. I can't guarantee the work of his replacements.

In contrast to the graceful deer dance there was the grotesque dance of the chapayekas. These dancers had cardboard or hide masks covering their whole heads. Each chapayeka held a rosary between his teeth under his mask, protecting him from the demon that accompanied him. The masks were often decorated with crude caricatures of icons of Anglo culture, Abraham Lincoln, for example. The identity of the demon had nothing to do with the person caricatured by the mask. The demons were feared. Protection from them involved certain rites. There was a procedure for leaving the dancing forum to go to the bathroom, for example. This involved lying down in the dirt to remove the mask and rosary after saying certain prayers.

The chapayekas' performance was a pantomime of filth. The demons behaved like Swift's Yahoos. A chapayeka might pantomime wiping himself with one of the sticks he carried and flinging the imaginary feces at one of the other chapayekas or hump another chapayekas's leg. The dancers' large sticks were erratically struck together, making a loud, eerie, echoing noise like the caw of a crow. The chapayekas portrayed some of the forces that put Jesus to death.

Few plants grew within the tight confines of the village. Bare dirt separated rudimentary adobe shanties and a small adobe church, open only on the end opposite the altar. The buildings poked up from the ground like the desert furniture. Most of the mesquite and creosote had been used for firewood or medicine ages ago and the cacti eaten. Along with the smell from stalls selling hot fried foods, a light dust springing from the dancers' feet seasoned the air. On Easter day, a group of small, colorfully dressed children, angels, chased the chapayekas away by throwing flower petals at them. It was beautiful.

The name of this, the largest of the three Yaqui settlements, was Pascua (Easter) Village. At one point, Anselmo appeared before my father, the City Magistrate at the time. I don't know what the legal problem was. He was pleased that my father addressed him as "Chief." Anselmo became an alcoholic some years later after his son died in a car wreck. Earlier, on Anselmo's advice, half the old village made a disastrous move to new digs far away from town at the remote, southern, weirdly saw-toothed end of the Tucson Mountains. It was a place as lonely as the tiny New Mexican village under the full, ghostly, twilight Moon in the famous Ansel Adams photo. But for a single dirt road, the new village was entirely enclosed by the strangely shaped mountains. I remember Anselmo, hung over, picking huge green worms from his tomato patch and complaining that he was now a worm-grower. He was no longer chief. He'd been deposed for his excessive drinking.

The Yaquis could cross over the border from Mexico easily. This was a lax time, long before millions of Mexicans began sneaking across. The Yaquis brought heroin from Mexico to sell in Tucson. Maybe that's why Anselmo attempted to move the tribe to a remote location.

I don't know what, if anything, the Yaquis really believe; pagan or Catholic, they have only stories. I don't know much of what I really believe either. Maybe I have only stories. I think few

75

people know many of their real beliefs. They have positions they assume because they think they look smart in them. Their positions are usually associated with their faction. Their faction may be their party, their class, their race, their religion or lack of it, etc. People rarely ask themselves if their faction's positions are true. They think up arguments for those positions, but they don't ask themselves if those are true either. The arguments are like cheers for the home team. My real beliefs are forced on me by experience, reason and the opinions of others. I can, of course, be an intent observer, thinker and questioner to increase my understanding. But that's not what I was, growing up. I was like the Cowardly Lion in the Wizard of Oz. "Oh! I *do* believe in spooks! I *do*! I *do*! I *do*!" I avoided sins against Faith with their terrifying consequences by holding onto the Faith that predicted those consequences.

Fear and imagination can bring about strange, cruel ideas that have little to do with experience. I remember walking home on a moonless night as a child. When I looked into the mesquite-forested entrance to our neighborhood, darker than the night, I froze. The blackness was stuffed with ghosts. I stood for an hour before I found the courage to enter. Can you fear things you don't believe exist? You bet. Watch a good horror movie. But persistent fear, especially if it involves you in ceremonies, wears away reason and can leave you truly believing truly absurd things.

Vanity and greed also foster unreasonable beliefs. A small, well-dressed man happened into an AA meeting for which I was the coffee maker decades ago. The man, a New Yorker by his accent, told the AA members that he was a talent scout for Paramount Studios. I would have guessed that no one would believe him, but over the course of a few weeks, he managed to persuade several young men who thought themselves handsome to give him $2,000 each as a "good faith payment" for finding them acting jobs in Hollywood. Then the talent scout disappeared.

Foolishness itself can inspire credulity. Eric von Däniken, Carlos Castañeda, and the priest, an "expert," brought to St. Ambrose grade school to teach us about the nine choirs of angels, all amazed and converted their audiences with the arcane improbability of their claims. My fear of Hell grew into sickness in this way.

Philosophers escape the problem of not believing in their own conclusions by saying that they "hold" those conclusions, for example, "We hold these truths to be self-evident." "Dedicated to the proposition…" is another excellent phrase. Theologians refer to unreasoned beliefs as "acts of faith," that is, moral acts. When challenged they often evince a belief simply by declaring, "It's a Mystery!" When philosophical ideas and ideals are contested the battle can be even more fiercely disingenuous and murderous than wars of religion. Self-righteousness and hatred often entirely replace any real belief when a man is passionate about a political cause. He sometimes becomes psychotic. I've been psychotic since I was a child, according to the doctors. Some of my opinions are passionate. However, I now know enough to spot and suspect my own vainglorious idealism, I think.

My friend Joe and I were on a bus headed for Washington, D.C. in 1963 in the summer of our first year in high school. We had a rest stop in Memphis, a town undergoing considerable racial strife at the time. When we approached the nearest lunch counter, there were three white men sitting at one end and one elderly black man sitting at the opposite extreme. The counter was quite long. There were, perhaps, fifteen stools. I had an idea. If we sat down next to the black man, we would have effectively integrated a lunch counter in the South. That was about the most idealistic thing you could do at the time. One of the four whites looked at Joe and me pleadingly as we stood there deciding where to sit. Then we saw that the black man had stopped eating and his hands were shaking. We gave up our plan to be heroes and sat near the whites. We did the right thing. We abandoned our "beliefs," and our ideals and exercised compassion.

"The art of writing is the art of discovering what you believe." Lest he be praised too highly it should be known that, at the end of his life, Flaubert, author of the words just quoted, said, "There is no truth. There are only ways of looking at things." The first quote urges intellectual honesty. The second quote is the height of intellectual dishonesty and the champion of lies.

A year-and-a-half ago, a Jaguar attacked me in the jungle outskirts of Oaxaca City. I saw it. It was looking at me. It came at me, threw me on my back and gnawed on my face for some seconds before it became bored and walked away. I hadn't tried to scare it away. There are two theories: (1) yell and run at the dangerous animal in the woods, or (2) stand stock-still. I chose the second, if freezing with fear is a choice.

One side of my face is quite scarred. I try a little to politely hide it by keeping my unscarred profile to interlocutors. When my brother Sammy came to visit me in Ixtec. He said several times, interrupting our conversation, " I can't *believe* you got mauled by a jaguar!" until I asked him not to say it anymore because it was making me sad.

I'm lying. I was never mauled by a jaguar. I just said that to show that I'm being truthful, the way God showed He didn't want human sacrifice by telling Abraham to kill Isaac. When the angel stopped Abraham's hand, Abraham had his revelation. Similarly, if I lie to you and then tell on myself, you will see that I'm truthful. I'm God. You're Abraham.

The Criteria for Losing Fights

The criteria for losing a fight vary. If you run, you lose. You lose if your opponent makes you cower and respect his demands, or if you're dead or unconscious. If you don't return the first punch, that often ends the fight if your opponent is kind. If someone else breaks up the fight after your opponent has thrown the last solid punch, you lose. Sometimes you can lose by saying "I give." That's less ambiguous and usually safer than pulling punches. You can lose by having a bloodier face than the other guy after a mutually agreed upon termination of the fight. Between being dead and "giving" there are a lot of gradations of losing. It may depend on what your opponent does to you while you're unconscious. "Sidewalk sandwiches" were fashionable in Tucson at one time. With some severe or gang beatings it's often impossible to know if you resisted. Are those beatings fights?

Many "fights," and many ways of losing are impossible to classify. Waldo, the father of Nick, the schoolmate of mine who took second place in the donut eating contest, opened a bar on Meyers Street in the poorest section of town where every few months someone was killed in a fight with straight razors. One night, the largest man in the bar told Waldo to get fucked. Grabbing the man by both arms to avoid a possible straight razor, Waldo managed to throw him out the door, which gained him the respect of his clientele, including the man he had thrown out. This took more courage than most fights, but was it a fight?

Conventional fights are less interesting. Years after he fell from the eucalyptus, when I was thirteen, Ernie and I were quarterbacks on opposite teams in a touch football game in his front yard. A girl, about nine, from next door asked us if she could play. We told her she could, and while we argued about which team would have to take her, she disappeared into her house, coming out three minutes later wearing a knotted jockstrap over her shorts. Half of us didn't know what it was.

Except for Ernie and I, the teams were made up entirely of smaller kids. My younger brother, Sammy, was one. Sammy liked to play football but was small and skinny. When he grew up he was six foot four inches and heavy. Ernie, like all the neighbor children my age, was better at sports than I. He kept taunting me. He pushed Sammy into some thorn bushes. I told him not to do that. He did it again. We fought. Ernie's parents came to the front door to watch. His much older brother shouted advice. I made a faint with one hand and bloodied Ernie's nose with the other. Then I asked him if he wanted to quit. He did. His older brother expressed his disgust and turned back to the car engine he was working on. Did the single delivered blow make this a fight?

There was an unwritten rule among the kids at St. Ambrose. You don't hit in the face. You could hurt someone and it was a deep insult. We fought rarely and only hit each other in the shoulders. One day a new kid hit me in the face. I couldn't hit him back. He backpedaled faster than I could run forward. I went to a nearby drinking fountain to wash away my tears of rage. A friend urged me to try again to hit the kid back, but it occurred to me that if the incident was my fault, I wouldn't have to do anything. So I walked up to him and apologized.

A high school friend, John Carletta, began stabbing me with the tip of a knife. He choked up on the blade, leaving only the point sticking out between his thumb and forefinger. He was Italian and was playing at being a gangster. He didn't want to cause real damage. After two or three painful stabs and curses, I hit him in the face.

When I hit him, in his shock, he wasn't sure he had been hit, but the most obnoxious moron at Salpointe saw it and insisted that I had hit Carletta *in the face*. The moron had muscles, and the violence visibly excited him. He looked around and saw frail Byron. The moron called Byron a "nigger" and asked him if he wanted to fight. The moron squared off. Byron threw his books at him and walked away. As I see it now, I lost a chance to protect Byron and perhaps pay the moral debt I owed him. But the moron was strong, so I didn't intervene. Was any of this a fight?

Charlie's courage and prowess grew as he got older. In high school, I was drunk in a crowded parking lot outside the restaurant that was the high school hangout of that time. The huge quarterback of the Salpointe football team was bullying me. I told him, as was my cowardly habit, to hit me. He was considering it. Then someone yelled, "Here comes his brother!" and the parking lot was emptied of five or ten people, including the quarterback, in about ten seconds. My brother came out of the restaurant grinning, looked at the empty parking lot and asked if I was ok. I said yes and he went back in. He went to the tough school, THS, and he was Charlie. He could fight.

Salpointe was the "good" alternative to "bad" THS. At my brother's school every male had to know how to fight or he would be humiliated or worse. At Salpointe, the fighters were a group of about ten candidates for the honor of being the toughest guy in school. They mostly picked on each other. Fred Thompson was the top hood in my class. He would fight anyone. Years later, I heard that, wielding a knife while drunk, he backed down a policeman who returned to his squad car and drove away. Did the policeman lose a fight?

I saw Fred or members of his crew fight only three times. Donald Crabtree, a tall skinny second lieutenant of the group, kicked a kid named Felix in the face. Felix was perhaps the friendliest kid at Salpointe. He wasn't at all aggressive and couldn't fight, but he struck a pose a little like John L. Sullivan. He wore heavy braces. It was a bloody mess. Fred stopped the beating, pushing Felix back by the shoulders in the manner prescribed for breaking up a fight between a stranger and a friend.

Another time, the shortest kid in Fred's crew kicked another kid, already defeated and on the ground, in the back of the head, skipping off his skull and rolling up a section of his scalp like a rug.

Once, when he had kicked a non-belligerent student in the testicles, Crabtree was apprehended and sent home. The kid with the kicked testicles had a friend, Mulvahill, reputedly the toughest kid in the class above ours. Crabtree being unavailable, Mulvahill fought Fred Thompson savagely. This fight was "refereed" by a football star who was a friend of Mulvahill. Every time Fred got a good hold on Mulvahill, the football player pushed them apart. Mulvahill's holds were allowed. Again and again, with his head locked under Mulvahill's left arm Fred was helplessly pummeled until he managed somehow to pry his head loose. When one of the priests came, the fighters ran but, while running, arranged to continue the fight at another location. Fred showed up but "gave" and the fight ended. Fred's face had several large red patches on it. Fred was lucky that "giving" could end a fight at Salpointe.

Charlie was the only other kid who beat up Fred. This was, of course, off campus. None of us in the family knew about the fight until much later. Charlie didn't need a "referee." Nowadays 69-year-old Charlie sends me photos of himself under water grabbing shark fins or moray eels in places like the coast of Madagascar or Phuket. I expect him to die one day in an explosion of blood. Will that have been a fight?

Mulvahill went to a school dance one weekend. When he left he found his beautiful, beloved, finely cared for car horribly dented with all the windows smashed. After some investigation, he found out that the likely culprits were a gang of pachucos from THS. We called the Mexican kids "pachucos," a term, in American Spanish, meaning, roughly, "hoods." Quite a few of the older Mexican kids really were pachucos. Mulvahill found out the address of their leader and the next night burst through the kid's front door, past the kid's mother and into a bedroom where he found the pachuco in bed. He took the golf club he had brought with him and beat the kid nearly to death. The kid had to be hospitalized for a long time. Was that a fight?

When, we were very young we feared older kids, especially the Mexicans from the other side of 22nd Street who bicycled through our neighborhood occasionally to see how the apparently rich lived. They never did anything to us. They couldn't have been much older than we were, but, when they engaged us in conversation, they eventually tried to bully us. Then Charlie would grab my hand and say, "Let's go home," and home we would go. My tendency was to freeze when I was scared, as I had frozen when that large hand closed around my ankle. I wouldn't have had the courage to get up and leave by myself. You should know how to run before you know how to fight.

The Mexican kids would often gather in gangs and, if they found a solitary Gringo boy, beat him up. They would beat up other Mexican children if they had a reason. A gang of pachucos kicked out all of Bobby Rodriguez's teeth one spring at THS because he studied hard, got good grades, took part in school activities, spoke both Spanish and English correctly, had some Gringo friends and dressed neatly in a non-pachuco manner (no lifted collar, *etc.*) I'm not sure it's possible to kick out all of someone's teeth without killing him, but "all" was what was reported. The only time I dislike Mexicans is when I remember the pachucos' cowardly ganging, and then I recall my Mexican godmother, my Mexican nephew, and my Mexican in-laws and the fact that they and the vast majority of Mexicans in Mexico, unless they're drug dealers, hate violence. The word "pachuco," in Mexican Spanish, means only "dandy."

Charlie and I were nearly beaten up by a gang of pachucos once. Charlie had arranged a football game with the pachucos at the park that had replaced the desert furniture. We had a washtub of old shoes at our house. Charlie marked the outlines of the designated playing area with those shoes. After the game I saw Charlie picking up the shoes alone. The pachucos saw him as they walked away. They turned and started back towards him. I found some courage and went back to the field to help him. The two adults who drove us to the park and our entire team were waiting near the cars. They were about forty yards away. They were watching us but made no move to help. Charlie showed grim determination and continued picking up the shoes. He had thrown a football into the back of the head of the largest pachuco during the game, and it was that pachuco who was nearest Charlie when he and I picked up the last shoes. For the first time Charlie noticed that I was standing by him. He told me not to say anything as we headed back to the cars with the washtub full of shoes and the football team at our backs. Charlie was "running" because I was there. He got me off the field but not before the gang's shortest member, the "jellybean," kicked me lightly in the butt. Charlie told me not to do anything. As we neared the cars and the pachucos drifted away, David, a boy Charlie's age, said to me, "I wouldn't let a punk like that kick me in the ass!" but I knew who the greater coward was.

The jellybean method of finding an excuse to beat somebody up has a lot of variations. The most common requires that the shortest kid in a gang pick a fight with a non-gang member. When the non-gang member fights back the whole gang beats him up for attacking someone smaller than himself. In a more recent variation, a black kid repeatedly pushes a white kid. When the white kid pushes back, the black kid's large white friend emerges from around a near corner, calls the white kid a racist and the two friends beat up the white kid. There are many craven ways of setting yourself up to be the "hero."

Charlie and I once went to a movie at the "Lyric," a theater our parents didn't like us to attend. It was the theater Mexicans attended. We sat under the balcony. In the darkness something wet fell on our heads. After a moment, we realized it was spit. We looked up and two heads drew back. I wanted to leave, but Charlie told me to stay seated. He got up and walked up to the dark balcony, the pachuco section of the theater, and came back. There was no more spitting. Was that a fight?

The coaches at Salpointe were tough. One, Coach Lutz, told us that, when he was in college football, some of the football players, after practice, entered the rushing shower naked together with leather straps and beat each other until there was only one player left in the shower. They played this game repeatedly. Coach Lutz said he always won. He had four daughters he raised like boys. They were said to be incapable of tears.

Another coach's son, who was also raised like a Spartan, was arrested in the performance of an armed robbery in a supermarket. The local television news filmed the "hostage situation" through the front glass wall. The shoppers and clerks were lying on their stomachs on the floor with their hands behind their heads. The robbers "gave" after the store was surrounded by police cars. Did they lose a fight?

One fight I was in took place in college. It occurred at a party that was thrown by a family that included a deranged man who had sequestered a bottle of Irish whiskey under a note that said, "Don't touch this. It belongs to Carl." I poured a drink from the bottle. Deranged Carl came up behind me and bit me hard on the shoulder. I hit him. Several friends of his at the party grabbed both of us and pinned us down. After a minute I was told that, if I could control myself, they would let me up. I said I could. As soon as I was let up I started swinging again. Someone punched me hard in the nose, and there were several other blows. I was thrown out the back door unconscious. Someone picked me up out of the barren, dry, dusty Tucson dirt and drove me to a hospital where I was treated. The nurse who treated me advised me to hire a thug to beat up my assailants. I didn't know any thugs at the time. My nose is slightly but permanently bent.

When Dad was a freshman at UA, he and a large number of his classmates entered into a brawl with a large number of the sophomores who had been initiating them. They fought their way into the UA's extensive cactus garden. He claimed that 30 students had to go to the infirmary to have the more intractable spines removed from their bodies. As I've indicated, some cactus thorns are thick, hooked, serrated, and viciously hard to remove. The number of wounded ended this fight. Dad told us the cactus garden story many times. It was the closest thing he had to a war story. He hadn't fought in WWII. The army, navy, coastguard and airforce had rejected him in succession because of his asthma. (How did they learn of his asthma?)

His much older and only brother, whom he idolized, had been killed in WWI in a fall from an airplane while dropping leaflets over France. No one knows what the leaflets said or how my uncle managed to fall out of the plane. He fell through a snow of leaflets. Mom told us this story. I went to see my uncle's name on a plaque in a chapel at Harvard decades later. My uncle's name appears there along with the names of several Harvard students killed in the war. The plaque says, "They sacrificed their lives," as though they died on purpose in a way that was holy. They presumably died with their integrity intact. Was my uncle's fall in war a fight?

On "The Friday Night Fights" Carmen Basilio was my favorite fighter. He almost always beat his opponents. He beat Sugar Ray Robinson who beat "The Raging Bull," Jake LaMotta. Boxing fans still argue about who would have won in a head-on contest between Carmen and LaMotta. Basilio won his fights because of his astonishing courage and ability to endure pain. He always looked worse at the end of a fight than the men he defeated.

I know of a bullfight which a courageous bull won. My mother and the rest of us were in Tijuana. The first fight had the bull vomiting blood. It was like water coming out of a faucet. It

85

took a long time and many sword thrusts for the crouching animal to die. It was disgusting. Someone had spilled beer down my back. I was hot and sticky. My mother started laughing, as she almost always did when things got difficult. At my urging, we all decided to go. On the way back to Long Beach the radio news announced that, in the second fight that day, for the first time in fifty years in the Tijuana bullring, a bull had been spared for its bravery.

Matadors can be as brave as bulls. One was gored in the groin recently in Mexico City. Limping heavily, he picked up his cape and sword and insisted on finishing the fight. He killed the bull cleanly. Then he fainted and was carried off on a stretcher. Word was sent from the infirmary that one of his testicles had been crushed and had to be removed.

As a boy, the closest I ever came to showing the courage expected of boys in the 50s was when I and my younger brothers sneaked into the semi-processed-sewage-water hazards on the golf course at night feeling for golf balls to sell back to the golfers the next day. The ball collecting stopped when we were caught in the beam of a security guard's flashlight. We squatted with only our eyes and noses above water for perhaps twenty minutes while the flashlight went round and round the hazard. We decided to fight the security guard, even though we knew he might have a gun. We jumped up screaming and ran at him. He ran away, and we slid through our hole in the fence. Was this a fight? The flashlight bearer turned out to be a neighbor boy playing a prank. We were stiff with cold. We stank. Whether we swam in the hazards or the arroyo, we were lucky we didn't get polio.

Was Emile's and my shoving match at camp a fight? Shortly afterwards, we began to hang out with each other. When we were fifteen Emile and I had become good friends, even though I still denied his assertions about bums in the arroyo. (Could the bums' sexual abuse of struggling children be considered a fight?) We stopped arguing, but, when he visited me, he would walk down Via Riachuelo, which followed the course of the arroyo, to my house. He usually walked with a thick stick of mesquite in his hand. He always hid it behind some cactus before he knocked at our front door.

Charlie was a great older brother. He always looked out for me, as I've shown. In fact, once, he let me beat him up. He was curious, I think, to see what I would do if he fell again and again before my blows. It took me a long time to realize that he was letting me win. Until then, I felt wonderfully powerful. Was that a fight?

School Days II

When my father died a eulogy appeared on the front page of Tucson's principal newspaper. It presented my father as the kind of <u>Last Hurrah</u>, old-timey politician whose favors kept poor people afloat and all the voting blocs in harmony. The article said my father frequently gave down-on-their-luck politicians handouts. In the end he could have used a few handouts himself. I dreamed he was secretly alive and living in a dingy, third-rate hotel, looking for work. He was in Purgatory. I would talk to him and tell my mother that I had seen him. She was always pleased, but I felt terribly sorry for him with his gray obscure existence. It seemed unfair after his earlier prominence.

I knew my father didn't wear a scapular, which would have allowed him to go straight to heaven. Instead he'd be living his drab afterlife for many, many years. I decided to make a Plenary Indulgence on my father's behalf. I set about performing the specified spiritual tasks in exchange for which, it was promised, all my father's remaining time in Purgatory would be cancelled. A priest, a good man, talked me out of it. This was Father Neal, known to be the toughest priest at Salpointe. We respected him enormously because he won a hand-to-hand fight with Coach Lutz. Father Neal fought him over an athlete who was supposed to be in detention, not on the practice field. The coach probably had fifty pounds on Father Neal.

Father Neal told me it was almost impossible to say with sufficient attentiveness the prayers that fulfilled a Plenary Indulgence. I stopped saying the prayers. A Plenary Indulgence was, apparently, like the tricky promise of the scapular for privileged entry into heaven. If a dying person is in mortal sin the scapular burns his flesh until he tears it off. Then he dies and goes to Hell.

These last two sentences are Catholic folklore, not Catholic doctrine. As Quoron explained, "What's the scapular for, if not to save sinners on their deathbeds?" Quoron also said that it was not possible for anyone to suffer complete solitude without ceasing to exist. I didn't understand, but I got a scapular from Father Towner and wore it continuously until Quoron took it from me many years later.

I was still afraid of the creatures. I suspected they were demons trying to undermine my faith and damn me. I asked Quoron if it was a demon. It didn't answer the question, but it claimed that it had no mean intentions. One Confession Saturday, before any of the priests or other parishioners had arrived, I saw Quoron and Artemis standing before the statue of Mary as I entered the church. They were discussing whether or not I should have what I wanted. Artemis said that I shouldn't. I was afraid that someone else would come into the church while Artemis was standing there naked. She saw me. She smiled and coyly put her right arm and hand over her breasts and her left hand over her pubis like Botticelli's Birth of Venus (reproduced in CGG), turned and walked out the door. Quoron told me that I should be careful of her because "If you touch her she will knock you down hard. Her object is to make you afraid to approach women." When I was alone in the church, still standing before the statue of the Virgin, I realized, temporarily, that Artemis and the children of animals didn't exist.

When I started high school my hallucinations became more sporadic. I was able to enter into some group activities. In the year in which I was on the high school debate team we argued the issue "Resolved: the United States should establish a Federal World Government," an outlandish proposal perfect for high school students. Later, I took up dramatic recitation, which didn't require me to speak extemporaneously or think. When I was a senior, I was the lead in the class play. The female lead was Barbara Wysch, the neighborhood girl with whom we had fist fights when we were toddlers.

I saw Sister Ann Marie, the director of the play and other high school speech activities, sometime after I graduated. She was running a bookstore. When I recognized her, she hushed me, telling me she didn't want her employees to know she was an ex-nun. We went outside to talk. It was a shock to find out that she had married. I didn't ask her if she still went to church.

Leaving the bookstore, thinking about her as I walked the next few blocks, I suddenly found myself under water. The same muted light one sees at the bottom of a swimming pool when the sun is shining brightly spread over me. I seemed to be walking as one walks through water or through a dream. The heat of the summer cooled notably. I looked up and saw a nearly complete twenty or thirty story office building covered with reflective glass opposite another shorter office building that reflected the light from the first building. The direct sunlight was blocked by the shorter building. I stood at the bottom of the well between the two buildings. A few days later the new glass building's windows began to break under the impact of birds fooled by the mirrored blue light.

I was the shadow of the waxwing slain
By the false azure of the windowpane.
I was the smudge of ashen fluff and I
Lived on, flew on, in the reflected sky.

Most imaginative people, like Nabokov, whose poem I just quoted, remain realistic in their personal lives. Brian Steen was the most imaginative kid at Salpointe, but he wasn't realistic. He had a million dreams and rarely tried to make any of them come true because he needed the time to have more dreams. One dream he did try to make happen was that of becoming a major league baseball player. He had no talent for baseball. He was not a member of the Salpointe team. Nor did he play in any of the leagues sponsored by the City. He hadn't even gone out for Little League when he was younger. But he did volunteer to be a batboy for the Cleveland Indians during their spring training in Tucson. If he hustled, he imagined, the manager of the Indians might notice him and admire his hustle and make him a member of the team.

Brian's mother had died when he was five. Brian's father, a wealthy lawyer, had no patience with all of the unrealistic ideas Brian came up with. Demonstrating his bitterness, Brian's father left a will that allowed Brian one hundred dollars a week forever. Being a lawyer, he was careful to leave no loopholes. He said in the will that its purpose was to give Brian an opportunity to find a job that suited him before inflation whittled away the meager inheritance.

When his father died Brian was incapable of holding a job and was soon unable to pay rent. He became one of the homeless. He tried to kill himself with some kind of sleeping pills. When he woke up he had lain on one of his arms so long that it was completely numb. He couldn't move it. He never regained the ability to do so. I don't know where Brian is or if he is alive or dead.

Jess, another friend from Salpointe immigrated to the United States from Mexico. His whole family picked fruit and vegetables in California for a while. The boss on one farm, a Greek, hated and abused Mexicans and backed Jess's father down in a prospective fight while the children watched. Jess hated white people. He told me so on more than one occasion. He scared me badly, until he explained that his idea of "white people" didn't include me. I wasn't complimented, but I was relieved.

Jess was from Sinaloa. He had come to the United States while in grammar school speaking no English at all. He spoke it fluently by the time I got to know him. The only sign of an accent was a slight nasal quality that he seemed to think was part of native English pronunciation. Jess was enrolled in Salpointe, but he also earned money doing odd jobs during school time for the priests. Among other things, he drove the school's ancient garbage truck, which he later told me humiliated him deeply. We didn't even notice him driving the truck and, if we had, we would have been impressed.

I was more like Brian than I was like Jess. Once, Jess was put in a paddy wagon after being arrested for shoplifting. Jess knew he was destined for Fort Grant if he couldn't find a way to escape. So he started cursing and spitting at the policemen through a wire mesh that separated the cab from the prisoners' carriage behind it. He cursed and spit for a long time. Finally the policemen stopped the paddy wagon under some palo verdes by the side of the road, pulled Jess out of the back into a dry arroyo, and beat him up so badly they were afraid to take him in.

He ended up in Fort Grant anyway a year later. Arthur, his close friend, preceded Jess into Fort Grant. When Jess arrived some of the inmates formed a circle around him, hitting and debasing him in various cruel ways. Arthur was in the circle, and, though he didn't hit Jess, he pretended he was enjoying the show. Three weeks before his release date Jess was planning an escape. He didn't follow through, but he told me of his escape plan as a way of showing me how awful Fort Grant was. Kids who misbehaved were beaten savagely. As I indicated, the kids hurt each other just for fun.

When they were free and using alcohol again, Jess and Arthur hung out with a middle-aged man named "Happy Hal." They allowed Happy Hal to suck their cocks in exchange for drugs. Sometimes, instead of the cock sucking, he would have them shove gerbils up his ass inside a small cardboard tube fitted with a cardboard plunger like a huge syringe. Jess told me that one of the priests in a nearby church had come to Happy Hal's house and asked for fellatio. The priest had presumably heard about Happy Hal in the confessional where priests often get useful information. Happy Hal was indignant and ordered the priest off his property. Jess got a steady girlfriend. He tried to convince her to watch Happy Hal suck his cock so that she could see the best way to do it. She refused.

Jess played the saxophone and was full of stories about the time he spent on the streets of New York where he went at the age of sixteen to try his hand at big time jazz, that is, avant-garde jazz. He lived on the street, running out on restaurant and delicatessen bills and breaking open parking meters with a crowbar for the change. He worked his way into some jazz circle headed by a famous musician and was eventually given his chance when the musician invited him to join in a set, telling him to jump in on a specified bar. Jess did not hear correctly and failed to jump in, waiting for a bar that did not show up before the piece was finished. The musician asked him why he didn't play. Jess explained. The musician invited him to jump in on the next piece. Jess was so embarrassed he declined the opportunity. That was the only chance he had in New York. Jess was very brave, but his pride crippled him. He could play beautiful, mellifluous music, but he chose to make peculiar and hair-raising sounds according to principles of coordination that were a mystery to me. Years later he took up drums. When he played, I was pleased to hear the sound of a rattling garbage truck.

Arthur was a painter, a good one. He sold paintings to Charlie and Happy Hal. Everyone who saw it was impressed with Arthur's work. He was also a composer and guitarist. He never played or painted again after he went back to heroin. He wasn't a Salpointer. He attended a very tough school, Pueblo, where he developed criminal attitudes that eventually led to his murder.

Byron had nearly flunked out of school. At some point in our senior year he became scornful of me and others in our group. I now think it was because his widowed mother was unable to send him to college where the rest of us were headed, but, at the time, my sore, ridiculously sensitive, lurking conscience told me it was because I hadn't invited him to my party four years before. Someone at Salpointe had scratched "Niger" in the paint on the roof of his tiny car in the school parking lot. The misspelling momentarily delighted Byron. However, he stayed angry and I stayed conscience-stricken for years.

In high school, the only girl I asked out was Sissy. In a taxi, she slid over next to me and I put my arm around her. That was as far as we got. I was struggling to be chaste. We went out regularly for a while, but I was drinking then. Slowly, I began to carouse with my drinking friends instead of going out with Sissy. When I was still going out with Sissy, I started to suffer from acne. When my acne wasn't blooming, I think I was handsome. I think I was more concerned about my appearance than most 13-year-old girls. I didn't at all like the way it looked, but, more significantly, I didn't like the way it felt. The sense that something filthy and unnatural was going on under my skin was almost intolerable. I couldn't go out with Sissy when my face was bad. As my acne became more persistent, I asked her out less and less, until she told me she was going to go out with other boys. When I hadn't gone out with Sissy for a long time, my mother asked me if I didn't like girls. This was in the unlit sunroom at night. The black and white television was on. We were watching the Friday Night Fights. Bobo Olsen was fighting Kid Gavilan, I think. The lights were out. What my mother had just said sounded so ominous that, remembering it, I feel like crying. I said, "Of course I like girls!"

I began drinking in high school. I knew alcohol was supposed to affect the way a person felt. That was an interesting mystery. My first drink, scotch in a clean jelly jar I carried to the arroyo under my shirt, affected the way I felt marvelously. I knew I'd be drinking again and again. At Salpointe I became famous for being drunk. I had an identity! I wasn't smart, but at least I was "the alcoholic." Kids came up to me in the hall, speaking abruptly and at length about their drunken weekends; I was the chosen person to receive boasts of drunkenness.

Just before graduation, it was the custom for the junior class to put on a skit at the senior class banquet lampooning members of the graduating senior class. A student pretending to be drunk stumbled onto the stage. Everybody knew it was supposed to be me. The audience was full of the nuns and priests who were our teachers. I was quite proud.

After we graduated from high school, Sissy announced that she and Byron were engaged to be married. Joe had been living with Sissy in a small apartment she had rented. Byron dropped by the apartment one night. He and Sissy went for a walk and she didn't return until late the next day. Joe left Sissy's apartment to live elsewhere. Byron took his place. Sissy made her announcement in a restaurant, our group's sometimes hangout. Others who already knew of the engagement sat close by. I was instantly painfully jealous, for I loved Sissy very much. I said, "You're going to marry that Nigger?!" and regretted it as I stood up and walked out. That was the beginning of my lovelorn years. The engagement was soon canceled, but that didn't give me the courage to approach Sissy, even when she began showing an interest.

Proust says the feelings of the lovelorn, when they are strong and persistent, are brought about by the lover imagining a vague, vast, pure, exalted world his beloved and other noble personages inhabit and that he is shut out of. That was to be my fate for a few awful years.

Byron called off the marriage when he decided to enter the army; he felt that, being in the army, he would face too much prejudice if he had a beautiful white wife. Back then he could very possibly have been killed and Sissy raped. Later I heard that he had become a religious fanatic and was on the psych ward of the Veterans' Hospital. Again, I blamed myself. I went to visit him. I reminded him of his obligation as a Christian to forgive me and apologized again for not having invited him to my party when we were in grade school six years earlier. He realized then that he had a hold over me. He hesitated. I reminded him again of his obligation, and he said, "I forgive you." It didn't do me any good, I soon discovered.

English Literature

When I entered the UA, my thinking was less confused for a little while. I had almost no hallucinations. I was frightened by Charlie's prior failure; Charlie drank himself out of school. I gave up alcohol and studied hard. I was admitted to the Honors English Program.

The Honors Program classes had an excellent teacher, Doctor Sean McCann, and were conducted like a seminar. There were only five students, and one was Sissy, who asked to sit in when she found out I was in the class. She asked if she could type one of my papers. I accepted her offer. She was paying a lot of attention to me, as though she were courting me, as I suppose she was. After Byron broke up with her, I think she desperately wanted to get married.

I always had the most extravagant ideas about the things we read, and Doctor McCann loved it. English Literature was like the mountains for me, Wordsworth especially. There were moments when I saw Beauty in an almost Platonic sense. I realized right away that we were being asked to read lots of bad poetry, that Wordsworth wrote lots of bad poetry, but for those moments of Beauty it was worth it. Doctor McCann told us, "If you aim high you have farther to fall. The best poets also tend to be the worst."

After achieving some success, I became less afraid of suffering Wayne's and Charlie's fate, both of whom dropped out of school and joined the Navy. I began using alcohol again. I used drugs for the first time. Drugs were fashionable. I liked amphetamines. There was a brand of nose drops sold over the counter, Sulfidex, which contained thirty-five milligrams of methamphetamine, the best of the amphetamines. The medicine was thick and snot-like. It tasted awful. I learned to shove a peeled banana into my mouth and mash and swallow it as soon as I had swallowed the Sulfidex. This usually drove away the revolting taste. For years, after they took Sulfidex off the shelves, I couldn't stand the taste of bananas. We used Y-amine asthma inhalers. We broke them open and swallowed the wet cotton inside. They produced an amphetamine-like high but left an uncomfortably medicinal, minty taste. We tried squeezing the cotton out into a spoon, and drawing the liquid into a homemade syringe. When we injected the Y-amine the same taste was there, but on the inside of our tongues. Either way, the Y-amine gave you gas. Both effects were as long lasting as the high. Of course, we had recourse to a variety of codeine cough syrups.

I was eventually addicted to amphetamines. Charlie used amphetamines. So did my mother. She used to ask me to go to the drugstore for her. I would pick up her time-release capsules of Dexedrine, open all the capsules, which were opaque on one end and transparent on the other, and spill their contents into a bowl, Then I would stuff a bit of cotton in the opaque end and repack the capsules with the time-release contents minus the halves left in the bowl, which I consumed. All the drugs I've mentioned diminished my fear of Hell and my hallucinations for a couple of hours. So did alcohol.

My mother relied on the counsel of priests. She often visited Monsignor Gramore, the Rector of St. Anthony and John's Church in the next parish. He was the one who got her through amphetamine withdrawal. Neither of them knew he was doing that. Back then, doctors prescribed amphetamines for everything from being overweight to being depressed. Mom suffered from a bitter resentment against my father for years. Monsignor Gramore helped her with this as well. He was a good man. Monsignor Hughes' advice from his death bed prevented my mother from selling our house at a disastrously low price. My mother's reliance on priests was a good thing. She did well by them.

My amphetamine addiction robbed me of my ability to write my senior essay. Luckily this was not a requirement for graduation. The amphetamines also cost me a three-year fellowship that I'd won. I resigned the fellowship because I was too crazy to go to school anymore. It was one of those fellowships instituted by the Federal government after Sputnik to help Americans catch up with the Russians educationally. English Literature, my fellowship area, didn't seem to have much to do with rocket science, but there it was. Now it was gone. However, I was about to graduate Phi Beta Kappa and with "Highest Honors," and that was enough proof that I was smart.

It was around this time that I first tried heroin. Jess gave me some. It was perfect, with no side effects, no discernible particle of compulsion or addiction after one use. It had a bitter metallic taste and smell, but they disappeared quickly. The heroin high completely erased my fear of Hell and my hallucinations for a full eight hours. I was a daily communicant throughout my college years. After I tried heroin, I stopped going to church, but I didn't stop believing.

Work

In a stunted try for independence the summer after I graduated from college, I moved out of the old house and took a job as night clerk at the Hotel Arizona, formerly the theater where "heladotin" was coined. There were ten rooms ranging in price from fifty cents to six dollars a night. My pay was that I got to live in one of the fifty-cent rooms. I ate old k-rations I'd been given by someone fresh out of the marines.

My first night at the desk, a handsome, young, neatly dressed cowboy came in and took the six-dollar room. Then he asked, with great *savoir-faire*, if we had any "young ladies." At first, I didn't understand what he was asking. I said we didn't have any that I knew of. Next, a nervous bald white man in a white suit came in, followed not too closely by a fat young black woman. The man shyly asked me if they could register as man and wife. He might as well have asked me to pee in a bathtub.

I righteously replied, "Only if you *are* man and wife." They left. If they had simply claimed that they were married I would have let them sign the register as a married couple, if we'd had a register. If I had procured for the cowboy or knowingly allowed the suited man to fuck a prostitute in one of the rooms it would have been a mortal sin. I told my boss the next night what had happened. He looked at me with pity. That was my second and last night on the job.

Jess and Arthur were my partners in crime. I was always careful to let them commit the crimes while I watched. They laughed at my Catholicism often, but my brief stint as night attendant at the Hotel Arizona kept them going for days.

Two weeks after I left the job, the new night attendant was murdered. Three men entered the hotel and told the attendant to open the cash box. The attendant explained that he didn't have the key. The robbers mashed him with a shotgun blast and ran off with the box. This seemed to justify my piety. It quieted Jess and Arthur.

After I moved back home, I got another job. I worked the night shift in a convenience store. I didn't do much. The night was punctuated by strange events and was otherwise a terrible bore. Every night I worked, retarded Raymond Edmund came in and talked at length about his dead parents and about being an Atheist. He thought it would be impossible for everybody to rise from the dead because the sky would be full of their bodies and they would get stuck in airplane propellers. That was his argument showing there was no God. He sure hoped his parents weren't up there, he said.

One morning, at about 1:30 a.m. two very tough looking men came in, walked to the back of the store where the beer was, picked out two stacks of cases, and walked out without paying, daring me to try to stop them, while, behind the counter, I shouted after them that it was after one o'clock and I couldn't sell them alcoholic beverages. I thought of Bobby Rodriguez and did nothing further. When I called the owner, he and his wife came down. I told them what had happened, and the wife, who was a police academy candidate, sneered at me. I blushed so hard I could feel my face.

When I was still in college, Ed's mother, with whom he lived, moved without leaving a note or address while Ed was spending a weekend away with a friend. He came home and found no one and nothing in the house. However, he could afford an apartment of his own. He had applied for and received Social Security Disability on the grounds that his years in a reformatory for stealing cars were the result of a permanent mental disturbance. I believe he found a cooperative psychiatrist. Until twenty some years ago, I was envious of Ed's not having to work.

I have never learned the correct mental attitude that allows work to be tolerable for any length of time. A job I had in college writing lectures for a professor was as intolerable as any of the other jobs I've had. So it didn't seem to me a matter or not whether I was intellectually challenged. I have been a cook in a drive-in theater snack bar, a gatherer and mover of clothing and accessories in a Lerner's clothing store, an unsuccessful real estate agent, several times a janitor, a printer, a packager for a mail order company, a paperboy, a house painter, twice a security guard, a proofreader for a rubber stamp company, a warehouse worker, and the copy editor of a book that proposed to teach English to Navajos, all minimum wage jobs. I was fired from most of the jobs I've listed here, including my job as a paperboy.

I've had other jobs that I'll discuss later. It was all like running in a sauna.

Hippydom

After I graduated from the University in 1967 and had been fired from my jobs, I began withdrawing from amphetamines, opiates and alcohol. I had been a scholastic and drug and alcohol recluse and had minimum social skills. Nevertheless, I went off to San Francisco to find Sissy and enter the new bohemian world. She had invited me in a letter, saying we could get an apartment together. She was staying with an old schoolmate, Sandy, whose apartment was across the Panhandle from the corner of Haight and Ashbury. When I got to San Francisco, I asked Sissy to make a "commitment" to me. Don't ask me what I expected her to do, declare her love, perhaps. She, of course, said no, and that seemed to be the end of the prospect of living carnally with her. Broke and incapable of making friends among the tens of thousands of hippies, I ended up walking the filthy streets bumming cigarettes and begging for change, but the days when panhandling could keep food in your mouth were long gone. I remember eating a wedge of cantaloupe that had fallen off a garbage truck.

Haight-Ashbury, where I lived, had become a dangerous place by then. One night, with some other folks, I walked out of a crowded store on Haight into a cloud of tear gas and a mass of people running down the street. The police chasing them turned and shouted to those of us standing on the sidewalk to go home. I walked back into the store. Outside, I thought I might be mistaken for a rioter. One hippy, who had thrown a bottle at the police, was running at top speed down the sidewalk with a cop on a motorcycle speeding down the sidewalk behind him.

Some drugged hippies with nothing better to do had started randomly breaking windows. The other hippies on the street that night decided to imitate them. Somebody supposed the hippies were demonstrating against an injustice. There was no injustice, real or imagined. There was no demonstration. When the crowd dispersed I finally obeyed the cops. I walked home, which for me was the front porch of a nearby apartment house. The newspapers the next day referred to the rioters as "demonstrators" but couldn't say what their cause was.

Two days later my mother sent me a check for Social Security funds I should have received while I was in school. My mother had managed to get the Social Security officials to issue my checks in her name while I was in college. She repented and sent the sum to Sandy's address, which I had given her before I left Tucson. Sissy managed to find me and give me the envelope with the check in it. Sissy didn't know what the envelope contained. She had her own apartment by then. She was apparently disturbed by the circumstances in which she found me and offered to put me up. I moved in with her. I never came near having enough courage to try to slip into her bed. Besides, she got a cold. She couldn't smell and kept asking me if the cat box smelled. I said no. Her cold lifted and she smelled the cat shit and kicked me out.

Some days after Sissy kicked me out, I was sitting alone in Sandy's apartment when the phone rang. It was Sissy. She said, "You know, every time someone meets you the first thing out of their mouths after you leave is 'Boy, that guy really needs to get laid.'" I screamed, "Whore!" and hung up. The image of Sissy as a purple sea anemone drawing in its arms in an instant reflex passed through my mind.

Nathan, an acquaintance of mine, was also in San Francisco. He was an unusual person. I had first known him at the UA. In San Francisco, I bumped into him on the street. He was involved in a project to get his fellow hippies to stop saying "Out of sight" and start saying "Outer sight" instead. I forget his reasons. After Sissy kicked me out, I moved in with Nathan. Nathan lived with his brother and his brother's friend, both students of ballet. We lived in San Francisco's tenderloin. It was full of prostitutes, pimps and male and female go-go dancers.

Nathan told me he had run across Sissy and she had said, in the course of their conversation, that she loved me but that I was sexless. He insisted that I not tell her what he had just told me. I said I wouldn't and immediately headed off to her apartment. It was not my intention to break my word to Nathan, and I didn't. I arrived very late and rang Sissy's buzzer. She stuck her head out the window two stories up, looked at me, shut the window and walked away. I called out her name loudly, which embarrassed her. Her neighbors would hear. She reopened the window, told me to stop shouting and buzzed me in. I walked up to her apartment and told her I was in love with her. She told me I had no chance. I said "Well, I guess I'll just have to forget about you then."

She said, "You won't be able to forget about me. You'll have to wait until it goes away."

"Maybe I can get a girlfriend," I said

"If you can find one," she said with sneering skepticism. It struck me that she was being pretty ugly.

Her reception of me and her gloating meanness convinced me that Nathan had called her to tell her I was coming and why. He didn't want anybody to think that he was uncool.

I avoided drugs in San Francisco because I was poor and frightened. They had begun to exacerbate my delusions instead of diminishing them. My desire to get away from drugs was much of the reason I was in San Francisco in the first place. Drugs, of course, were plentiful there, but I was afraid of the hippies selling them. I even avoided drugs after I got my check. However, I bought a flute. I tried to figure out how to play it, with some success. Later, I had a teacher, Jess.

The Draft

I left San Francisco the first time because I received a forwarded letter ordering me to take my draft physical in Phoenix . In Phoenix all the potential draftees were housed in a YMCA on cots spread across a large hall. I and a black who played the song "Bugaloo Down Broadway" over and over again on a portable record player were avoiding the boisterous group of white youths trading tales of manliness and crime in the center of the hall. I was by myself on a cot set in a leftover space beneath the wall clock. There were no other cots near it. The black was across the room, also alone. I was lying on my cot with my face to the wall unable to sleep by reason of the loud talk and repetitive music. Suddenly, I felt my cot jar violently and leaped out of bed. One of the manly crowd was standing on the head rail of my cot pretending to do something to the clock. He was taunting me, a loner.

Unlike most young men I hadn't discussed escaping the draft with anyone. As I said, I had been an obsessively studious, antisocial university student for the previous four years. Now I had to face questions I'd simply ignored before. Surprisingly, as a war protester, I'd never once imagined myself facing the draft. If the young men in the center of the room had been discussing draft evasion, and I had had the courage to try to join in their discussion, I might have gotten some ideas. Instead, all I got was a forecast of myself as the isolated, taunted resident of an army barracks.

The next day, after breakfast, I and a couple of others who hadn't gotten enough sleep were lying down on the waiting room benches before our physicals. A very mean looking officer screamed in our faces, "Sit up!" It was like being jerked up by a rope. My Lai had happened but hadn't hit the papers yet. However, returning veterans were spreading that story and numerous other detailed horror stories about events in Vietnam. One returning soldier bragged to Jess that he had helped "cut off a Gook's kneecaps." Jess told the soldier to get out of the house. Most young men knew that something awful was going on. The mean looking officer's order seized me so suddenly and violently that I realized I would almost certainly do anything I was ordered to do in the army. I realized that my cowardice would control me utterly. Moreover, I feared that by being in Vietnam, helping to kill Vietnamese, I would be in a constant state of mortal sin. At the same time, I would be at an abnormally high risk of corporeal death. Dying in mortal sin would put me in Hell. Evading the draft, as far as I could tell, was not a mortal sin, and it would remove me from physical danger. A week before my session with the draft board, I had a devastating revelation on a San Francisco bus that if I served in Vietnam, I, alone, would be responsible for the Vietnam War.

Those were my motives for deciding to dodge the draft. But I didn't know how I was going to do it. As a prelude to the physical, we were given a short psychological inventory to fill out. Among other things, it asked respondents if they were homosexuals. I knew that homosexuals weren't allowed in the army, but the presence and forthrightness of the question surprised me. "Are you a homosexual?" it said. I was even more surprised when I checked "yes." The act carried much more guilt then than it might now, but many draft candidates escaped in this manner. Because I avoided induction in such a degrading way, I would never, I hoped, be able to pretend that my behavior was the product of idealism. The idealism, the intellectualized hatred and self-righteousness of the war protestors with whom I had marched, disturbed me. I knew I might be tempted to engage in homosexual acts to try to legitimize my lie. To avoid this I renewed my lifelong vow of celibacy, the seriousness of which had waned with time, though I had honored it with respect to copulation theretofore. The temptation to become a homosexual stayed with me through the years and was almost overwhelming when homosexuals gained victim status.

When we got to the physical part of the exam, we took off our clothes. We all had bodies that were much too fat or much too skinny. Many of us had numerous blemishes on our backs and chests. We were ugly naked, except for one Mexican who apparently worked out, a rarity in those days. We went through the humiliation of bending over and pulling our buttocks apart as the examiners looked up our anuses. They took blood samples and took our blood pressure. Finally we arrived at a table where several doctors reviewed with us the forms we had filled out that morning. The doctor who interviewed me looked at me with disgust, told me I'd receive notice of the draft board's decision in the mail, and dismissed me. It was an odd sort of relief I felt a week later when I received the letter telling me I had been exempted from the draft. I knew that what I had done would mortify me for a long time.

My brother, Sammy, beat the draft without subterfuge. He answered the call to the medical examination but defied the examiners, telling them his opinion of the war and refusing to fill out the written inventory. Back in Tucson, several weeks after the ordeal, he received notice of his draft exemption. Apparently the army was having a lot of trouble with rebellious war opponents in their ranks and did not want another. Memo followed the same route, obediently showing up for the examination but then showing open defiance. My draft dodging crippled me. Their draft avoidance didn't cripple them. What they did was not the same as what I had done.

When I was teaching, my kids suspected me of homosexuality, especially the aggressive sluts who occasionally approached my desk after class. I felt like Clint Walker in "Paint your Wagon." He plays the part of the Sheriff. Kim Novak, the hussy, comes up to him and asks in a forlorn voice, "Don't you like me, Sheriff?"

Clint Walker answers, "Just 'cause I uphold the law, Ma'am, don't mean I'm peculiar."

I believe God doesn't hold me to account for being peculiar, if I am such, because I haven't committed any peculiar acts. However, he may well hold me accountable for evading the draft. Most of the guilt I felt before I set about killing my conscience came from the thought that someone went in my place. Perhaps I, a college graduate, would have been put to work as an officer's clerk. If so my draft dodging may have allowed some soldier to escape combat by becoming a clerk in my place. None of the many scenarios I dreamed up to excuse myself was helpful. I no longer pretend there was some specific person who filled the vacancy that I created by my draft evasion. No doubt a large group of draft dodgers and avoiders necessitated the call-up of a large group of new candidates for the draft, and among the latter, some died. That conclusion wasn't helpful either, of course. What was helpful was the knowledge that the law required men to go into the army, but the facts didn't. The ease with which I, Sammy and Memo beat the draft proved it. We all had an opportunity to step out of line and took it.

And how is my horror of Communism to be reconciled with my evasion of the draft during the Vietnam War? Do I oppose violence generally whichever side engages in it? No. Am I a hypocrite? I don't care. I stand by what I did then and what I believe now.

Forth and Back Again and Again

When I returned to San Francisco a few weeks after my physical, I was steadily psychotic. Byron, with severe mental problems of his own, accompanied me. We hitchhiked from Tucson. Rides were hard to come by then. We had to sleep one freezing night in a gardeners' closet just outside the military base at San Luis Obispo. I used a frozen, coiled hose for a mattress. The next day a man picked us up and propositioned us. When we turned him down, he stopped and let us off. I hadn't felt the slightest temptation to have sex with Byron and the man.

When we reached Salinas, Byron tried to talk me into hopping a freight to Canada. I didn't want to go to Canada. Byron insisted that I go to Canada to escape the draft. I told him I'd already escaped the draft. Still, he insisted. I refused several more times before we resumed hitchhiking to San Francisco.

We got another ride. About 60 miles outside San Francisco Byron became very sick. Our ride took us to a hospital. After Byron and I were dropped off at the hospital, Byron immediately ceased to be sick. I think Byron was trying to keep me away from Sissy. In response to my call Sandy drove the sixty miles to pick us up and bring us to San Francisco.

When Sandy was dying of cancer in Tucson some years later, she told me she was angry because she felt people had used her all her life. She said other people hadn't shown the same interest in her that she had in them. She said this was something she had never complained about before, but now that she was dying she was bitter. I suggested that she hadn't been courageous enough to complain, that her San Francisco-style generosity was the product of cowardice. Then I tried to convert her to Christianity. I was not a Christian at the time.

I left San Francisco again a few months after Sandy picked us up, because Artemis commanded me to go home. I don't know if the girl in the park who called herself "Artemis" was real or imagined. She was naked and beautiful. Among hippies a naked public appearance wouldn't have been that unlikely, only a little more likely than public fucking. I obeyed her.

I arrived in Tucson and left again two weeks later. This time I traveled to San Francisco with Jess and his innocent Anglo girlfriend. Jess got a "drive back" car. He was to deliver the car to somebody in Oakland. When we got on the highway, Jess suddenly lost control of the car. There was something seriously wrong with the power steering, which turned the car on its own, leaving it to drift for perhaps a second between the moment when the driver turned the steering wheel to correct the car's direction and the moment when the car resumed its course. At my insistence we continued our trip. Jess found he could keep the car under control if he rocked the steering wheel a few inches back and forth continuously. Despite this, a screeching brody left the car parked sideways in the middle of the Pacific Coast Highway near Long Beach. Again I insisted that we continue. Neither Jess nor his girlfriend realized there was something wrong with me. We arrived in San Francisco safely.

One evening in Sissy's apartment in San Francisco, when I visited her with Byron and Jess, Sissy drew Byron, with whom she had long since broken up, behind the open bathroom door and kissed him. Jess later told me that he'd seen her peeking through the juncture of the doorjamb and door to see how I was reacting. When Jess told me this we were on the street. I immediately walked away from him and stopped a stranger who was walking in the opposite direction. I asked the stranger if he was Jesus. He brushed past me wordlessly, which proved he was Jesus and proved He had rejected me. During this period in San Francisco, I became ever lonelier in my delusions. But having Jess there helped. Arthur came to town and that helped too.

After two months in San Francisco with Arthur and me, Jess decided he wanted to return to Tucson. He put his girlfriend on a bus, and he and Arthur began hitchhiking. They didn't have enough money to take a bus themselves. They were taking amphetamines. Jess, who had a bad heart, apparently had some kind of heart attack. Their ride let them off at a hospital in Riverside. Jess, still swooning, told the doctor about the amphetamines. The doctor refused him treatment. Arthur called the doctor a "heartless faggot." The police were called and they took Jess to jail, heart condition and all. Jess was given a hearing without a jury and the judge sentenced him to six months for violation of some county drug ordinance. Jess spent the first day of his sentence writing a long letter to the judge explaining that the sentence would prevent him from entering school in Tucson as he had planned, a lie. In Jess's jail cell there were several prisoners, including two young, well-muscled inmates who were brothers. One day, one of the brothers was telling a story of having anally raped a teenage prisoner so violently that the teenager bled. The others in the cell were laughing. Jess didn't laugh, and the prisoner telling the story noticed and asked why. Jess growled that he didn't think it was funny.

The prisoner surmised that Jess was "one of them" and said, "Tomorrow you're gonna suck my cock." The other prisoners expressed interest and the storyteller told them they could "have some, too."

The next morning, after breakfast, Jess was separated from the other prisoners for his required haircut. When the barber turned his back Jess grabbed and pocketed a pair of sharp-pointed scissors. After the haircut, he was led back to his cell where the other prisoners were sitting on their bunks grinning at him. Before Jess had a chance to show his scissors, a guard came and told him to get his things. While getting his things Jess slipped the scissors under his mattress. The guard told him the judge was having him released because of his letter. Jess left the jail and finished hitchhiking back to Tucson.

I spent my last six months in San Francisco in a mental institution and a Pentecostal church by turns. I had been walking aimlessly by the Norwalk Neuropsychiatric Institute. I saw the sign, entered, asked to see a psychiatrist, talked to one for about two minutes and was admitted to a ward full of hippies who were the subjects of a study.

The Institute was an appendage of the medical school of The University of California at Berkley. The accommodations, food and staff were great. Sterling Hayden visited our ward. He was accompanied by his girlfriend who told us she used to go on safaris but was now interested in the hippy way of life. The ward was richly financed. It even had its own television and film studio to allow us to get a look at ourselves. We made awful movies and closed circuit TV productions.

When I worked up the courage I described how sissy treated me to one of the younger psychiatrists at the Institute. He verified my impression by wincing and then tried to hide it with a yawn. I needed verification because, although I often understood the motives of other people, I had no confidence in my conclusions because I wasn't sure other people existed. I was lucky I talked to the young psychiatrist about it. The older ones were practiced in the then fashionable technique of showing no emotional reaction whatsoever to what a patient was telling them, and if they said things to the patient those things were a sort of testing, as though they were prodding him with sticks.

The younger staff, on the other hand, was very personal. They taught, along with some first generation psychobabble, San Francisco-style left-wing politics. This was when I first heard that I was "to own actions" for which I seemed not to be responsible. Such treatment wasn't in the medical textbooks and wouldn't have won the approval of the older psychiatrists.

Numerous creatures pursued me into the Institute. I never told anyone about them. I hoped they were hallucinations, and I didn't want anyone else to tell me he could see them, too. They revealed themselves by their resplendent, turbulent, golden faces. As Lorus explained, the creatures were the children of animals, but not animals themselves. They did what they wanted, but they couldn't choose what they wanted. They were awake, but their behavior wasn't their own. When the creatures became too frightening I could escape them by getting a pass and going to my apartment for a couple of hours. I still had the apartment I'd rented before being hospitalized.

The most familiar creature and sometimes the most frightening was Lorus, itself. It had been with me at the tower and during my earliest episodes of blasphemous thoughts. It urged me to mutter rapid, repeated prayers. My prayers made the creatures laugh loudly. The creatures continued to embarrass me in any way they could. I sometimes hid from them in the

112

concrete utility closet at the top of the stairwell. The closet contained many worms. I noticed that the number of worms grew when I stared at them, so I never stayed in the utility closet for very long, and I usually kept my eyes closed once inside. Lorus told me to stay away from the worms entirely because they caused remorse which would make me deny things outside myself. Lorus picked out two worms that were clinging to me in folds of my wrinkled shirt, threw them to the ground and crushed them. The flattened corpses and stains looked like small, thin, three-fingered hand prints, palm up as though asking for change. There were no more worms or remorse for the rest of the day. Still, I thought that Lorus might be a demon.

I had a rosary I'd found on the sidewalk the week before I was admitted to Norwalk. Whenever I began to suspect that the creatures were demons, I carried the rosary around the ward between my teeth, which made the creatures laugh, embarrassing me again. I clenched down too hard on the frail chain. It broke, a near blasphemy. I felt the holiness leak out over my tongue through the break. I abandoned the rosary.

I was usually still a solipsist. I think that was the only reason why the admitting psychiatrist admitted me. (I didn't tell him about my creatures.) As I said, I believed at times that I was forever alone, that I was everything that existed and that my "senses' presented me with nothing but illusions. I was the only God of the only universe. "Reality" was a churning collection of meretricious fantasies hiding black nothingness. This was Hell, the selfsame fact as my self-centeredness. My solipsism was terrifying when I believed it, far more terrifying than the creatures.

The remotest possibility that a scary idea is fact, its self-consistency, is often enough to convince psychotics of its truth. Believing the possibility is like a revelation: "I see it all now! It all fits! Everybody but me really is a robot!" Only deductive arguments can dissuade a psychotic from his delusions. A psychotic can't adopt contradictory delusions in the same moment. When I thought that the creatures were real my solipsism wasn't credible.

Lorus introduced me to the rest of the creatures as he had introduced me to Aworac and Quoron. There were about thirty. I struggled to give them all names, but they kept distracting and embarrassing me. Their expressions constantly changed. They never looked the same as any of their fellows. Sometimes they made me laugh, and then the names I had so far given them fell out of my head like dandruff. I asked Lorus why the creatures had no names. "We don't use names because we don't have identities or faces," it said, "We only have compliant masks. If we stop mugging we're exactly alike. We can't stand to be alike."

Perhaps I clung to my psychosis because the hallucinations were exciting. I've seen other mentally ill people do this. God commanded a friend of mine to kill a prostitute. He stabbed her twelve times with a large knife. A drug was found that defeated his psychosis, but he often skipped this very effective medication because his delusions were more entertaining than the world. Even when he did take his morning dose he often watched Christian television, which stimulated his imagination and overcame the salubrious effects of the drug. He was frightening at those times. I made him break his UHF dial. I myself liked Christian television, but it wasn't one of the things that called forth my delusions.

Fear of Hell assailed me more and more in Norwalk. A Hindu nurse sat me down and told me that he had had a religious upbringing "even more terrifying" than mine and had gotten over it. His declaration was encouraging because I knew something of the horrors of Eastern religions, unlike most hippies, who ignorantly embraced the various American romantic versions.

A little more helpful was my sudden memory of Hume's refutation of Berkley. If I only know others and other things as ideas, I only know myself as an idea, too. The thought of myself has no more reality or substantiality than any other thought. On the ward at night when I couldn't sleep, I sometimes shouted "I don't exist!" scaring the nurses. All the patients slept in a single dormitory. Some of them always giggled, embarrassing me. Some cursed me, also embarrassing me.

We had occupational therapy three times a week. I made two small round pots streaked and glazed to look like Jupiter. The accidental effects of the mixed glazes were spectacular and not at all like Jupiter. After three sparsely attended writing classes given by a graduate student from Berkeley, I wrote a kind of nursery rhyme and a vignette to cure my frightening egocentricity:

The Huge Head

Once, I feared that everything and you
Were only images in my head.
I told you. You said
If that was so
I was only an image in my head also.
You confounded an image in my head that wasn't true,
A huge head I thought surrounded me and you.

The Case of Maria

There was a case some years ago of a seven-year-old Hindu girl, Maria, who had been raised in a Catholic orphanage in Calcutta. She suddenly started speaking Portuguese. A Brazilian nun at the orphanage identified the language and translated. Maria was claiming to be the Brazilian nun's dead grandmother. The Brazilian nun verified the accuracy of Maria's "memories." The nuns immediately tied the girl to her bed and arranged for an exorcism. Local Hindus got wind of what was going on and protested. They said this was clearly a case of a remembered past incarnation, and exorcism would be blasphemy. The tension between the two groups mounted dangerously. A bystander suggested they ask the "grandmother" whether she was a demon or a past incarnation of Maria.

Now, it is an article of faith that a possessing demon can't lie to a chaste inquisitor. The nuns had consulted the prospective exorcist, a very old priest, who informed them of this truth. The priest interrogated the Brazilian nun and, finding that she did not know about the birds and the bees, agreed to let her ask the question. To be doubly sure of the demon's veracity the nuns insisted on putting a rosary around Maria's neck and drenching her with holy water before the inquisition began. The Hindus consented to this procedure on the condition that they be allowed to place a statue of Ganesh at the foot of the girl's bed. Maria was drenched and a huge statue of the elephant god, which had to be chiseled to fit through the doorway, was set before her. In accordance with the agreed upon formula, the Portuguese nun asked the "grandmother" if she was a demon or a previous incarnation of Maria. After a pause, looking very puzzled, the "grandmother" said, "How would I know?" Five minutes later the babbling girl could no longer speak Portuguese. The nuns untied her.

I stopped shouting, "I don't exist" after I wrote "The Huge Head" and "The Case of Maria," but the poem and story didn't much help my efforts to live outside my head until I reread them years later.

Pilgrim Temple

On Sunday mornings, when nothing was happening at Norwalk, I'd get a pass. Because none of the staff knew about the creatures or worms, I got passes easily. I'd head off to the Pentecostal church in Oakland. On Wednesday evenings, too, there were church services. I'd again head off to Oakland. Whichever day it was, I hitchhiked over the bridge and, getting out on the other side, walked 70 blocks to Pilgrim Temple, otherwise known as Brother Dixon's Assembly.

I visited it the first time on a Sunday. I went there because Byron had told me the congregation didn't believe in Hell, and my attempts to escape my religious fears at the Institute were only moderately and temporarily successful. At Pilgrim Temple, the people believed that, unless you were saved, when you died, you died. Immortality was for those who believed. There were no other alternatives. You either ceased to be or you went to Heaven. I heard Brother Dixon say that belief in Hell was comic. He described savages who had never heard of Christianity jumping up and down, screaming on the burning marl forever. Saying this, Brother Dixon broke into bright laughter, while an itinerant, visiting minister stood by scandalized. The people at Pilgrim Temple took the time to show me that the passages in the New Testament usually thought to refer to Hell were misinterpreted. The church members' case was persuasive. For example, the "worm dieth not" Isaiah 66:24, Mark 9:44 was a description of the finality of death, the "worm" being the corpse worm. I had been raised to believe St Thomas Aquinas, the 13th century theologian recognized as preeminent by the Catholic Church. Aquinas held that the "worm" was a metaphor for eternal remorse, one among many tortures of the damned.

Summa Theologica, Supplement, Question 97 The punishment of the damned, Article 2 The worm of the damned is not corporeal. **Objection 1, Reply to Objection 1**

The people at Pilgrim Temple told me that the story of Dives and Lazarus Luke 16:19 in which Dives goes to Hell was a parable and not intended to be a report of actual events or existing places. Without knowing it, the Pilgrim Temple members reinforced my hope in death; one way or another my pain would end someday, I hoped.

The people at Pilgrim Temple also taught that, "We are saved by faith, and that by grace and not by works, lest any man should boast." Ephesians 2:89. Catholics, contrarily, say, "Faith without works is dead," James 2:26, which means to traditional Protestants, "If you have the gift of faith it will show in your behavior." I hoped the Protestants had it right, but I couldn't lastingly adhere to Pilgrim Temple's position in any of these matters. My religious beliefs weren't susceptible of either reason or desire. I didn't know that I was still a Catholic.

When I was wandering the streets of San Francisco, before I was hospitalized there, I began stopping people and asking them if they believed in Hell. Of those who answered, all without exception said approximately, "No. There's no Hell, unless it's_____ forever." You can fill in the blank with the name of any potentially eternal form of suffering that interests you. It's like room 101 in 1984. I think most people believe in Hell. The people at Pilgrim Temple didn't.

Brother Dixon, an old somewhat tired Southerner, couldn't attend the services in their entirety, but he began each service with a long practical sermon about problems, usually financial, that the church was confronting. Then he would outline some aspect of doctrine, such as avoiding vain ceremony and "the idolatrous filth of Methodism." Then he would give a brief lesson on Church History, for example, "The four canonical gospels were all probably written within living memory of Jesus. None of the Apocrypha was," which was true, I found out when I was no longer a Christian again.

Pilgrim Temple contradicted my Catholicism in many ways. The congregation at Pilgrim Temple used the name "Jesus," for example. Catholics are often embarrassed to say "Jesus." They like to say "Christ" instead. It reminds me of the movie version of Who's Afraid of Virginia Wolf? The producers changed the phrase "angel tits," as written in the stage play, to "angel boobs," in the movie, "angel boobs" being less suggestive of nipples. "Jesus" is a person. He has nipples. "Christ" is an abstraction. "Christ" originally meant "The Anointed." Catholics are similarly averse to using the title "Holy Ghost." Nowadays, usually, Catholic clergy insist that the term "Holy Spirit" be used instead. Fundamentalists usually use "Jesus," "Christ," "Holy Spirit" and "Holy Ghost," without consistency or clear preference. "I ain't ashamed of Jesus! I aint!" I heard a burly, countrified member of Pilgrim Temple declare.

> "Whoever is ashamed of me and my words, the Son of Man will be ashamed of them when he comes in his glory and in the glory of the Father and of the holy angels."
> Luke 9:26

After Brother Dixon finished his sermon and left the church, the real service began; people "got the Holy Ghost." They began with a simple song:

> Victory, oh victory shall be mine.
> Victory, oh victory shall be mine.
> If I hold my peace,
> The Lord will fight my battle.
> Victory, oh victory shall be mine.

They repeated whatever song they picked over and over with their arms raised high in the air, until, in the back of the church odd noises would mix with the singing. The singing would diminish and the odd noises would grow like a mounting wave moving slowly towards the front of the church. Men and women would gyrate and fall to the ground, pronouncing distinct, spellable nonsense, "henini," for example, in long fluid chains. A few women who had not gotten the Holy Ghost that day would move about between the writhing figures on the floor, throwing coats over exposed thighs.

At first, I was imitating those around me, holding my arms high in the air, trying to feel the Spirit overhead. As I heard, for the first time, the sound of glossolalia rolling towards my back, I became afraid and pulled my arms down. "God doesn't like the stiff-necked or those who draw back," I was pointedly told.

After the group convulsion had subsided, a newcomer would be invited up to the front of the podium, "the altar," to pray until he got the Holy Ghost. At the altar, he would be told to kneel down on the uncarpeted concrete floor, raise his arms in the air and pray amidst a

119

confusion of prompters, each urging a different prayer. It was a position that soon became very painful both psychologically and physically, and the pain would build. "Say, 'Thank you Jesus!' Say, 'Praise Jesus!' Say, 'Sweet Jesus!'" The novice would try to repeat the overlapping phrases. Then the "saints" would begin to insert meaningless syllables: "Say, 'Henini!' to the Lord. Say, 'Nola!' Say 'Jeshuar whilow!'" After an exhausting and embarrassing ten minutes of repeating such things, the novice's tongue would begin to produce meaningless sounds spasmodically and automatically. He had the Holy Ghost.

I eventually got the Holy Ghost. At least those I knew among the congregation thought so. I didn't believe it. There was no inner transformation, no new knowledge, and I had been assured there would be. There was a quiet argument between two members of the congregation the day I went up to the altar. One asserted that he had been speaking Chinese, "in the Spirit," the day he got saved. He said he knew it was Chinese because he had heard two Chinamen speaking to each other where he worked and recognized the sounds coming out of his mouth when he spoke in tongues.

His opponent thought that wasn't credible or dignified, and she remonstrated, "Most of us speak the language of the angels." But both tried to convince me that I had spoken in tongues, whatever the language. It was the "Christ," "Jesus," "Holy Spirit," "Holy Ghost" contention again. Chinese was the real language, the "language of the angels" a high abstraction. The woman who favored the "language of the angels" turned out to be well-educated.

One Sunday, at the break for lunch between the morning and afternoon services, two of the assistant preachers sacrificed their meals to preach on the sidewalk and invite passersby to attend service. After about half an hour, they brought into the church cafeteria a blind homeless man who was obviously taken aback by the attention. He was as filthy as the wolf boy. They washed him, dressed him in clean clothes from the church's store of donations, gave him something to eat, and while he was devouring his food, explained to him church doctrine and the hope of being saved. He wanted what they described, and when he had finished eating, they led him to the altar and subjected him to their procedure. He prayed

120

fervently for a while, but when they started asking him to repeat nonsense syllables, he roared "No!" several times very loudly, swirling his outstretched arms around him in a full circle without getting off his knees. This drove the closely pressing crowd back. Then he continued praying in English, as the faithful, one by one, drifted off. I don't know how long he continued praying, because I drifted off too, ashamed that such a person had more integrity than I.

I don't mean to criticize the people at Pilgrim Temple. I'm confident that most of them were sincere, simple, good people. Their glossolalia reminds me now of Mass Latin. When we asked what the words meant, the nun assigned to teach prospective altar boys their responses told us it wasn't important. I think she didn't know what the words meant either. That the Latin sounded cool was enough for us and there were translations of the phrases on the cards we sometimes had recourse to during Mass. With two altar boys at each Mass, it was always a contest to see who could first finish the long Confiteor we were supposed to be saying in unison. It must have sounded a lot like glossolalia. There were rarely used missals in every pew that translated the Latin for the congregation.

Pilgrim Temple's congregation in 1967 was the only fully integrated group I had ever run across. They even had as many black as white ministers. Black or white, I thought of most of them as hillbillies. I'm grateful to the congregation and Brother Dixon. They relieved me of my fears of Hell more effectively than Norwalk and for longer. The relief lasted almost seven months. But after the affair of the blind bum, I took the church less seriously. At one point, an old, black member of the church told me that he had seen fifteen drunken sailors come into church on a Wednesday night, and all of them went up to the altar, and all of them got the Holy Ghost. I was amazed by his naïveté.

When I told some of the church members immoral things I had done, they informed me that confession wasn't a part of Christianity, but the same old black man collared me privately after service and told me immoral things he had done that were very like the things I had disclosed. He told me he had evaded the draft in WWII by pretending that he thought he was a chicken (I swear!). The draft officials who interviewed him laughed at length and toyed with him, but let him go because they didn't want a coward in the army. He was so simple it didn't occur to him to justify himself by reviling his country, though Jim Crow was still in full effect during the war. Once, when a black member of the congregation said God had killed the Kennedys for leading people away from Jesus, the old man started crying and left the church. The old man, I thought, was an extraordinarily compassionate hillbilly. (No slur intended.)

A few days later a black, female guard loudmouthed me in the de Young Museum. I objected. I told her I wanted to speak with her supervisor. In response to her phone call, another black guard arrived and asked me what was wrong. I said the woman, who stood near us, had shown disrespect by bellowing at me. He said, "That's the way she talks. It's part of black culture."

I said, "That's absurd."

She joined in, "Yah. It's just the way we talk. You must be prejudice."

I said to the supervisor, "Well, I'll leave you to deal with this hillbilly." (Slur intended.)

The woman charged me, but her supervisor grabbed her. I turned and walked away.

Despite my skepticism, I decided to get baptized in Pilgrim Temple. I was baptized along with two or three other novices. We walked into the waist high water dressed in long white robes. The water was in a big glass tank at the front of the church. We were instructed to hold our noses. Two of the assistant preachers leaned our rigid bodies backwards into the water. Everybody could see us under the surface with our white robes flailing in the sudden current like angel wings.

One of the things that persuaded me to join Pilgrim Temple was the congregation's distaste for vanity. For example, church members regularly wrote songs and sang them during service. If the people weren't taught a refrain before the song began, their silence became a rebuke. When an educated church member mentioned in conversation in the cafeteria the Epicurean Philosophy as an example of sinful pleasure seeking, it stopped the conversation. Admiration for the Kennedys, solitary song, and education were all considered vanities. I heard a returned African Missionary excuse his teaching his African initiates to read by insisting, twice over, that it was only to allow them to read the Bible.

Brother Dixon taught that the tongue was the hardest part of one's body to govern. I don't know how that teaching bore upon his belief in the mutterings of the Holy Ghost. He didn't ever speak of our spirits. How God could keep us alive until the Resurrection after our bodies were given to corruption was a mystery beyond human understanding, according to Brother Dixon. He didn't think that memory, thoughts and sensations were separable parts of a person. He put me in mind of John Milton and Ludwig Wittgenstein.

He thought, perhaps contradictorily, that the Holy Ghost was a physical being. He would probably have agreed with the skeptic's sentiment: "If I thought that, after I died, someone would put my atoms together again and put me in fire, I wouldn't move."

Brother Dixon used to say, "God loves even the unlovely," another miracle it was supposedly impossible for people to understand. The sentence reminded me of Saul Bellow's parody of Biblical verse. "The forgiveness of sins is perpetual and righteousness first is not required" Henderson the Rain King."

The congregation at Pilgrim Temple didn't believe people had the power to change except by God's grace. The staff at Norwalk believed people could change for the better with or without religion. There was a handwriting expert associated with the Institute who gave me lessons on changing my handwriting whereby I was supposed to change and improve my character. The changes I made in my handwriting are with me to this day, but my thinking didn't change until God took hold of me. So I agree mostly with the people at Pilgrim Temple. In my character there was a sort of escapement that made changing for the better impossibly difficult, but changing for the worse was as easy as falling.

Hells

At Norwalk, we sometimes were allowed to go up on the roof in small groups. A high, chain-link fence topped with barbed wire surrounded the area. One day, lying flat on the roof was a clean, round mirror something over three feet in diameter. One of the patients, who had leaned over and stared into the mirror, called it to our attention. We began to lean over it, one at a time. When it was my turn, a bright, white, even sky rose to encompass me. It looked as though I were falling backwards into "the white radiance of eternity." Suddenly I feared I was on the brink of being lost forever. I panicked, began to lose my balance and had to look away. When I looked away, I knew I had sinned. "God doesn't like … those who draw back," I remembered. Though there was no image of Hell corresponding to this sin yet, I was terrified.

I was still going to church, though with less fervor. I refused to return to the altar to "reaffirm" my "Baptism in the Spirit." and the members of the congregation who had been close to me were no longer so close. One Sunday, a boy, perhaps 12 years old, dressed in his Sunday best, came into the church. He talked to me. People who are adrift socially often do. I think they see my loneliness. He was not at all shy. He described to me the string of churches he had attended. Most recently he had been a "First Church of Christer." It was clear that churches were his social forums. It was strange to see a kid come to church without the urging or accompaniment of adults. He lived with an aunt. His parents were dead. But he was quite cheerful. He was very much at home.

A member of the congregation drew me aside and told me that, when it came time, I should take the boy to the altar to receive the Holy Ghost. I was being asked to pay my dues. Awhile later, I asked the boy if he wanted to go to the altar. He said "No" pleasantly. I felt crummy, not because he wouldn't go but because I'd asked such a young and vulnerable person to do such a thing. I'd recently been told of the miracle of a four-year-old girl who went up to the altar. The Holy Ghost threw her into convulsions and it was half-an-hour before she quieted down. I thought that the boy might have such an experience. I thought he was too innocent to defend himself against the force of Pilgrim Temple.

From time to time, since I was a child, scenes of damnation have revealed themselves to me. I'd guess that I have had 2,000 such scenes since my nothingness dreams. They are complete and instantaneous. I don't have to add a thing. The wrongs I've done to call them forth are often so trivial most people would deny they were wrongs at all. In one Hell, the dead gather in a limitless, close garden. It's the desert in summer, after the first torrential rains, in the warm, piquant morning when the air swarms in the yellow light. The sharp sweet smell of insects and flowering trees, the cactus blossoms, the sprouting leaves, the fields of ambrosia, the refreshed, humid air, the copper arroyo, and the sun over the looming mountains make the desert a thick, golden-green, sparkling meadow.

> Full many a glorious morning have I seen
> Flatter the mountaintops with sovereign eye
> Kissing with golden face the meadows green
> Gilding pale streams with heavenly alchemy.

Shakespeare's quatrain describes this Hell almost perfectly, except the arroyo's shining water has stopped flowing and is heavy with multitudinous, small life.

Multitudinous larvae burrow under my skin as I plod and fall crossing the nearly gelatinous arroyo. I have no coin. Entering the garden is unbearably painful. Something like an intense allergy takes hold of me. The crowded, tangled, pullulating growth presses in on me and burns unconsumed. The redeemed glory in it, as though they are enjoying their own *autos da fe*. I draw back from them. In the end they are trying to speak to me through loud flames. When I can't hear or see them, I fall into my fiery self. The redeemed disappear as though they have never been.

This Hell was the pain beauty brings to those who fear beauty, my most common sin. More specifically, the Hell was a punishment for my failure to go up to the Institute's roof again so that I could get a better view of a spectacular Aztec sunset. Looking west through the barred ward window, I had seen in the sunset the stylized figure of ancient, Xiuhtecuhtli, Lord of Turquoise, Lord of Day and Lord of Fire, whose sacrificial victims were roasted alive. We had a carelessly painted ceramic bas-relief of Xiuhtecuhtli, opalescent where the glazes mixed. Beneath the figure, a thickly varnished paper legend in poor English explained the god. I bought the bas-relief during a family shopping excursion to Nogales, Sonora, and hung it on a wall in the games room with our other totems and trophies. In San Francisco, where sunsets are rare, the god's outline was traced in the cyan narrows between the scattered pink islands in the archipelago above the setting sun. It was amazing, but the day's humiliations hadn't left me enough strength to stand under that magnificent sky, and the momentary cloud-picture of Xiuhtecuhtli frightened me. I lay down on my bed and looked up at the ceiling. Then the Hell I've just described revealed itself to me.

"God doesn't like... those who draw back." I had sinned by drawing back at least three times: drawing down my arms when the Holy Ghost came near in Pilgrim Temple; drawing back from the mirror on Norwalk's roof; and drawing back from Xiuhtecuhtli's sunset. The Hell somehow "resembled" all three of the sins that had brought it forth. The resemblance proved the Hell was real. I hadn't yet gotten the ability or permission to argue disingenuously against my own beliefs.

For two decades, that Hell and far worse could seize me without warning, and I couldn't turn away. The Hells grew progressively more frightening and often occurred in rapid series. Toward the end they were accompanied by visions of the enormous Tucson sunsets that could cover almost the entire sky and seemed to trap the world beneath a ceiling of flame. After that, my Hells held darkness with no hint of beauty, only my sickening self.

Byron

With an all-day pass from Norwalk, I went back to my apartment one Sunday after service at Pilgrim Temple. At the door, I thought I heard the television. I walked in on Byron, then the occupant of my apartment. He was sitting in a chair in the dark with his eyes closed repeating the syllables, "Yama, yama, yama," almost humming them. Speaking in tongues wasn't something Byron had to go to church to do. It amused him.

In fact, Byron dared not go to church. I had talked to Brother Anthony, my closest friend in Pilgrim Temple, about the difficulty of living with Byron's peculiarities. Byron was always trying to get me to be his follower. Brother Anthony said, "How can you live with such a person," which was a relief because it meant my troubles with Byron weren't my fault. Brother Anthony told me that Byron had been "so high in the Spirit people thought he might make the Bride." "The Bride of Christ" was the 144,000 who would rule with Jesus in Eternity, an elite among the Blessed. "When you fall from being high in the spirit, you fall farther and lower than you would otherwise," Brother Anthony said. From then on I knew Byron had fallen from grace. I began to be afraid of him. His aunt Shelby, a staunch church member, was the only one who spoke favorably of him. However, she didn't like the fact that Byron and I lived in my small apartment together; it was clear that she suspected us of having a sexual relationship.

Byron's dead mother had doted on him. When he became an adult Byron found out that he had been adopted. Byron began calling his mother "Mrs. Washington" instead of "Mother" or "Mom." His stepfather accused Byron of having killed her.

One Friday, Byron and I went to his stepfather's house. We found his stepfather and several of his stepfather's friends in a drunken craps game. One of the participants was trying to borrow money to continue in the game after having lost his entire paycheck.

"She's gonna beat the hell out of you," Byron's stepfather said as the man stumbled out the door.

After the craps game ended, Byron announced to his stepfather a plan to hitchhike with me to Corpus Christi, Texas, and do some street preaching. Byron's stepfather encouraged us in this plan. It was new to me. After we left his stepfather's house, Byron said it wasn't until his stepfather encouraged us to go to Corpus Christi that he realized how dangerous it would have been for a white and black to preach together in such a place. His stepfather was mean, Byron concluded, and the plan was dropped.

Shortly thereafter Byron began washing raw hamburger meat before he cooked it. This was his idea of a diet derived from Biblical dietary law. I told him that the early Christians had rejected Jewish dietary law and that he was clogging up the sink. Byron was only rarely capable of changing any course of action he decided upon. Giving up his plans for a mission in Corpus Christi must have been hard for him. He continued to wash his meat until he moved back into his stepfather's house. He moved because I wouldn't obey.

One afternoon, I found Artemis and Lorus arguing fiercely in the "panhandle" in front of my apartment building about whether or not I had gotten the Holy Ghost. "Nonsense," she said. She saw me. Her gargling voice was unintelligible but sounded very much like glossolalia as she walked away, her perfect buttocks ever so slightly trembling. Lorus told me he was sure I was saved.

We Were Degenerates

For several days, I stopped going to Pilgrim Temple and Norwalk, where I was now an outpatient. I resumed wandering the filthy streets among the other self-indulgent, wretched hippies. One day on Haight Street, I watched a young man with his pants and underwear pulled down around his ankles tug at the locked door of a car full of scared tourists caught in traffic. He ended by pressing his pubic area flat against the back window of the car where two gray-haired old women cringed. The surrounding hippies laughed and cheered. An older man looked at me and said, "I don't think God wants people to act that way, do you?" I agreed. I knew that, "to act that way" meant "to deliberately attack the sensibilities of innocent people for mean fun," something the television-obedient like to do in subtler ways. By "television-obedient" I mean people who reflexively credit televised stereotypes or opinion and have few other criteria for determining the truth of an opinion than its appearance on TV.

Walking back to Norwalk I saw a large worm in the grass in the Panhandle.

A few days later, I saw a girl in Golden Gate Park bare herself and let her German shepherd fuck her from behind in front of fifteen or twenty cheering hippies.

A couple of days later, a young man was stabbed to death on Haight in a fight while a dozen hippies watched without any attempt to intervene. This was prominently reported in the newspapers, sending the whole of Haight-Ashbury into a fit of excuses: "They must have been paralyzed by shock at the sight of such violence." No, they were enjoying the show.

"I can't sleep without my shiv!" said a distraught hippy on the Panhandle as he ransacked his belongings for the third time looking for what had been stolen and a crew of helpful fellow hippies searched the near grass for the shine of metal. If they'd found the knife they would have stolen it.

Awhile later, some people were slashed to death in Los Angeles. Those arrested, whites, were, by their dress and hair, hippies. There was another, longer period of justification. San Francisco hippies opined that the perpetrators were insane and, therefore, "not really hippies."

Nonsense. Lots of hippies were ambulatory psychotics whose psychoses didn't disqualify them as hippies. The murderers may or may not have been insane but their statements were certainly loony. That was the problem. Crazy or not, hippies didn't live in reality. They lived on the mental plane of the Ouija Board and the I Ching and wild, ever-changing "theories" about any matter that occurred to them. The hippies pretended to believe that their theories, hallucinations and delusions were part of a "superior reality." The accused murderers in Los Angeles had such theories.

I began seeing more worms in the patches of exposed dirt of Golden Gate Park and on the nearby sidewalks and streets.

In San Francisco, a party of black bohemian activists had begun leaping out of cars, jumping white joggers and stabbing them to death on the sidewalks. They left notices on the bodies describing their group as a liberation movement "dedicated to the mutilation and murder of whites." The city was in a panic. The nearest witnesses could only describe the afros.

I remembered this when I read the following thought experiment in a newspaper. Suppose you are walking late at night in downtown Cleveland. There is no one around. Suddenly a raucous group of black youths turns the corner a block ahead of you and starts walking towards you. When they see you, they're suddenly silent. They continue walking towards you. What difference does it make in the way you feel if you know they have just gotten out of Evening Bible Study? Your answer to that question is your opinion of Christianity.

A hippy friend I read this thought experiment to told me that being afraid of a group of raucous black youths in the circumstances described was "prejudice." It's not prejudiced to conclude that there is a greater chance of being hurt by a group of black teenagers than by other groups. My friend was rejecting the thought experiment because he wanted to continue to condemn Christianity for its supposed bigotry. He was the one who was prejudiced. Intolerance isn't where the stereotype of intolerance says it is.

I found worms in the toilet tank and sink of my apartment.

Hippy comic books, of which there were many, revealed the new age sensibilities best. I remember one called "Lesbian Cowgirls at War," in which Lesbians who practiced bestiality struggled in anguish to decide between their girlfriends and their horses while fighting Nazis. Another, "Binky Brown Meets the Blessed Virgin Mary" told the story of a man whose fingers and toes turned into penises that flashed obscene rays all around him as he walked. A third, "The Druggist" told of a dwarf pharmacist who had a crush on a beautiful female addict to whom he sold intoxicating drugs. When she spurned him, he concocted a pill that would cause his sex organs to enlarge enormously and suddenly. Then he required the girl to fuck him, withholding her drugs until she agreed to do so, and took the pill he had concocted just as he reached orgasm. His instantly expanding penis tore the girl's head off and a huge load of sperm shot through the hole in her neck. There were many such publications.

In a restaurant, I found many small worms in a sandwich when I tried to salt it.

The Test for Inverts

The question of my sexuality came up when I returned to Norwalk. We patients were required at one point to take the Minnesota Multiphasic Personality Inventory (MMPI), which was a long series of questions selected because people with specific diagnoses typically answered the questions in specific ways for unknown reasons. The staff psychologist told me my results. He said, among other things, that the test showed that I was an invert. I asked him what an invert was. He said an invert was a homosexual. I wasn't an invert, I told him. I couldn't walk down the street past a pretty girl without getting at least the beginning of an erection. He didn't give my denial any credence at all. He spoke to me as to a person who was having trouble accepting the truth about himself. I wandered around in a slight daze for a day thinking that, if it were true that I was an invert, I wouldn't be a draft dodger; I would just be an accidental truth teller. But, "Sin is in the will," the nun had said.

When you're not sure other people exist, sex is a problem. I was a twenty-one year old virgin, spurned by Sissy, my very sexually active true love. In San Francisco, in the counterculture, of course, chastity was a joke and promiscuity and perversion a virtue. I had been under the influence of sixteen years of fervent Catholicism. However, in contrast to my Catholic guilt about sexual matters, I had begun to think of my virginity as the punishment of the White Goddess— Robert Graves' White Goddess. I decided my unwillingness to risk my pride by approaching women angered the Goddess. At the same time, I wondered if the White Goddess was Satan. I thought Satan was a woman – the Sataness. I yearned hopelessly to bring my sexual isolation to an end.

My desperation was partly caused by my recurrent self-centeredness but also by the sex prophets whose astonishingly dishonest conclusions were dogma for the young beginning in the 1960s. Hippies who didn't read said things like "You're sexually repressed" or "Sexual morality is relative."

Before he came up with his doctrine that neurotics were sexually repressed, Sigmund Freud conducted bloody and disfiguring operations on peoples' sinuses following another entirely untested theory that this would rid his patients of their neuroses. The Notable Names Database, Sigmund Freud, nndb.com. Freud, like the hippies, *pretended* that his ideas were true. He had no real evidence for them. He was a true quack.

Margaret Mead, the first Neo-feminist, was another fraud. Some of her interviewees survived until the 1970's. According to them, when Mead interviewed them in Samoa in 1925 she asked them the same questions over and over again until they gave her the answers she seemed to want. Grant McCall, Australian Journal of Anthropology, April 2001. Then she left them alone, having proved that sexual morality was entirely relative. I saw an Anthropologist on television defend Mead by saying, "I've done the same thing myself!" as though that made falsifying research results better rather than worse.

Similarly, Alfred Kinsey interviewed *prisoners* about their sexual practices and concluded that 10% of all males were homosexuals. *The Lancet* wrote that Kinsey "questioned an unrepresentative proportion of prison inmates and sex offenders in a survey of normal sexual behavior." The Lancet, March 2, 1991.

The three specious doctrines cited above were core elements of the sexual revolution which killed so many.

What happened to the recommendation of Madame Curie that we hold our theories loosely so that we can release them if they conflict with the results of our experiments?

One morning, the staff at Norwalk arranged an outing for us at a secluded beach near San Francisco. When we arrived, I took a stroll down the beach mulling over my miseries. Suddenly, there on the beach at my feet was a marijuana cigarette. I picked it up and walked over to the only person from the ward who was also off by himself. I showed him what I had found.

By the time we'd finished the marijuana cigarette, the sky seemed to be opening. A great vortex reached down to me from the blue, letting me know that I was in the presence of God.

"I'm afraid to do anything," I confessed.

"Just choose. Make any decision at all, It doesn't matter what," my marijuana companion advised. This particular person, whose name I have forgotten, was an existentialist.

"Ok," I said, obeying God and abandoning my oath of celibacy. At that moment, I determined that I would ask the one girl on the outing to sleep with me. I decided to ask her before the outing ended. I had my apartment, so we had a place to go if she agreed.

Now on the ward I had no friends because I was so shy, but I had money and, therefore, cigarettes. In the mental hospital, cigarettes were prized. I gave out cigarettes freely, each gift being a primitive sort of communication that cut through my loneliness.

Deserting the existentialist, I went back to the area where the rest of the group was looking out to sea. The girl I was to proposition was holding a fat, gluey, transparent jellyfish. It covered her whole hand like the still small blob in an early scene in the movie, "The Blob." The girl was chasing a particularly effeminate fellow patient who ran from her to avoid being touched by the jellyfish. I wondered how I might arrange things so that I was alone with the girl and could ask her to sleep with me. I planned to walk with her when we went back to the van at the end of the outing. It was a long walk and I pictured the patients spreading out along the trail, thereby providing me with enough privacy to ask the question. When we were told it was time to leave, most of the other patients formed a clot around the girl, and I became terrified that I wasn't going to be able to carry through with my resolution. I knew I wouldn't have the courage to ask the question in front of other patients.

Suddenly, there at the girl's feet, was a whole, perfect cigarette, and when she stopped and bent to pick it up, the clot of patients moved a couple of steps ahead. I stayed back with the girl. Then there was another cigarette and another and another. There must have been most of a pack strung out along the beach. By the time we picked up the last of them, the group was far ahead of us. I asked the girl if she would sleep with me. "Will you sleep with me?

We can go to my apartment." The girl expressed surprise but agreed. Everything was working out.

The girl's passes were limited because she was so unpredictable. However, two days after the outing, she was able to get a pass on some excuse and we headed for my apartment. I had allowed a friend to use it while I was in the hospital and had given him the key. It was locked. No one was at home. Desperate, I asked the girl if we could try again the next day. She said "Maybe." The next day I caught my friend, got the keys and angrily asked him to vacate. He vacated and the girl and I returned. It was grinding labor. She didn't want foreplay. I was put off by her wetness, which I understood only by virtue of one of the crude hippy comic books. I came and I think she did, too. It was over quickly. The best part for me was finding out that sex wasn't transcendental, that it was simply another organic function, not a brave new world I was prohibited from entering. The experience was like my experience with tongues, disappointing. However I still couldn't walk down the street past a pretty girl without the beginning of an erection.

I described what had happened and talked about how commonplace it seemed at the next group therapy session at the Institute. Afterwards, the squarest of the nurses came up to me and said: "I know it must have been hard for you to say that in front of her, but she needed to hear it."

I said, "No. It wasn't hard at all." It hadn't occurred to me that the girl might be offended. One of her other lovers approached me and confessed his earlier liaison. He said he was disappointed because she had separated herself from him as soon as she came, leaving him without an orgasm.

It turned out the girl was in love with one of the other patients, the beautiful boy she had been chasing with the jellyfish on the beach. He later tried to seduce me. The girl confessed her love for the boy at a group therapy session. The boy said, "Oh dear!" The girl tried to kill herself, was confined to a locked ward and put under a suicide watch. My sexual desperation was gone for the time being. I wasn't subject to the White Goddess's displeasure anymore.

I wasn't accepted as a hippy. I was psychotic, but that wasn't the reason I was rejected. A bedraggled hippy entered an apartment off Stanyan Street one night where I was visiting Shelley, a friend. The hippy asked my friend if he could sleep on the porch. Shelley, a short, ugly hippy who sometimes dressed as a clown, said no. The intruding hippy persisted. Shelley got angry and ordered him out. Still the hippy persisted.

I intervened: "You can stay in my apartment."

"Yah! You can stay in his apartment," Shelley said.

The hippy looked at me for a moment and said, "I don't crash with straight people." The most authentic bohemian in the room had decided that I was not a flower child.

In the early years of the hippy movement, Shelley had come to San Francisco on a "Saint Francis trip." He came from a neighborhood in Kansas City where he would walk out on his front lawn naked and act retarded and spastic to avenge himself on the neighbors. He imagined they looked down on him, his sister and his parents for being poor Jews. At first, he made his way in San Francisco by begging, "like St. Francis." When he discovered he was making thirty dollars a day, a large amount in those days, certainly more than the salaries of some working people, and certainly more than St. Francis, he doubted his ideals.

He took LSD and hallucinated the end of the world by atomic destruction. He took another dose of LSD a few weeks later and hallucinated the end of the world by atomic destruction again. He used to say he wished everybody would die so he "could go into their houses and take their stuff." He came to embrace a kind of religion of meanness. He stopped using drugs and became absolutely cynical. For philosophical reasons, he liked to hurt people. Hurting people was "real." He ended up in Norwalk with me for a while. He slept with the same girl I slept with. When she tried to commit suicide, he imagined that she did it because she was monumentally disgusted by the sex she'd had with him. Of course, we were all blaming ourselves, but Shelley's reason showed us we were all ridiculous.

Later, he was my roommate, but his imagination was too frightening to live with. In my apartment one night he stood up, as though at attention, when the TV broadcast the news that a young girl had been seized and blinded by an unknown assailant. Apparently the assailant drew a knife in a deep cut and curve across her face just under her brow like a violinist drawing his bow over all the strings in succession. The police could suggest no motive for the crime. Suddenly Shelley declared, "I take full responsibility for blinding that girl. I chose to do it." I didn't believe him, but I asked him to vacate the next morning. I was relieved when he did.

Another strange hippy patient at Norwalk followed women. He hallucinated come-hither looks. He tried to follow a strange woman into her house. From what I gather the resulting scene was hair-raising. The police brought him straight to Norwalk.

The blind man, the First Church of Christer, Byron in the outer darkness, and my growing doubts about the validity of my experience with tongues, were bringing me closer and closer to complete disillusionment with Brother Dixon's Assembly. When Wayne and Memo drove Wayne's van into San Francisco to take a look at the hippies, I told Wayne about Pilgrim Temple and he went with me to church. We attended the Wednesday night service. Wayne just sat in the pew with an angry look on his face while the convulsing went on around him.

I could take no more of the exhausting craziness and degeneracy of San Francisco. Besides, I was broke and scared. I asked Wayne if I could ride with him back to Tucson. He said I could. I didn't bother to say goodbye to the folks at church or at the Institute, where I was still a patient.

Wayne had picked a winding route home. First we headed toward the Eel River, north of San Francisco. Byron came, too. I was desperate. I was unable to escape. San Francisco was going home with me. Wayne stopped to camp and have lunch in the woods. I tried to stay away from Byron, but he followed me wherever I walked, making dark hints that Pilgrim Temple's doctrines were wrong and there really was a Hell. I ended up screaming at him to get away. I was in tears. After lunch, Wayne took Byron back to the city. Byron stayed there. I left with Wayne. I don't know what Wayne said to Byron, but, as we were driving off, I saw Byron staring at me with dedicated hatred.

When we got to the river, I went swimming. The air was wonderful. The river seemed to wash off a filthy crust Byron and San Francisco had deposited on me. I was free. I could swing my arms and jump and splash like a two year old in the broad, shallow water. The water ran like the desert after a cloud burst, but the water in the Eel River was clear, and the smell was pine, not creosote.

On the way back to Tucson, we stopped at Yosemite and the Grand Canyon. They were too grand to believe. I'd seen too many pictures of them. They seemed painted on the inside of my skull. I wasn't able to marvel at them. On the contrary, I feared my solipsism was impending and had to look away. Two short moments of fear were all I felt of awe.

Some Christians say the Biblical phrase "Fear God" means only "Be in awe of God." Aworac says God doesn't want either my fear or my awe; I can never sound any part of Him. All I can do is accept His condescending I love.

I believe I made the round trip from Tucson to San Francisco and back three times during hippy days. I'm not sure. I'm not sure about the order of events in San Francisco and Oakland. Some events may not have taken place in San Francisco or Oakland at all. Some may not have taken place.

Sissy was back in Tucson by the time I returned. In college she had gone through Joe, Byron and Barney, and those are just the ones who had been friends of mine. She dated freely in San Francisco and, after returning to Tucson, had short affairs with quite a number of young men, including Memo.

Memo

From our childhood on, my parents and I made periodic trips to Nogales, Sonora, sixty miles south of Tucson. Rows and rows of shops sold cheap trinkets, pottery, and jewelry. If some item sold well in one shop one month, every shop would stock it in profusion the next. Onyx chess sets went through this cycle. So did bongos, conga drums and ceramic plaques. Later, lurid paintings on black velvet became fashionable, a poor man's Caravaggio.

Nogales had an interesting restaurant built in a rock cave that had been used by Pancho Villa to hold prisoners. The menu was excellent. You could get turtle soup, turtle steak, dove and quail, among other things. I loved the turtle. The restaurant was destroyed in a fire and not rebuilt. Now it's just a cave again.

Nogales had a thriving red-light district.

When we were young we mostly wanted firecrackers, which had to be smuggled back across the border. They were altogether illegal in Arizona. Dad, who had probably sponsored the bill that made them illegal, would hide them for us in the car. It was fun being smugglers and thinking up good places to hide the contraband, but Dad's places were always better.

As teenagers we wanted tequila and traveled to Nogales to get it. As adults, my friends and I sought drugs. Wayne became an addict on Nogales heroin.

Unbeknownst to our parents, Memo and I, when we were both thirteen and I had just met him, took the Greyhound bus to Nogales. Memo bought a pint of tequila and smuggled it back across the line in his pants. On the bus back to Tucson, he took a few swigs but wouldn't give me a sip. At that age, he was extremely obnoxious. He bragged about everything and had an erratic, clumsy manner that made you feel you were being knocked about.

There was something wrong with Memo. He had attended Mansfield, the public junior high school. At Mansfield, the dominant pachuco had kicked at his crotch in the cafeteria line. Memo had grabbed the boy's foot, always a danger when you kick, and backed him out through the cafeteria door and down the steps. Then he let go, and the bully beat him up with the full force of his frustration at having been held helpless for a few seconds. Thereafter, the pachuco friends of the bully beat Memo and humiliated him every day for most of the rest of the school year. He finally reacted by clowning. That seemed to satisfy them. They left him alone. During the time of the beatings, each day, when Memo got home, he used a bullwhip on a post of the veranda in his back yard. The bullwhip came from his family's rich collection of Western and Spanish memorabilia. He had his choice of any number of weapons, but repeated lashings with the bullwhip worked off his anger best.

Two years after his bullying at Mansfield, on the bus home from Salpointe, Memo overheard some gossip. An Anglo boy was saying that a Mexican student at THS had drowned during a late summer flood. Memo remarked, "It serves the stupid Mexican right." I think he believed it was an impressive thing to say. Two of the Mexican girls who went to Salpointe and were friends of the drowned boy heard Memo. They told the drowned boy's tough friends at THS. Two of the friends were waiting for Memo the next day at a bus transfer point. Memo denied the remark. After challenging him for a long time while he refused to fight either of them, they left him alone. I sat nearby doing nothing.

Memo's performance at Salpointe was so bad that his father sent him off to a military school, which was, of course, very strict, but the boys in their dorm in their free time, played sex games, circle jerks and the like. After military school, Memo was sent to THS, but the pachucos, treated him decently.

Memo liked to take us, me Norman Nielson and Walter Adam, the son of an executed Nazi war criminal, in Memo's father's jeep out onto the Papago reservation where he would speed and bounce wildly over very uneven desert pursuing jackrabbits. I saw him pick a large airborne segment of cholla out of his upper lip without in the least slowing down. At night, we hunted the jackrabbits with more success. We cruised slowly along, combing the brush with our flashlight beams until they landed on a rabbit confused by the light. I don't know why deer and jackrabbits freeze in a beam of light and most other animals don't. We were usually able to hold the rabbit motionless long enough for the jeep to come to a bouncing halt. Then my companions shot it with their 22s. The rabbits' ears were always full of ticks. My friends wouldn't lend me their 22s to take a shot, reminding me of Memo's unshared pint of tequila.

What we got we took to Norman's mother. Norman was the son of Norwegian immigrants. His father was a doctor who got into the United States by agreeing to be one of the physicians for the Papagos. The Nielsons had excellent, government-paid housing in a compound reserved for Anglos. The compound was designed to complement San Xavier del Bac, the most beautiful of all the old Spanish missions, which was also on the Papago reservation. Norman's mother would dress and cook the jackrabbits. Cooking, they smelled exactly like rotting flesh. The smell permeated the house. The first time I walked into that smell I was aghast. I had never smelled that smell before, except in conjunction with road kill. I froze and stared at Norman's mother as though she were a cannibal caught in the act. My companions actually ate some of the jackrabbit. It was a test of courage I failed. I think of it now whenever I see one of those TV shows where people eat nauseating substances to win money.

One afternoon, Memo's jeep broke down on the Papago reservation. Norman and I hiked and hitchhiked back to his house. By then it was dark. Norman surreptitiously got the keys to his parents' shiny new Buick and drove it slowly in the dark over two miles of rough arroyo ribbed desert with the headlights shining, scaring away badgers and other wildlife. Norman drove very slowly. The suspension was terrific. We barely felt or heard the bumps beneath us. The radio played classical music. It was quite beautiful until we got to Memo and Adam where we had left them four hours before. They cursed us a little and then got in the car. We left the jeep. The Buick wasn't so damaged that Norman's parents noticed.

By the time he was in high school, Memo spoke good colloquial Spanish. Going with him to the red light district in Nogales was an especially interesting experience. The prettiest whores would come up to us when they realized he could talk to them easily in Spanish. Memo would tell them outlandish lies about us and they would laugh uproariously. The laughter of whores is uniquely refreshing. They plunge into it as though it were a sort of swimming hole, probably because they relish diversion in their unfortunate circumstances.

Jess was always testing Gringos who claimed to speak Spanish. He did this by throwing a lot of slang at them. Memo was the only Gringo who passed the test. He responded with slang. He had had the benefit of growing up with a succession of non-English speaking, uneducated Mexican maids attending to his needs. That's how he came to be called Memo (William = Guillermo = Memo). It was odd that Memo had a Mexican nickname and Jess had Anglicized his.

Educated Mexicans, however, were aghast at Memo's miserable grammar. It never improved, despite the two years Memo spent as a student at the Universidad Nacional Autonoma de Mexico (UNAM). He was one of those people who simply can't study. In a way, UNAM was perfect for him; most of the professors there didn't bother coming to class. They posted reading lists at the beginning of the semester and only showed up to pass out the final exam.

Memo dropped out of UNAM, and, with a friend, hitchhiked to the Amazon. He never told any of us the story of his adventures. Before he left, he said he wanted to come back so hardened that he could "skewer a baby" without contrition. (Women who get abortions often act tough, too.) Memo became tough for a time during the next few years.

About the time Anselmo was picking worms out of his tomatoes, Memo, back in Tucson, set up a forge behind his mother's house. The house was huge, the center of an old, former ranch that had encompassed what is now downtown Tucson. The sprawling house had a century of additions and an enormous yard, all that was left of the once extensive ranch land. Black, thick, oily smoke poured out of the forge chimney as Memo learned to make horseshoes and shoe horses. He had no horses. He got hold of a horse's hoof from some rendering plant. It stunk worse than the forge smoke. It smelled exactly like Mrs. Nielson's jackrabbit.

Then Memo, using his forge and several rare woods, started making elaborate furniture for a café Joe and he had decided to set up. When it opened Joe and Memo worked alternate shifts. Memo was unreliable, largely as a result of drinking. Memo's little sister would sometimes take his place out of pure charity. Memo and Joe had a bitter fight over Memo's absences and reached a settlement. For a small amount of money, Memo gave up his share and obligations in the café and his friendship with Joe. The money he got he gave to his parents as proof that he could make money.

In addition to the Amazon trip, Memo spent a year in various countries in Europe, again bumming his way. He lived much of the time off his girlfriend, Sloane, a Tucsonan in medical school in Geneva. She ended up dropping out of school and going with him on a few of his treks. She later came to hate him for "doing that to [her]."

Memo's most interesting adventure was in the Far East. He traveled on a convoy through Laos. The convoy was stopped and searched by the Khmer Rouge. Memo was questioned but convinced the Khmer Rouge he was French. He had somehow acquired a French passport. I don't know how vicious the Khmer Rouge were at that time. This adventure came after Memo had avoided the draft and was probably a way of proving his courage.

Freed from the cafe business, Memo outfitted an old school bus, put his forge in it and set off for New Mexico to become a traveling farrier for the ranches. The bus was too expensive to operate. It got three miles per gallon. So Memo took up residence in his bus on top of a 7,000-foot mountain. He connected his bus to a rudimentary cabin he built. He lived on the mountain for a few years with a woman who apparently wanted to marry him. Memo was a confirmed bachelor like me but for different reasons. In the end the frustrated woman screamed something at Memo that wounded his pride and self-confidence. I don't know what it was. Then she left him.

Memo moved, for about a year, to a lonely motel outside a small New Mexican town on the high plains under a wide sky. He became completely incommunicado after a while. His mother sent the motel manager monthly checks and occasionally called to ask the manager how Memo was doing. Deserting his forge, bus and accumulated stuff at the top of the mountain, Memo left the motel and headed back to Tucson and the family home. Shortly thereafter, a strange gray-haired, tough-looking woman came to the house. Memo ignored her. The woman seemed to believe she was Memo's wife. His mother let her stay. She got nowhere with Memo and after a few days, went away.

On a visit to some rather new, drug-using friends, Memo found himself accused of being a narc. The accusation was unjust, but Memo couldn't talk his way out of it. Other acquaintances heard it. Memo was rabid to clear his name and couldn't. The accusation that Memo was a police informant and whatever happened on the mountain in New Mexico put Memo in a state of deep resentment and anguish. He continued to withdraw from all his former Tucson friends. One day he spoke to me in gibberish of a kind that he and Joe used when they were smoking marijuana. They called it "free association." They traded nonsense back and forth. One might say "Avoid saluting when you burn a nest for your party." The other might respond, "Sam Houston faced tree surgery in a banana ring Circus." It was a game I never understood because it wasn't solitary. They seemed to understand each other. Maybe it was something like pig-Latin, susceptible of translation. When Memo tried to play the gibberish game with me, I asked him what he was trying to say. He became so angry that he hit me, hard. That's when I first realized that something was wrong. He became increasingly silent. He wouldn't shave, comb his hair or bathe. He beat up and reportedly tried to rape his littlest sister when she got angry with him. She was about 16 years old and had lost patience with his smell. She tells me she is still afraid of him. So am I. All he has done for the past thirty years is sit in his house alone, entombed in his own silence. He was a courageous adventurer utterly defeated by inconsequential words. Thirty years ago his father died and his mother broke her hip and moved into the house of Memo's older brother. Then she died. Memo's siblings go into the house periodically just to bring groceries and clean up. Of course, Memo won't answer the phone.

Debts of Guilt and Hate

I got a job as a proofreader for the UA Press after I left San Francisco with Wayne and Memo and was back in Tucson. My proof reading, poor at the outset, deteriorated. I began writing sarcastic and obscene remarks in the galleys. They couldn't fire me. My job had come at the behest of a family friend who was a high official at the UA. They tried to help me by giving me interesting material to proofread. The best was <u>Blessing Way</u>, a Jesuit's translation of one of two long cardinal poems/ceremonies of the Navajos. The poem evoked many colorful gods. "Corn Flower Girl" was my favorite. She was beneficent. All the gods in the poem were beneficent. The other poem was called <u>Enemy Way</u>. I suspect the gods in it were not so beneficent, but I may be wrong. Quoron told me it was about healing not war.

The Navajos were a relatively peaceful tribe, though they had slaves, presumably gotten in war. In a public area of the Arizona State Capitol there is a wall with aging photographs taken in the late 19th century. The Navajos, even more than the Yaquis, were a handsome tribe. One photograph shows three beautiful Navajo women in their Indian blouses and wide skirts with high, complex Indian coiffures, vaguely resembling American women's Civil War hairdos and dress. The Navajo women are serene, sitting at first twilight, a distant tottering mesa to their right, while, to their left, "boundless and bare, the lone and level sands stretch far away." The women couldn't have appeared more alien if they had been on Mars.

Another book I liked was a history of Victorio's fugitive band of Apaches, who are, except for ugly Geronimo, even handsomer than the Navajos. The history is told by an Apache who, as a child, had been a member of the group. The hunted band had fled the reservation. The narrator described a squaw bulldogging a steer, holding on by biting its ear and grabbing one of its horns while she flew through the air and slit its throat with her free arm. It was not her habit to do such things; she had never killed a steer before; she did it because the children in the band were hungry and the men were off fighting and misleading the pursuing troops. "Native American squaws and braves were magnificent, and we destroyed them," said a member of the staff at a halfway house where I was a patient when I told him of this incident. He knew nothing about Indians.

Political guilt, the kind I learned in several institutions, can usually be cured by facts and reason. Counselors, as I said, call this "rationalizing." Researchers don't normally pray, but I was so upset at having been repeatedly told that I should "own actions" for which I could not possibly have been responsible that I prayed to preserve my objectivity when I began investigating the subjects that follow.

Two weeks after I finished the book about Victorio's band, the scholar hired to check the book's accuracy returned the galleys with serious criticisms. Among other problems, he pointed out that Victorio tortured captives mercilessly. The narrator had not said a word about that. The torture of captives was a common practice among Indians. The tortures practiced by the Apaches were horrifying, but not especially so. The parents of Apache children encouraged them to capture and torture small animals in preparation for torturing people. The Iroquois and Comanches were the most vicious practitioners.

Indians killed two of my ancestors, Thomas Kimball and Hannah Kimball in 1676 and 1697 respectively. They were killed in the northern reaches of the Iroquois Empire. That's all that's certain. If Iroquois captured them before killing them, Thomas and Hannah would have been tortured to death hideously then eaten. They would have been eaten in any case. I don't grieve the fate of these distant ancestors. They are personally unknown to me. Nor do I bear any ill will towards Indians. No living Indian had anything to do with these events. My intention here is to show that dealing out blame on the basis of race is mistaken as well as bigoted.

The Aztec Empire, the Inca Empire, and the Pawnees, among others, practiced human sacrifice. One Aztec codex boasts that during the four-day celebration dedicating the Great Pyramid in Tenochtitlan in 1487, 80,400 human beings were sacrificed.

Many tribes were adept at conquest. There were 30,000 Hurons in about 1600. The Iroquois extended their already large empire by hunting the Hurons until the Hurons numbered only about 500 individuals chased hundreds of miles from their homeland. The Comanche empire was always up to the business of extending the vast frontiers of its dark realm. Indians attacked and killed or drove off other Indians to such a degree that, at the time of Columbus, probably no Indians occupied lands of which their ancestors were the original human inhabitants. Europeans didn't initiate conquest and murder in the New World.

Slavery existed among many Indian tribes and included inter-tribal slave markets. This and the facts above are rarely mentioned. What is often mentioned is the claim that Europeans deliberately distributed smallpox infected blankets to the Indians and taught the Indians to scalp people. The first of these stories is unproven and disputed. The second is provably false. Europeans treated Indians badly but they treated Indians better than Indians treated each other.

Nor were Indians environmentalists:

> As everyone except a handful of Native American fundamentalists now accepts, the bison herds were in terminal decline even before the arrival of white hunters. There had originally been seven million 'buffalo' on the southern plains but by the 1860s, before the frenzy of the white bison hunters, half of these had already been killed by the Indians.
> Frank McLynn, "Literary Review," Spartans of the Plains, The Comanche Empire, Pekka Hämäläinen (Yale University Press, 2008).

In our doping circle there was a young man who occasionally played non-speaking parts of Indians in Westerns. The young man had a dramatic, Indian-like appearance. He liked to describe his fantasy of murdering all the whites and winning back the land for himself and the other Indians. "Give me a break, *Salvatore*," one of us said to him one day. He was the son of two Italian immigrants.

On the other hand, some Indians need real help. An anthropologist, a friend of mine, investigating an increased rate of Indian suicides in the U.S., told me that the suicide victims were almost all teenagers and that, while there was no favorite method of suicide among the boys, the girls overwhelmingly chose self-immolation.

I remember watching a small circle of Indian teenagers on the dirt in front of the Indian School on Indian School Road in Phoenix. Surrounded by office buildings, they beat on their tom toms, which were empty coffee cans. They might have learned the stereotypical four-stroke rhythm from movies and TV. One at a time they each got up and danced in the center of the drumming circle. The dancers all skipped in place, tamping the dirt. They kept their backs and heads bent in an arc over their pumping knees. Each danced in this same simple way, which they also might have learned from movies. Even from across the street their shyness in each other's presence was evident. The scene was deeply touching. I wanted to find some blameworthy or at least blamable person and take self-righteous vengeance on him. Fashionable sensibilities are that sophomoric, and the most sentimental lead to hate. I owe no debt of guilt and hate to Indians. I feel no remorse.

I owe no debt of guilt to women. Neo-feminists claim that the dependence of women on their husbands makes those women victims. In the recent past, jobs had little or nothing to do with creativity or fulfillment, and they certainly weren't performed by pecking away at a pc keyboard. A list of the jobs almost exclusively taken by men before extensive automation would typically include coal or other miner, construction worker, farmer, steelworker, factory worker (before robots), fisherman, logger, sawmill operator, teamster, shipbuilder, soldier, oil worker, boilermaker, sailor, mechanic, stevedore, ironworker, ranch hand, welder, plumber, ditch digger, policeman (before Tasers), garbage man when men had to lift and empty garbage cans by hand, etc. Only a very small proportion of men ever had a chance to be executives, lawyers, doctors, or politicians, the type of jobs most Neo-feminists are after. Married men normally took brutal and dangerous jobs to support their families. It isn't even a close question who was exploiting whom. Men still suffer 92% of all work-related fatalities. But women have preempted the status of victims. When I was at the University of Virginia (UVA) in the 1990s affluent young American women drove their shiny cars about campus imagining they were the wretched of the earth. There has never been more absurd pretension.

148

Neither are men more violent than women. Violent acts are almost always directed against someone weaker. Some men sometimes harm some women, who are usually weaker. But women abuse children, who are weaker still, twice as often as men. And women have famously surpassed men in the savagery of their treatment of bound captives. In the hands of Indian women the torture of a single captive could continue for days. This kind of thing has been going on for a very long time; a carving on Trajan's column shows Dacian women torturing Roman captives.

As national leaders, women have been just as warlike as men. Consider Tomyris, Hatchepsut, probably Semiramis, Ahhotep I, Nefertari, Cleopatra, Boadicia, Mawia, Xenobia, Trung Trac, Isabella, Mary Queen of Scots, Elizabeth I, Jinga of Angola, Catherine the Great, Maria Theresa, Rani, Indira Ghandi, Golda Meir, Margaret Thatcher and many others. If women leaders went to war less often than male leaders, it's only because there were fewer women leaders.

Nowadays, false rape charges resulting in the long term imprisonment of innocent men, a feminine form of extreme violence, have become common. Using DNA evidence, the Innocence Project had won the release of, by 2004, 124 prisoners falsely convicted of rape. They were convicted on the basis of "eyewitness misidentification." (How do you misidentify the man raping you?) The men "misidentified" spent as many as 34 years in prison.

Of course, American mothers killing their children and the recourse of tens of millions of American women to abortion make all other measures of female violence seem insignificant.

Women aren't categorical victims and men aren't categorical villains. Any other conclusion is bigotry. But many women want the role of victim badly enough to become bigots. They want to be morally superior to men, to browbeat men, and to have men owe them.

One other fact contradicts the supposed victim status of women. Women have been the majority of those eligible to register to vote in the U.S. for 70 years. How is it that men are to blame for the condition of women? Betty Friedan, the founder of Neo-feminism, rebuked her colleagues, saying, "Men were not the enemy.... The real enemy is women's denigration of themselves." I don't owe women remorse.

Neither do I owe a debt of guilt and hate to American blacks. Slavery and the sale of slaves were rampant in Africa long before America got into the act. In fact, many of those who were enslaved survived because of slavery. In the constant intertribal wars of Africa, the conquering tribe enslaved women and children captives but killed adult, male captives until chiefs learned they could sell their male slaves to Arab and European slavers. The idea that black slavery was exclusively or even mostly the fault of whites is not true. The majority of slaves brought from Africa to the United States were initially enslaved by blacks. Most of the slavery that exists today is still the result of Africans capturing and selling other Africans. More importantly, no living American has ever been a slave or a slaveholder.

The present comparative poverty of blacks, supposed, falsely, to be the result of slavery, is no more so than Appalachian poverty is the result of devastating defeat in the Civil War and of longstanding contempt for "hillbillies" and the people we call "rednecks" and "crackers." There are abundant intervening causes for black and Appalachian poverty, for example, welfare dependency of various kinds, especially deliberate out-of-wedlock pregnancies to qualify for Aid to Families with Dependent Children. Present day blacks are not victims of anyone so much as themselves.

In 1963, in the Salpointe cafeteria, when racial violence in the South dominated the national news, Joe, my drinking buddy, and I discussed the best way to disperse an angry crowd of white segregationist Southerners. With relish we spoke of Thompson submachine guns, hand grenades and finally settled on shotguns loaded with rock salt.

I owe blacks no remorse.

I owe no moral debt for colonialism. From New Guinea east to India, savagery was the rule before Europeans ever arrived. The Europeans more often than not tried to put a stop to it. For example, on one annual feast, Hindus sacrificed their infants by throwing them alive into a shark infested confluence of the Ganges off Sagar Island. The British ended this practice and

150

other forms of human sacrifice. The British ended Indian slavery. At one point there may have been as many as nine million slaves on the Indian subcontinent. The Royal Navy began a campaign to stop the international slave trade in 1807 and was successful. When they ended sati, the British saved tens of thousands of Indian woman from being burned alive. Sati was the widespread Indian custom of immolating a widow on her husband's funeral pyre. A succession of European colonial powers that were active in the area tried to stop headhunting and cannibalism in New Guinea. Now the British are gone. Slavery is resurgent in African countries and cannibalism in New Guinea. Human sacrifice may be making a comeback in India. Still, the Third World condemns colonialism and reviles the West, claiming victimhood as an excuse for the Third World's failure to develop. I owe them no debt of remorse.

I owe no debt of guilt to Jews. When I was a child, a new Jewish couple moved into our neighborhood. The wife was extraordinarily beautiful and kind to us gentile children. Both the husband and wife spoke several languages. He had fled Germany before the war. Free himself, he arranged for the flight of other German Jews before all avenues of escape were closed. The family kindly adopted my mother, the widow, and invited her to their parties. At one party she met a group of Jews who were formerly Germans. They said they had voted for Hitler. They liked him until they were forced to take his anti-Semitism seriously. My mother asked, "Wasn't his anti-Semitism obvious and serious from the beginning?"

One of the ex-Germans replied, "We didn't think he was talking about us. We thought he was talking about vulgar Jews." The horrible mass murder of Jews took place in a land far away, before I was born. I owe no remorse to Jews.

Nor do I owe a debt of guilt and hate to homosexuals. Telling homosexuals that they should let it all hang out, that they have a right to do their own thing, that their behavior is natural, that they should be "who they are," is *nice*, but it's not one bit *kind*. Telling them that sodomy and promiscuity spread death is kind. I disapprove of homosexual behavior, *and* I don't owe homosexuals remorse.

I also stopped paying the painful debt of guilt I felt toward my country. And so I don't hate my country.

If your criterion for truth isn't the pain that it causes ("The truth hurts"), remorse can sometimes be reasoned away. As I have shown, I eventually reasoned away guilt with respect to all the political claims of victimhood mentioned above. Of course, my personal escape from this kind of guilt won't stop the television-obedient from condemning generations yet unborn to remorse for their race, religion, nationality or sex.

Guilt for past "wrongs" isn't the only means by which people can be made to feel culturally inferior. A Buddhist scholar I knew was puzzled by the appeal Buddhism had for hippies. He tried to explain to his hippy classes that "Nirvana" didn't mean heaven. It meant "put out the light," the end of an individual's existence, in other words, death. Traditional Buddhists are death worshippers. They believe that: life is pain; pain comes from desire; indifference destroys desire; and perfect indifference is annihilation. I'm a death worshipper myself. I sympathize with Buddhism. Westerners who want to romanticize things Eastern translate "Nirvana" as, for example, "absorption into the undifferentiated oneness of Being," which, seems to reserve a place for glory. For me, such phrases have less meaning than, "Rolled round in earth's diurnal course /with rocks and stones and trees," an unromantic sentiment from the Prince of the Romantics. Westerners invented Romanticism, but I don't see why we have to paste it over everything like grocery clerks stamping prices on cans. Often the screwy purpose of romanticizing distant cultures is to denigrate our own.

I remember being in a Chinese literature class. The young teacher described an ornate set of conventions that governed the writing of every line of a poem by Wang Wei, an eighth century Chinese Buddhist. The teacher read the poem and led the class in discussion. The class concluded that the poem was spontaneous and natural, unlike artificial Western poetry. The teacher agreed.

The first time I lived in D.C. one minor but depressing event occurred in the Smithsonian. During an exhibition of European and Far Eastern paintings from the time of Columbus, a young Smithsonian staffer was guiding an elderly couple through the exhibits, browbeating them with apocryphal and speculative "facts." He told them "Scientific logic has failed," "The West is in decline," and "Columbus killed and enslaved all the Indians." Obviously, he was trying to make his grandparents feel culturally and politically inferior. It looked like he was succeeding. Trashing one's own culture and country, in one respect or another, is a favorite pastime of millions of Americans. It allows them to feel superior to their countrymen.

My childhood friend, Ed, will lash out violently at anyone who says anything good about the West. He comes from a violent family. His two brothers, when they still lived at home, got into a fight over which of them had contributed most to the household. Each started breaking and tearing up the items he had bought for his mother. Since they had bought many things they continued breaking and tearing until their mother's house had little left in it that remained whole. All the while Ed and his mother stood silently by, knowing better than to try to intervene. I guess the point of Ed's siblings' destroying their mother's belongings was to somehow demonstrate their superiority.

Ed's violence is only verbal, but the intensity of his hatred makes it unmistakable. He condemns his country, his culture, his race, his sex and all that pertains to them. When he visited me in D.C. at my invitation, he refused to go to the National Gallery because the art in it was European. When he called me from Tucson to ask if he could stay with me for a second visit, I said no. I just couldn't take his invective anymore.

In the last twenty years, as I and one or two others in the old gang achieved some measure of success, I think Ed began to feel guilty about doing so little with his life. As I explained, Ed hasn't worked in fifty years. He came to believe that he had wasted his life. His cynical denigration of the West served a purpose. He had "dropped out" fifty years ago and so now what he dropped out of has to be evil to justify his dropping out. Ed also denigrates Western culture because, despite his denigration of it, he believes it *is* superior to other

153

cultures, *and that's unfair*. Lately Ed has decided that truth is unfair. He has adopted oriental culture. From romanticized Buddhism to Indian incense to kimono bathrobes, he has surrounded himself with it.

Drugs and Guns

When Joe first tried marijuana, he stayed high for hours. He loved it. That's when he went to San Francisco, where he tried every other drug. When he returned, he settled into the Tucson dope scene as the patriarch of its white contingent. He got arrested for possession of a relatively large amount of pure methamphetamine destined for sale. Joe didn't use amphetamines; he always favored marijuana. His reputable father was able to influence the district attorney. Joe was to go into the Navy. He was stationed in San Diego. There he was able to persuade Wayne, who was also in the Navy in San Diego, to stash some marijuana in Wayne's car. When the marijuana was discovered, Wayne was frightened by his interrogators into telling them where the marijuana came from. That he had ratted was common knowledge in Tucson's doping circles. Wayne never got over it. It was the pivotal shame of his life, as draft dodging was of mine. We each lost our self-respect. Joe was arrested again and was also discharged dishonorably. He came back to Tucson and resumed his patriarchal role.

Joe hurt people. He urged people to take drugs, but his principal means of hurting them was to give them stupid advice while they were high. I suppose he felt important when drugged people took his counsel. He was like Allen Ginsberg. If Joe had had as wide an audience he would have hurt as many people.

Stan was, perhaps, the most normal member of our company. He eventually became a UA fine arts professor. He launched his career sending in a drawing to the "Draw Me" match cover address. He took Joe's advice seriously. When Stan's wife was past the ninth month of pregnancy, she developed a condition that was dangerous to the child. The doctor urgently recommended inducing delivery to save the child. He needed the parents' consent. Joe talked Stan and his wife into denying the doctor permission because the delivery wouldn't be "holistic" if it was induced. The doctor probably wanted to hurry delivery because he had a golf game he wanted to get to, Joe said. Stan followed Joe's advice, but was in anguish. He asked me what I thought. I asked him if he had any specific reason to distrust the doctor. He said he didn't. I said, "Then you should do what the doctor advised." Stan gave the doctor permission. After the delivery, the doctor showed Stan the placenta, which had peculiar spots all over it, and said that was the condition he was referring to. It dawned on me then that Joe was truly a fool. You're a fool when your soul is stupid. It's not a nice thing to say of someone.

Whoever shall say, "Thou fool," shall be in danger of the fire of Gehenna. Matthew 5:22

The best parody of pompous unwisdom is old Granfer Cantle in Return of the Native advising a credulous teenager, "A man ought either to marry or go for a soldier....Neither to raise men nor lay 'em low... bespeaks a poor do nothing spirit indeed."

Another time, two sailors who wanted to be hippies had come back to Tucson on leave. Joe talked them into deserting. Kale, Memo's mother who was land rich, had some farmland outside of town that needed care. Joe offered the two sailors as tenants. Kale accepted them. Kale allowed them to live free on the farm in exchange for maintaining it. Joe didn't reveal to Kale the deserter's circumstances. The deserters grew bored in the country and walked away from the farm, which had pigs and cattle, without telling anyone. I don't know what became of the two young men or the pigs and cattle. There was a forest of spineless prickly pear around the farm. So the cattle and pigs had plenty to eat.

Joe took another drug-bent hippy under his wing. The hippy was obviously disturbed. He said he was in telepathic contact with Bob Dylan and claimed that he had had sex with Joan Baez telepathically. Joe kept handing the young man lit marijuana cigarettes on the theory that marijuana was a kind of therapy that could cure delusional thinking. It has the opposite effect. One day, when Joe had two attractive young women visiting him, the hippy, after several minutes of trance-like silence, smiled at one of the women lasciviously and said, "That was great! Let's do that again!" I believe he thought that if he had the audacity to fantasize publicly his fantasies would come true. I don't know what happened to him either. I do know that marijuana wraps around you like the layers of a mummy's gauze. Marijuana catches you by ideas.

When I came back from San Francisco, where I had been clean, I began using drugs again. At that time, Wayne, my roommate, also started using hard drugs. Wayne and I liked heroin. Late one night, Arthur, now an addict and dealer, came into our house after I had gone to sleep. He gave Wayne, who was already quite drunk, a big hit. I was suddenly awakened by Arthur's shout:

"Bobby, wake up. Get in here."

I wrapped a sheet around me and stumbled into the living room. Wayne was lying on the floor. His face was gray-blue. He wasn't breathing. Arthur said Wayne's heart had stopped. I immediately resented the fact that I hadn't been offered some of the heroin. I also thought, "I hope his mother doesn't blame me," a thought that dismayed me as soon as it entered my mind. Wayne and I had been friends since first grade, and I knew his family well. Arthur was kneeling over Wayne administering the usual lifesaving procedures. Arthur ordered me to find a phone and call for an ambulance. I ran out into the alley and started pounding and screaming at the doors of nearby houses trying to get someone to call an ambulance. Finally, without opening his door, a man asked for the address to which he should send the ambulance. I told him and headed back. When I walked into the apartment to tell Arthur an ambulance was coming, Wayne was standing up stretching as though he had awakened from a long sleep. He said:

"What a rush!"

No ambulance ever showed up. A police car slowly drove by.

After that I put up a cardboard sign prohibiting drugs in the house. Wayne moved out. Ed became my roommate. Ed and his thuggish friends defied my prohibition. Ed overdosed. His friends took him to a hospital and dumped him off at the emergency room door. It was quite a task. Ed weighed over 300 lbs. He lived. Overdosing is easy on heroin; you never know the strength of what you buy until you try it. Everybody wants to get as high as they can as fast as they can.

It is remarkable to me that Arthur stayed to save Wayne's life. No one but Wayne knew he was there. Most heavy heroin addicts like Arthur would have simply walked out, leaving Wayne's pulseless, breathless body on the floor. Heroin makes a person with even a light habit extremely selfish.

About this time, guns came to be involved in our lives. Wayne, Arthur and I all had guns. Wayne's was for protection. Mine was for committing suicide should I ever have the courage to do so. Arthur's was for robberies.

Arthur's return to heroin occurred after a horrendous withdrawal succeeded by two years of abstinence. Arthur told me at the end of those two years that he just couldn't feel free without trying heroin one more time and then quitting before he got hooked. He said he would always be afraid of the drug otherwise. Arthur soon developed such a habit he had to become a dealer to support it. In the conventional way of dealers, Arthur tried to get people addicted so he could more easily support his own habit.

He did worse things. Arthur, at the direction of the police, had purchased some heroin from Chente, an Indian famous for never losing his composure. Then Arthur ratted on him. Arthur and the police entered Chente's place of work, a state agency that dealt with juveniles. The police arrested Chente there when Arthur pointed him out in front of Chente's co-workers. Everybody liked Chente, including some serious criminals. One of them paid a nighttime visit to Jess and asked where Arthur was and if Jess was Arthur's friend. Jess said that he didn't know Arthur's whereabouts and was no longer Arthur's friend. That satisfied the thug.

In the end, Arthur tried to do still more dangerous things. He was murdered without his pistol, which he threw down when one of his proposed victims fearlessly pulled out his own gun and shot the now unarmed Arthur in a sham drug sale Arthur had arranged. Arthur was in the wrong trade if he was too kind to shoot someone.

The police made sure Arthur's acquaintances knew that he was killed in a fake drug sale so that they wouldn't think his murder was vengeance for ratting on Chente. They didn't want people to think they didn't protect their informants.

Prison

After I quit the UA press, I was night attendant at the Broadway Animal Hospital. I was afraid of the dogs and cats. I had returned to school to get a teaching certificate so that I could use my education to earn more than minimum wage. When I began taking the insipid Education courses, I looked for compatible work. The only compatible work was the job at the animal hospital. As it turned out, it was also the only work that prepared me for teaching. I later learned to approach the kids as I had approached the animals at the hospital. The veterinarian gave me a room with a kitchen, a bathroom and a small salary. My duties were simple. Only once did clients make use of my nighttime services. A couple, worried about their wheezing Chihuahua, brought him in for oxygen.

My job at the animal hospital left me time to practice the flute I'd purchased in San Francisco. I had a good teacher, my closest friend at the time, Jess. This was two years before he "cut me loose."

At the animal hospital, my routine was as follows: At 5:30 p.m., I would lock the front doors, put on a smock and go to the examination table where I relieved whoever was assisting the doctor, usually Dennis, a tall, strong blond with slightly crossed blue eyes, who, in contrast to me, had no fear at all of the animals. After Dennis left, the doctor would hand me a numbered tag. I could tell by the number whether it was a cat or dog. If it was a cat, I would grab a towel from a stack of towels as I headed into the kennels. I would take the cat out of its cage, wrapping its hindquarters in the towel, grasping and crossing its front legs in my right hand and tucking the wrapped rear end and legs under my left armpit, I would walk the cat back to the waiting doctor. The cats had the high numbers at the far end of the kennels. The kennels were two-tiered concrete cells standing against concrete walls on both sides of the concrete walkway under the low concrete ceiling. This meant I had to walk the cat back through the front section of the kennels where the dogs, no more than two feet away on each side, howled with incredible resonance and pitch into the long, echoing tunnel. If the cat stiffened, I readied myself for an escape attempt. Dennis didn't use a towel. All the other attendants did. The problem with holding the cat in either case was that the pliant neck and head were within range of my right hand. No cat ever bit me. They never thought of it, apparently, or, perhaps, they thought of me as protection, since there was no clear way to escape the howling dogs.

With the dogs we used a leash. The little dogs could be nasty. The big dogs were easy, especially Dobermans. The doctor, however, would not board any Doberman for more than three days because they rebuilt their sense of territoriality within that time, and then they became dangerous. The doctor never boarded pit bulls because they immediately killed any other dogs in their company. Sometimes the doctor would have me hold an animal he didn't want to anesthetize. He asked me to hold the largest German Shepherd I have ever seen while he cut something out of its testicles. It remained placid throughout the operation.

Each night, after the doctor finished with the last dog or cat, I would clean up. Usually there was a bloody mess. When the cleaning was done, I would drink two sixteen-ounce cans of malt liquor and practice my flute. I practiced in Jess's absence but under his written direction for three hours every night without fail for six months.

After six months, Jess began to show me more complicated series of notes to practice. He expected me to see how these "sevenths" or "elevenths," if I remember the names correctly, related to each other and to scales. I couldn't. I realized that I would have to forgo the two cans of malt liquor if I was going to advance in my flute playing. I gave up practice for a few days. Then I got drunk and sold the flute for fifty dollars. I began to devote myself to poetry. You can write poetry when you're drunk. Jess was furious with me for selling my flute.

I remember Dennis with some affection. He and I were roommates at the animal hospital. He was uneducated. He may not have been able to read. He had one friend who only came to see him when that friend needed backing in a fight involving more than two people. Dennis had served in Vietnam, where he killed a man, unsure whether the man was a Vietcong or civilian until he found the dead man's body next to a rifle. He said he was afraid and so didn't check before shooting the man. Later I made some remark implying that he had seen the rifle before he shot. Dennis wouldn't have it. He corrected me. From boredom, Dennis got drunk almost every night.

When I think what Dennis or the doctor might have done if they had known I was stealing the hospital morphine, I shiver. The doctor was an ex-WWII bomber pilot with 1950's attitudes. A drug addict was scum. The friend of another employee had stolen morphine when Dennis was present some months before I went to work at the hospital. Dennis hadn't known what was happening at the time, but he knew later when the absence of morphine was discovered. He expressed the hope that the thief would someday return to the hospital. Dennis was morally upstanding. He would never have used drugs, but he relished the possibility that he might someday beat up the thief.

I tried using the wide gauge needles we used for the animals to inject the morphine, but the needles were too big. I swallowed the morphine, which reduced its effect. So I had to take more.

It had been my task to wake up about 7:00 a.m. and give the dogs that were being operated on that day a shot of morphine in the scruff of the neck. The morphine would make the dog vomit. It's dangerous to operate on a dog with food still in its stomach. The morphine was in a box in a cabinet that was always unlocked. The box was shaped like the box a pizza comes in, only slightly thinner. Inside, there were about a hundred small, portioned-off cardboard squares. Each one held a small bottle of about ten small pills. Each of the bottles was sealed with a band something like the band they used to put on cigarette packs to indicate that the taxes had been paid. It was after I sold my flute, that I began stealing the morphine. I was afraid to tell my friends, because they would have tried to coax me into stealing dozens of bottles of the stuff.

In the morning, after the injected dogs threw up, I took them back to their kennels and cleaned up the vomit. If it was a Saturday, I worked during the day until noon. The first time I worked Saturday morning, the doctor sent me back for a dog. I opened its kennel and it rushed out past me, snarling horribly. Dennis apologized to me for not having warned me that the dog had been bitten by a rattlesnake, was in terrible pain and was crazy. We got lots of animals wounded in the desert, mostly because they had tried to fight the much tougher coyotes or chase javalina. The javalina cut them up badly.

We had a margay in the hospital for a little while. Though the doctor didn't usually accept wild animals, he had accepted this one as a special favor to an old customer. It was beautiful, a small, sleek leopard, a long, liquid house cat. It moved with such grace that Dennis would watch it for hours on one of those rare nights when he didn't go out drinking. Always seeking the high ground, it would walk up Dennis's arm, across the back of his neck and up his other, outstretched arm and then turn and walk back the other way when Dennis tilted his rigid arms like airplane wings in the other direction.

A man brought a housecat in late at night. The cat was very nasty, he said. It was huge, long like the margay rather than stocky, and it was obviously terrified. It escaped his arms and bloodied him in the process. When he caught it, I let him take it back into the kennels and place it in a cage, which was against the doctor's rules, but I didn't want to try to tackle the thing myself. I forgot to warn Dennis, who later admonished me, but was unhurt.

Once, the doctor sent me to get another enormous cat that looked absolutely round. When I pulled it out of its cage I realized that it was solid muscle. There was almost no flaccidity in its composition. Its fur was very short, a butch. I noticed that it had many scars and large parts of both ears were missing. The cat peacefully folded itself up in my arms and showed no nervousness whatsoever as I walked it through the tiers of howling dogs. That cat could probably have killed any dog in the kennels.

There was a beautiful Australian Shepherd that someone had boarded then abandoned. The doctor used it for blood transfusions. Dogs can be given any other dog's blood without regard to blood type. The Shepherd had its blood taken a bag at a time until it died. The doctor liked the dog, which was always friendly. The dog's corpse went into a huge freezer whose contents were periodically carried off by the county to be burned. Usually, a large pile of frozen corpses was on hand for collection.

One Saturday, when I walked into the operating room, the doctor had one of his son's friends on the table and was cutting a wen out of his cheek. The doctor looked at me as I passed by. He seemed to be trying to guess whether or not I would rat. He continued the operation. When I finished school I quit the animal hospital. I got my teaching certificate and moved back in with my mother.

I first taught in a mining camp, Morenci, Arizona. Morenci, including the churches, was entirely owned by Phelps Dodge. The miners were paid much more than the teachers. Some of the miners didn't like teachers. The teachers made the miners feel dumb. There was at least one fist fight. The teachers were good, hard-working, moral people, except for me and two others. One seduced her male students. The other married a whore from Agua Prieta who tried to convince her husband's visiting male friends to have group sex. I used drugs.

I don't know how the other teachers ended up in Morenci. I ended up there because Jimmy was arrested in Hermosillo on drug charges. We had gotten a call late at night in Tucson. The caller told us, in broken, heavily accented English, that Jimmy was in prison in Hermosillo. When my mother and I arrived in Hermosillo to track down Jimmy, we went to the local jail. Through a large window in the Commandant's office we could see a whole crowd of prisoners, mostly young Americans shouting and asking us from the roof of the adjacent building to inform relatives or friends of their situation. In their midst was Jimmy waving his shirt. He managed to communicate to us the message that we should deny that some scuba tanks next to us in the commandant's office were his. They were his. They contained false bottoms and were full of marijuana. Most of the jovial young Americans in the jail were probably set free within a couple of days. Jimmy was sent to the state penitentiary in the same city. That's when I knew I had to get a job to help pay the costs of getting him out.

When my brother arrived at the penitentiary, the prisoners were having a party with a large vat of home brew. They were extremely noisy and there were a lot of them. The partiers were the prisoners that ran the inside of the prison. They were called "cabos" ("corporals"). They formed a gauntlet when the new prisoners were released among them. The cabos treated the new prisoners to various humiliations. A huge Mexican prisoner confronted my brother. He told Jimmy to kiss him on the cheek or he would beat him up. Jimmy did and was called a "joto" ("fag") for a few days. In an American prison he would have been cruelly treated for the rest of his incarceration. The Sonorans allowed conjugal visits, including visits from prostitutes male and female. There wasn't any rape in the prison.

My brother's prison in Hermosillo was an impressive place. It was a huge stone castle with turrets and crenels and merlons, dark and damp, totally out of place in the Sonoran Desert. The cells were concrete closets with concrete platforms for beds. The cells dug into the walls like animal burrows. The toilets were holes next to faucets with buckets hanging from the faucets. I needed to urinate when I went in, but lost the need utterly when I saw the facilities. I didn't understand how they were to be used and they looked unsanitary.

There was a fight between two of the prisoners in the courtyard during my first visit. A thin, quick young man managed to keep out of the way of a stocky hirsute bruiser who looked like the head bandit in "Treasure of the Sierra Madres."

Jimmy told me there was an old man in the prison who had captured little boys, cut off their scrotums, cured the emptied scrotums and sold them for change purses.

He told me that three Americans had escaped briefly a month before. One of them, before making his way through the sawed off bars of a small window and down the rope the escapees had made, managed to steal the heroin of the cabos, who were in the business of selling it to the other prisoners. The police caught the three fugitives and brought them back to the prison. The cabos tied them up so they couldn't move more than a couple of inches. One by one, the cabos took running jumps, jamming their knees into the fugitives' chests, over and over again until the Americans were vomiting blood and begging the cabos to stop. When the cabos let them go, they couldn't walk. They crawled around for a couple of days and then died.

An old man committed suicide the night before my visit by tilting his rigid body over the second tier railing, then sliding and landing ten feet down on the concrete on his head. When Jimmy woke up he saw the pool of blood and the corpse. I only saw the blood.

The prisoners who had money prepared their own food. The rest ate in a large, crudely furnished room where all meals were the same. A pig donated by the diocese each day was cooked, chopped into fine pieces and served with rice. Jimmy said he found a small piece of jawbone with a tooth in it in his bowl. He wouldn't eat the communal meals after that if he could avoid it.

The first day Jimmy was in the prison, my mother and I were still in Hermosillo. We found that, if we called the prison, the official would bring Jimmy to the phone. So we kept calling with one last message or another until the official said, "This is not a hotel" and hung up.

I found the job in Morenci to earn money to pay a bribe or hire a lawyer for Jimmy. I arrived in Morenci drunk, throwing my last beer can out of the car onto the side of the road. Morenci was on the rising ground in Greenlee County, a moderate distance from the White Mountains. There were two huge smokestacks from which the sulfurous smoke sometimes swept downward across the plateau, enveloping the housing, the churches, the company stores and the classrooms. It was thick, but we taught through it.

The land around Morenci, when the smoke rose, was all pale blue and pink pastels in undulant layers, melting into the sky, like some Indian paintings. Three miles below Morenci in a canyon was Clifton, the left over town of a long defunct mine. Clifton could have served as a movie set, a town in the Old West. There was a dirt main street bordered by wooden stores sharing a wooden veranda over a wooden walkway raised a foot or two above the dirt street. People in Clifton liked to fight and had guns; this was only slightly less true of Morenci.

I went to the first Morenci home football game two weeks after my arrival. The whole town was there. I was quite drunk and attempted to pass my pint around to the kids I recognized from my classes. I thought they'd think I was cool. They got one of the local policemen at the game to drive me home. I remember things like that about my drinking and am still ashamed decades later, which is helpful. Other than the habit of screaming at myself, I have no psychological screen against my more humiliating memories. "I was drunk" doesn't help. It was the real me. But I found that embarrassment was a reprieve from my leaden solipsism, which is considerably more painful.

I got drunk every night while in Morenci, and as often as I could I bought codeine cough syrup from the druggist the next morning. He was a member of the school board. I liked some of the kids but I couldn't confront discipline problems in class. No real teaching went on.

Once I was able to keep my kids within bounds by looking absurd. One whiskey evening it entered my mind to cut my own hair. I did a thorough if awful job. The next day in all my classes the students were subdued. I had embarrassed myself again, but I frightened them. I cut my own hair from then on and still do today. When anybody suggests I pay for a haircut (haircuts are only $4.00 here in Ixtec) I say to him, "I would, but I can't find a barber who will cut it like this." The Mexicans call people who have hacked-up hair "trasquilados" ("hacked-ups"), a term that still applies to me.

During my second visit to Jimmy's prison, Jimmy proposed a scheme for escaping wherein I would give him my visitor's pass. With the pass, he would leave in a disguise he had created; I would stay behind until he was safely gone and then leave myself, explaining on the way that I couldn't find the pass they had given me. I said I wouldn't do it. Half way through the school year, after a bribe was paid, my brother got out of prison. His ineffectual lawyer became Governor of Sonora. That means he was influential enough to have gotten my brother out at any time.

I was in Tucson with the family and a friend of Jimmy's the night Jimmy returned. We congregated in the games room. Jimmy's friend pulled out a marijuana cigarette and started

166

passing it around. There was an almost immediate fight with my older brother, Charlie, who went to the phone to call the police. I ripped the cord out of the wall. He grabbed me by the neck with one hand. He let me go and went into the drive and grabbed Jimmy by the neck. I tried to intervene but couldn't. We were all screaming. Charlie finally let Jimmy go. Neighbors had come out of their houses to watch. Charlie drove off and didn't speak to the rest of us for some years. I don't blame him.

More Nose Drops

I finished my contract, but that was all. I determined I would never teach again and, when school ended, went back to Tucson where I worked more dead-end jobs for a few years. First, I became a security guard at Tucson General Hospital (TGH). I had the graveyard shift, which allowed me to drink. I was usually drunk at work. Hangovers became very hard for me. The sense of guilt and humiliation caused by whatever I had done when I was drunk and the fear of possible consequences were often agony the next day. If I ran out of liquor during the night, I would use my keys to get into areas of the hospital forbidden to me to find drugs with which to calm my writhing withdrawal from alcohol. In case of fire or other emergencies, I had the keys for every room except the pharmacy. I tried surgery but only found local anesthetics. The secretaries sometimes had drugs for their personal use, Darvon, for example, that they kept in their unlocked desks. I ate all the painkillers I could find. I didn't leave any. I didn't care that they noticed the theft. Opiates cure hangovers. I was never caught. When I had stolen all the opiates I could find, and there were no more, I came across a bottle of nose drops. I read the ingredients. No intoxicant I knew of was mentioned. There was one ingredient I didn't recognize at all, so I drank the whole bottle on the off chance it would get me high. I vomited for a while.

One evening, I took a friend, Chuck, a dedicated heroin addict, to the hospital. We stole a large, expensive television set from the guard shack, a trailer where they had a classroom for nurses' continuing education, but which only the guards had access to at night. It was an incredibly stupid theft. Chuck drove off in my mother's car with the television in the back to see if his dealer would accept it in exchange for some heroin. As soon as he drove off, I jumped to the conclusion that it was the car he would trade for heroin and that I would never see it again. It was easy to trade a stolen car for heroin in Nogales, Sonora. I was thinking up excuses to give my mother, "Someone stole the car while I was making my rounds," when Chuck drove back with no television and no heroin. He said the dealer would only give a dime, ten dollar, bag of heroin for the television, and we would only get that tomorrow. I was so relieved to get the car that I didn't argue. Chuck had undoubtedly pocketed much more than a dime bag of heroin to use over the next few hours and planned on giving me half a dime bag the next day for my trouble. The half bag was cut to almost nothing when I got it. Over the next three days no one noticed that the enormous television wasn't there. Over those same days, air-conditioning repairmen were given access to the trailer. When the television was found to be missing, it was concluded that the repairmen had taken it.

Chuck later staged a drug burn. A kid with mafia connections (Joe Bonano and his family lived in Tucson) was selling large amounts of marijuana. Chuck arranged a meeting between the kid and certain "customers." When the customers showed up they had knives. They tied everyone up. They said they were going to rape a girl who was there. They stayed about an hour, all the while making other grisly threats and clearly enjoying themselves. Then they took the marijuana and left. The kid's mafia connections deduced that Chuck had set up the burn and offered to kill him. The kid met with Chuck. The kid decided Chuck was not guilty. While the questioning was going on, Ed and I were in the next room listening. I wanted to intervene. Ed stopped me. Several months later Chuck told me he had set up the burn, though he hadn't anticipated such menace. Chuck was letting me know that I couldn't trust him, a generous act.

I got away with a lot while I worked at TGH. Sometimes, when I came to after a night's drunk and drug use and could remember that I had done nothing dangerous or criminal the night before, I would shake with fear because I knew it was luck. It terrified me to know that my life was a roll of the dice. Once, a nurse happened upon me while I was trying to break into the pharmacy. She apparently didn't understand what I was doing. She just smiled, said hello and went her way.

Toward the end of my drinking I got into the habit of imagining a button on any near wall. I imagined that the button, if pushed, would rid me of whatever evil I was feeling conscience-stricken about, usually an evil that had made itself apparent during the previous night's drunk. As remorse deepened I would imagine myself pressing the imaginary button. Pressing the

169

button I crushed a small vulnerable life, a worm, too slow to escape. The relief in this exercise came from knowing that I at least *wanted* to be free of the evil in me. Later, I began saying to myself, "Well at least I don't ..." whenever I had done something awful. For example, I might say, "Well at least I don't steal from my family," the morning after I had robbed a church poor box. Then, the next time, I would steal from my family and have to set another lower standard. Years later, during the first week I was clean and sober, I watched a businesswoman standing ahead of me in a bank line accept a huge stack of $50 bills from the cashier. I knew that if I was still drinking and drugging I would have followed that woman out of the bank and hurt her in any way necessary to get her money.

While working at TGH, I usually lived with my mother who had also become an alcoholic. One day she was already drunk when I returned from my security guard shift at about 7:20 a.m. I always bought two quarts of Colt 45 Malt Liquor and four ounces of codeine cough syrup on my way home from the hospital. I drank one of the Colt 45 bottles while she finished her unbelievably foul tasting, dollar-a-bottle wine. This time, when she had finished, she began rocking in her chair. She began to chant: "You bum. You queer," slowly, over and over again. With increasing fury, I told her to stop. Then, suddenly, to my surprise, I threw the full quart of Colt 45 at her head as hard as I could. She dodged it. The bottle took a chip out of the brick wall behind her and splattered. She paused for two or three seconds and then continued: "You bum. You queer." I went over to her and started slapping her face, hard. She stopped chanting and I stopped slapping. She said: "You realize this is the end, don't you." I responded with another series of blows until she said: "Ok! Ok!" Then I rushed out of the house. When I went back that afternoon, my mother was sober and had just awakened. She said that whatever it was she had done must have been terrible but that I must never slap her. That was how I knew I was still welcome to stay in her house.

When my mother was about 65 years old, she decided to have plastic surgery. She had her face lifted, and, later, she had breast implants. One morning after my security shift at TGH, my mother's new face started coming off. There was no bleeding. A long, deep, red slit appeared in front of her ear. When I saw it, I became upset. I pointed it out to her. She was drunk. She went to the mirror and looked at herself, but shrugged it off and said she'd see the doctor the next day. I went to bed wondering if her new breasts were falling off, too.

At TGH there was a hospital car the security guards sometimes used. There was an alcohol rehabilitation center run by the hospital about half a mile away, which was why we had the car keys. When I was called to pick up and deliver a drunk to the rehab, the alcoholic rehab nurses and counselors didn't notice my condition. I was drunker than the drunk I delivered.

I delivered the drunk some months after a weak first suicide attempt. I had taken a full bottle of my mother's tranquilizers. They didn't work. They just made me itch terribly deep inside my joints where I couldn't reach to scratch. When it became clear I wasn't going to die, I told my mother what I had done. She was disgusted. She drove me to the hospital where they gave me an emetic. I remember a young nurse looking at me with contempt. I said, "If you knew how I feel you wouldn't look at me that way."

My second suicide attempt, while still feeble, was not as feeble as the first. My mother had taken too many of her pain pills, Darvon, and gone without sleep for a day, which is an effect opiates, especially synthetic opiates, can have. She continued to take the Darvon, thinking it would help her sleep. She went without sleep for several more days and started to say nutty things. Jimmy and I were living with her at the time. I told Jimmy we should watch her constantly, relieving each other in eight-hour shifts. He didn't take me seriously and didn't show up for his shift. I got angry with him when he got home. He said that the idea was stupid, that mother didn't need watching. I suggested he go into her bedroom and try to talk to her. He did and came out stunned. We traded shifts and, after a few more days, called her doctor. I explained to the doctor what I thought had happened. He thought I was probably right and asked for the bottle of Darvon to see how many she had taken. I told him I had flushed the remaining pills down the toilet. He looked at me strangely. Of course, I had taken the remaining pills myself. He wrote a prescription for Sodium Amytal, the strongest sleeping potion. The doctor warned me not to give my mother more than one every several hours. I did as the doctor asked. My mother went to sleep and woke up coherent. In the meantime, I had the rest of the Sodium Amytal.

I was deeply depressed a few months later. I took all of the Sodium Amytal. There weren't many, seven I think. So I also took some Thorazine I had and a bottle of schnapps. I went to sleep for thirty-six hours. My mother was out of town. Nothing ever came of this second weak suicide attempt, and no person but me ever knew about it. I had scheduled my attempt for a time when I had a couple of days off work. I hadn't wanted to lose my job in case I failed again at suicide.

Artemis came into my apartment. She calmly reprimanded me for my suicide attempt, but when I asked, she told me I wouldn't have gone to Hell if I had succeeded. (Next time, I could try to kill myself without fear!) I asked Artemis if Lorus was a demon. She said it wasn't. Then I asked her if she was a demon. She advised me not to ask constantly for reassurance. As she walked out through the door she turned her upper torso and head back towards me showing a breast and her bottom and smiled like Betty Grable but without the bathing suit.

Later, when I asked Lorus what she was like. It said, "She's unrealistic."

Orange Light

A few weeks later I visited a free psychotherapist and told him how the orange light of the afternoons oppressed me, making me nauseous and claustrophobic. He cut off the interview and had me hospitalized for that. He apparently thought I was hallucinating. I wasn't sure, though the orange light I referred to invaded my aching head and stuck like dried paint.

The UA hospital psych ward, where he sent me, had none of the comfort and relief from tension that I felt at Norwalk. It seemed to increase the patients' anxiety. I asked for a pass the first weekend. Despite the atmosphere on the ward, I was feeling a bit better. I hadn't told the doctors about Lorus and the others. The doctors agreed to give me a pass, but then changed their minds. One told me, "Extremely depressed people often aren't able to commit suicide because they see no hope in death; they wait until they feel good." I was miserable because I feared I could never die. If I'd had a firm conviction that someday I would die, I would have felt wonderful. Some lines from one of Nájera's poems describe my depression best:

Saturn, I know well that no one you have created
Can ever cease to be.
But spare, I beg you, the as yet uncreated
From the black fate of being.

Saturn, the God to whom Nájera prays, ate his own children and vomited them back up again, whole and well.

Though I'm no longer hopelessly depressed, I'm still determined never to create an immortal life.

After three weeks in the UA hospital as a patient, I was given nighttime passes to return to my job as security guard on the graveyard shift at TGH, where I could sleep or get drunk or get drugged or all three. I continued stealing things. Sometimes I was already drunk when I arrived at work. Once, the security guard I was relieving handed me the keys. As the door to the guard shack slammed shut behind him, I fell over on the floor and passed out for seven

173

hours, waking up at about 6:00 a.m. in time to fill out a false log of events occurring on my watch. I returned the keys to the switchboard operator and went home. If I arrived at work too drunk and happened to be relieving Sammy or Jimmy, who also worked as guards at TGH, they would take my place to keep me from being fired.

One evening I was called into one of the TGH treatment rooms. There was a man suffering a heart attack, lying on a gurney, trying to sit up. I was told to take the place of the nurses holding him down. He kept begging me to let him sit up. The doctor and nurses were all fooling with different pieces of equipment. I asked the doctor if I couldn't let the man sit up for a second. He thought about it and said I could. I did, and the man sat up and fell back down dead. As he prepared to apply resuscitative measures, the doctor looked at me and said, "You can go now."

The only other time I was called to help with a patient, I was more useful. When I arrived at the ward indicated, an old ranch woman with that rare but still extant Arizona accent, a little like an East Texas accent, was wrestling with the nurses who were attempting to treat her. The old woman was using the worst language I'd ever heard a woman use. It embarrassed me terribly. The old woman noticed and ceased struggling. She said something friendly and, again, I was allowed to leave. When I left, for a little while, I wasn't a solipsist.

We patients on the ward in the UA hospital, to which I returned each morning, had group therapy in a large room with a wall of one-way mirrors behind which sat medical students and sometimes visitors. We were assured that there was almost never anyone behind the mirrors. We soon forgot the mirrors and lost any inhibitions they might have caused. During one group session I described my sexual habits in detail. My sexual desperation had returned during the long abstinence since I'd lost my virginity at Norwalk. In group therapy at the UA hospital my description of my sex life and attitudes was unrestrained and excruciatingly detailed. I discussed my vow and distrust of women, wept profusely and came close to collapsing.

After my catharsis on the ward, I discovered that an entire class of student nurses had heard my revelations from the observation room behind the one-way mirrors. The student nurses were there on the ward when we got back. I suppose there were ten of them wandering around the ward interviewing different patients. None of them bothered to talk to me. One of them, a beautiful girl with a fine figure, looked at me seductively, went into one of the vacant group therapy rooms and closed the door. I was talking to one of the medical students who urged me repeatedly to go in after her. I knew the door to the room couldn't be locked. I felt manipulated. My vow and my puritanical streak took control of me; the staff of a psych ward shouldn't be acting as a procurer! I couldn't do it. I couldn't follow the girl into the room. Maybe I was deluded; maybe what I was imagining simply wasn't going on.

I was diagnosed on the UA psych ward as having obsessive/compulsive disorder. "Obsessive compulsive" sounded familiar to me. When I was ten, in my frenzied attempts to avoid blasphemy, I had some ceremonies I engaged in. The principal one involved complex maneuvers to avoid pointing my penis in the direction of the church, in case I intended to blaspheme. I figured that was "obsessive/compulsive." I was "schizophrenic" and "bipolar" at the Institute. I have, in addition, been diagnosed as having "pseudo-dementia." I was twice diagnosed as "homosexual," before the American Psychiatric Association voted to eliminate that condition from its list of disorders. I don't think my diagnoses were real medical conditions. The mental health facilities I was in were only hiding places.

There was another patient on the UA psych ward I couldn't help but notice. He was monstrously ugly. He was always anxious. The first time I saw him we were having group therapy in one of the smaller rooms on one side of the ward. Just as the meeting started, he stood up, pointed to one of the male therapists and said, "I want to fight you, but first I want to have all my teeth taken out." One evening, when a new patient came onto the ward, the monster challenged him to fight. He liked people to laugh when he did these things, but when any of the patients talked down to him (patients tend to imitate therapists) he got angry.

He was not just ugly. He was like a character in a horror movie. His face was very angular; he had very dark bushy eyebrows that emphasized an already protruding brow, a Frankenstein forehead. He had huge buckteeth jutting out from a prognathous muzzle. His cheekbones stood up and stretched the skin of his jowls. Nevertheless, he was able to make friends with a mildly attractive female patient. They chased each other around the ward laughing, until a vulgar, extremely fat older Jewish woman, a rich patient from New York, loudly teased them about their "romance," at which point they were paralyzed with self-consciousness.

Jerome was the staff psychologist. At my request and at risk to himself, he showed me the forty dissecting tables with their corpses in the medical school dissecting room. At first look, I thought the drained, embalmed corpses were plastic training dummies.

After about two weeks on the psych ward, I was discharged into the care of the Papago County Mental Health Halfway House. I was sent there as a result of an assessment by psychiatrists on the ward that I had a strong determination to get better. I was the only patient from the ward to be admitted, although Jerome joined the staff at the halfway house. So at least there was one friendly face. I still worked the graveyard shift at TGH.

I stayed at the halfway house for about six months and only left when I concluded that the staff was insane. It was full of uncertified hipster counselors who preached responsibility, which is typical of mental institutions. Less typically, the hipster counselors claimed you determined everything that affected your life, from your emotions to your parents.

You selected your parents in the afterlife when you were in the process of either achieving Nirvana or being born again. As you drifted through the nether world, monsters that were your personified sins terrorized you. At the end of that gauntlet you had a vision of two people fucking. If you stared, captivated by the vision, then those two people turned out to be your parents in your next incarnation and the scene you witnessed was your own conception. If you didn't stare, but were indifferent, you got Nirvana. All this was supposedly part of the Tibetan [Buddhist] Book of the Dead, which is a hell of a thing to be teaching crazies in a state financed mental institution.

I believe there is a tendency in many human beings to blame themselves whenever they are in serious emotional pain. Reasoning your way out of guilt and blame is usually called "rationalization," which has popularly come to mean, "Lying to yourself." The counselors at the halfway house told us we were lying to ourselves whenever we struggled against guilt. Without realizing it, they were teaching us that all guilt was justified. Though they didn't intend to, the staff, being hip, casually promoted political guilt, like the counselors at Norwalk, as well. Several of us hadn't known that the U.S. was despicable. Most of the clients at the halfway house, like most mental patients, were passive and automatically adopted the opinions of the staff. We were told to "own" actions for which we had no obvious responsibility. "If we own our choices, we can change," the staff urged. They couldn't rekindle the political guilt I had been at such pains to extinguish, but the councilors, their Tibetan Book of the Dead and their peculiar psychological doctrines burdened me with a weight of responsibility almost as great as my Catholicism. My Catholicism had taught me that the consequences of my willful acts were infinite.

Jerome was different from the other counselors at the halfway house. He didn't try to catch you. He had no fast retorts. The other counselors thought they were showing insight if they made cracks as you spoke to them. They would have called them observations, but they were just cracks that made you feel small. They were rarely true. "If you want to change you have to face up to yourself" or "You have to own yourself if you want to get better," they sometimes said if you complained. The counselors made you feel like they were the know-it-alls of your soul, but they didn't know anything. Sometimes their cracks were so inane no reply was possible.

The idea was that you were there in the halfway house because there was something "wrong" with you; therefore, finding "faults" to correct was the counselors' job. The most formidable cracks and retorts came from the Director of the place. Her name was Sheila and she was the second worst bitch I've ever known. All the clients in the halfway house were assigned to one or another of the counselors of which there were probably eight, including part-timers. The counselors engaged their clients in one-on-one sessions a couple of times a week. I was assigned to Sheila. For a while, I combated her, usually giving as good as I got. I think she would have tried another tack if she'd had another tack to try. She had no insight of any kind that I could detect. Like the other counselors, she didn't even have realistic criteria for determining when she might have been right. As far as she was concerned, she'd hit the mark when she reduced someone to cringing passivity. She was fast with her remarks because she said the first thing that came into her head when she was providing a client with therapy. We were called "clients" rather than "patients" because the former title was thought to confer dignity, but the halfway house wasn't about conferring dignity. One of the clients, an insecure sixteen-year-old rape victim, told me of this conversation:

Client: "I'm afraid you're going to kick me out."
Sheila: "We won't kick you out. We might ask you to leave, but we won't kick you out."

A string of such replies left you not knowing what to say, at which point Sheila acted as though she had hit a lot of home truths and ended the session, leaving you to study the home truths. After a while, I couldn't keep pace with Sheila. I started to clam up so as not to give her any leverage. Nevertheless, her comments were insufferable. I dreamed of finding a hypnotist who would hypnotize me and tell me that, whenever I was offended, I would think it was hilariously funny and laugh until the offender went away.

I didn't find a hypnotist. Since my experience at camp, I didn't really believe in them, but, after a few months in the halfway house, I found another way to produce a similar effect. I began to score some heroin before each session. With heroin in my bloodstream I was able to just sit and smile as Sheila bitched. It was what I had wanted from a hypnotist, only, probably, less expensive. This disturbed Sheila and she clamed up too. I ended up with a small habit. Later, I confessed my heroin use to Jerome. He asked me how much I was using. I told him twenty dollars on the days I had a session with Sheila and ten dollars on other days. He advised me to cut down the amount. Of course, he told Sheila, who decided to quit her job and go to California. Her best friend among the counselors hated me after that. He had told us in one session that sometimes a patient was able to break a therapist's confidence. Then the therapist would quit and the client would triumph. I sure was in a contest with Sheila, and I sure felt like I triumphed. How much insight could Sheila think she had if she couldn't tell that a client was doped up on heroin?

About that time, a halfway house counselor took several of us clients to a nearby bar. I got very drunk. I tried to dance but was too self-conscious to move my feet. People made comic cracks about my stationary gyrations. When we returned to the halfway house, I sneaked into one of the other client's rooms looking for some prescription painkillers I knew he had. He was a champion rodeo bull rider and was broken up pretty badly. One of his housemates caught me. I told some inane lie and went to bed.

When I woke up the next day at four P.M., it was my turn to wash the lunch dishes. Doing those dishes that afternoon was the hardest work I have ever done. Later, I put on my TGH security guard uniform and paced the hospital corridors crying aloud and talking to myself all night, terrified I was going to be humiliated, perhaps beaten up by the bull rider, and turned out of the halfway house. That night was one of the few times I made my rounds faithfully throughout my shift. No one noticed. When I went back to the halfway house, I gave the absurd excuses I had prepared to the bull rider, and he accepted them with some skepticism.

I showed Jerome my shiny blue satin security guard's jacket with excessive padding to make the wearer look more muscular, sewn-on badges and insignias, gold braid and a brass identification pin. Jerome burst into laughter. I didn't mind. But sometimes, to lend dignity to my job, I called myself a "night watchman."

When I was at the halfway house, I and one of the other clients, a huge ex-football player named Keith, attended a session of "bioenergetics" together. This mode of therapy required the participant to stand and stretch his arms straight out in front of him, bend his knees at about a 45-degree angle, and raise himself on his tiptoes. His head had to face forward, not down. He was to remain rigid in this position, which was extremely uncomfortable and became rapidly more uncomfortable as time passed. It was referred to as "the stress position." As you stood this way, usually trembling, the therapist would stand next to you and touch you in various places and pronounce judgments on the reflexes called forth. Keith maintained the stress position without interruption for as long as I was there. The therapist touched Keith on the cheek. When Keith drew back, the therapist asked him if he was beaten as a child. Keith said he had been. This went on, with many of the guesses being correct. When it was my turn it was impossible for me to maintain the position for more than a few seconds. The experience reminded me of kneeling on the concrete floor before the altar at Pilgrim Temple with my hands stretched into the air, while the faithful prodded me with glossolalia. The therapist sent me away when it became apparent that I didn't have the courage to suffer. I still wonder what Keith's psychological problem was. He had been at Kent State when the killings took place. He was the chess champion of Colorado.

One day, the same therapist who conducted bioenergetics, a bearded, bell-bottomed mild young man whose goal in life seemed to be to remain unperturbed no matter what happened, invited all the clients of the halfway house to a therapy session at his home in the Tucson Mountains. The therapist lived in a foam dome he had constructed himself. We all inspected the one-room dome and were shocked to find the unenclosed toilet in the center. The therapist explained that he wanted his children, who were off at somebody else's house, to feel unselfconscious about their bodily functions. We lay down on the floor around the toilet and started the session with some relaxation exercises. Then Keith got up and said, "I have diarrhea. I *have* to go to the bathroom." Perhaps he thought we would all step outside, but the therapist reacted with indifference. I would have gone outside and shit in the desert.

The exercises went on. Keith pulled down his pants, sat down on the toilet in the midst of us and began shitting with the usual diarrheic smells and sound effects while the therapist intoned: "Imagine you are lying on a beach. A light breeze is blowing through your hair....etc." After a time, Keith rejoined us.

Keith shitting in front of us all was the major topic of conversation at the halfway house the next day. It was the consensus that he had shown great courage. His courage in the bioenergetics class and in his fecal predicament reminded me of an obscure saint's story.

Courage

Prospective Catholic martyrs in Japan in the 16th and early 17th centuries were presented with the fumi, an image of the Virgin and Child. They were subjected to various tortures, having boiling water poured over them, for example. This was to make them apostatize by stepping or spitting on the fumi. All the Jesuit missionaries, manly men at the time, and many of their peasant converts refused to apostatize. Their Japanese persecutors sought ever more dreadful forms of torture. The final torture they devised broke the resistance of even the Jesuits, all of them. The peculiar torture consisted in suspending a person upside down in a pit filled with feces and corpses. The victim was tightly wound with many turns of rope, like the long socket of a hangman's noose. The backs of his ears and his forehead were slit to drain the accumulation of blood and keep the victim from fainting. Slowly the pain built. No one subjected to this torture was able to endure it for more than four hours. They said the pain was worse than burning. I don't know the mechanism that made this torture so painful.

Finally, a peasant girl whom the authorities suspected of being a Christian was told to step on the fumi. She wouldn't. She died upside down in the pit after hanging for thirteen days. She never signaled a willingness to apostatize. I, who am a coward, sometimes pray to her because of her superhuman courage. She is a martyr and enormously superior to me in all important ways. No one is sure of her given name. She was canonized as Magdalene of Nagasaki.

Many envious people hate courage because they know they have none. They call it "macho," with a sneer. Most Saints, both women and men, were astonishingly courageous. The sisters raised us to emulate them. In my case they failed, but, at least, I don't hate courage. I don't obey television.

Halfway house clients other than Keith showed courage. Randy, another brave client, had fought back against over-aggressive policemen and been beaten by them. They had clubbed him and knocked out his front teeth. He was always laughing and always wanted beer. Everybody liked him, except Sara, who thought he wasn't serious enough.

Sara was a Communist. She governed the other clients of the halfway house like a tank boss. She could bitch at you with the effectiveness of a physical assault. She could stand up to anyone except Sheila. I tried to stay on her good side. I succeeded so well that she invited me to bed. I didn't want to go to bed with her. She was too bony.

The bull rider forgave me for trying to steal the medication he used to anesthetize his broken body. He had served in combat in Vietnam where he was unhurt.

One client, Steven, had made up a complex religion encompassing everything spiritual that he wanted to be true. The religion included a rigorous self-discipline for spiritual growth. When he felt he was not growing fast enough, he disciplined himself by attempting to cut off his foot with a machete. After a few strokes, surprised by how much it hurt, he quit, but he had a ghastly scar on his ankle that he showed me. Steven became a moderately successful Fuller Brush salesman and spent most of his time away from the halfway house.

Larry, an almost catatonic client, was a cowboy from a ranch in another county. He dressed neatly, always in cowboy clothes. He never washed his bedclothes or his hair. There was a thick, black, ugly stain on his pillow. He had risked the wrath of his extremely strict parents by falling into forbidden love with an Indian girl. His parents had him hospitalized. That, apparently, was what triggered his condition.

When I had been at the halfway house for a few months an amazing new client was admitted. She was pretty. She befriended another new client whose nose had been cut off. She was kind to him. He was soon obeying her. It was a sort of Esmeralda-Quasimodo affair. She listened carefully to the counselors and was soon imitating their jargon quite well. During her fifth night at the halfway house, she gathered four recent admissions and had them sit on the floor in one of the living rooms. She divided them into pairs, asking the members of each pair to hold hands with their partners, stare into their partners' eyes for two minutes, and then close their eyes and try to imagine what their partners would look like if they were attractive.

While they were holding hands, she walked a figure eight around the two pairs reciting a kind of litany:

> There are no accidents.
> Everything is just the way it's supposed to be.
> We all have an inner parent and an inner child.
> We each have an inner man and an inner woman.
> We each have inner grandparents.
> We each create our own reality.
> There are no misunderstandings.

I should have intervened. I remember watching her advise a new client who mistook her for a counselor. He was completely absorbed. She was the craziest client at the halfway house. Those of us who had seen her when she was first admitted knew it. We finally took it upon ourselves to let the new folks know. I rebuked her one day for "pretending to be a counselor." Some moments later her noseless protégé thrust his face to within inches of mine to punish me for hurting her feelings. Her peculiar looniness came to the attention of the counselors sometime later, and she was gotten rid of. It was decided she needed to be in a hospital. I can't help but think her persistent act required courage.

At the halfway house, my conscience was crippling. Every personal decision I made had a moral aspect. I was in the same position as Lara, another client. Lara said her voices told her that, if she killed herself, she would go to heaven, and then, as soon as she took thirty barbiturates, the voices laughed and said that they had been lying and that she was really going to Hell. My conscience vacillated like that. No matter what decision I made, it was going to put me in Hell, and if I changed my decision, my conscience changed with it.

Actually Lara believed in reincarnation, as well as Heaven and Hell. I espoused atheism at the time. I was trying, unsuccessfully, to keep my fears of Hell at a distance. We had an argument in which I said I resented her metaphysics because it meant I would have to live forever, and I desperately looked forward to dying. She said she resented my atheism because it meant she had to die forever. She wanted to live; she showed courage that I didn't have.

I believed that Lara wanted to sleep with me. I asked her out, feeling that a formal date was required first. I borrowed my mother's car. After I drove her back to the halfway house, we were talking at the kitchen table in her dorm. We were alone. I was trying to work up the courage to ask the girl to bed. I didn't know if her voices were becoming involved. I determined to speak very loudly. Suddenly Karen, a counselor, came in and abruptly told us that "clients should not sleep together while at the halfway house." Then she walked out. It was a surprising entrance and exit, a puzzling coincidence. I think she may have sized up the situation and was at a loss for something to say. Karen believed in free love. Her remark did not accord with her opinions at all. But her sudden appearance and words had mystical qualities. Lara was indifferent. She was a very willful and brave girl. Karen's remark was excuse enough to allow me to give up my already painful attempt to seduce Lara. I kept my vow of celibacy. After that Lara lost her confidence.

One day, at the halfway house, all the clients were told to attend a meeting in the large meeting room. All the counselors were there and the meeting was turned over to an almost hysterically stern girl, Sara, the Communist I mentioned. The meeting proceeded with a denunciation, couched in therapy jargon, of a counselor and a client who were caught sleeping together in one of the houses. The counselor and his client-girlfriend were sitting in the middle of the room. I raised my hand and asked the counselor and his girlfriend if they had consented to the meeting. They said no, and I said, "Then I think this stinks." The meeting was brought to a quick conclusion after that. The counselor was fired. His girlfriend continued on. Like Lara, the girl who slept with the counselor was pretty as well as brave. She made a few comments in my direction that let me know that she wanted to sleep with me. I didn't have the courage to do anything, of course.

Those were all the clients that I knew. There were five or six other clients in the halfway house.

Not only did I chase Sheila away. I once made a new counselor so uncomfortable, she quit after her first night on the job. It hadn't been my intention. Her name was Gina. She had been talking to a client in the living room as I sat there. She expressed her belief that people didn't die until they were spiritually ready. I saw the client withdraw into himself. I could see a thin, semi-translucent shade draw down over his eyes. He ceased focusing on external things. He was "tripping."

I said, when the new counselor made her remark, "If it were true that people only died when they were ready, there sure would be a lot of old people."

She said, staring deep into my eyes to emphasize her profundity, "There are a lot of old people."

I said that her idea reminded me of the old saw, "Only the good die young." The refutation was perfect, not in the least logical. It just made her belief corny. That's the only way to undermine hippy metaphysics. The client relaxed and his eyes stared outward again. The counselor quit, she said, because she was unqualified. She was, but so were all the other counselors. She came back to the halfway house when she had a date with the rodeo cowboy. After she returned she came to my residence. We were sitting next to each other. She seemed to be signaling that she would be willing to date me, but my cowardice, my uncertainty about signals, and my desire to avoid creating an immortal life kept me from asking.

When Gina left, outside the screen door, I could see Artemis and Aworac talking to her. Artemis said "Leave him alone. He doesn't want any of that."

Aworac said, "He doesn't really know what he wants. You should ask him"

Artemis turned to Aworac and said angrily, "He might ask her to fuck him, you idiot."

Aworac replied, "She'll say no, and he'll have humiliated himself.

She and Aworac began shouting at each other while Gina walked away as though she'd never heard them. When Gina had gone Artemis broke off her argument and turned and stared into my eyes seductively through the screen door as though we were sharing the same lewd thoughts.

Sex

One day, Wayne, newly clean, invited me to a party at Sissy's house. I didn't know it, but this was to be the occasion of their engagement announcement. When Wayne informed me they were to be married, I surprised myself; I offered hearty, sincere congratulations and insisted on being best man. Sissy, who was hoping for a different reaction, became extremely angry. She started screaming at me to get out. Wayne tried to calm her down, but I had to leave to put an end to the scene. I don't understand why Sissy wanted me to be a rejected, suffering suitor. What was in it for her?

After Wayne had been married for about a year his marriage lost its shine. He had reverted to his old drug habits. Sissy told me she couldn't climax when they had sex. Wayne had started forging her name on checks to cash to buy heroin. She assumed she was a total incompetent who couldn't balance her checkbook. The feeling of incompetence was doubly hurtful to her because she'd just finished a semester of student teaching at one of the local high schools and was so horrified by the meanness of the students that she'd quit teaching forever. So when she found out Wayne was forging checks to buy heroin she asked for a divorce. She'd had her first child some months before and was delighted with it. She kicked Wayne out of the house. I felt guilty because I had known all along what Wayne was doing with the checks and had often shared in the heroin.

After he divorced Sissy, Wayne began smuggling heroin from Nogales into Tucson. Suddenly he quit drugs altogether and remarried. He still drank heavily. His new wife was stupid, but, like me, she studied to be smart. She was a psychologist. She had her doctorate. She was a Neo-feminist. Her nickname, she bragged, was "Macho." She browbeat Wayne. She criticized him for trying to be "macho" every time he showed any spirit. I despised her. After she divorced him for his drinking, they kept coming back together momentarily for sex. I saw that she was still able to beat him down during those brief periods. I shouted at him one evening that she was an awful person and that she was hurting him. He was oblivious. There had been a time when he was emotive and intelligent.

He was six foot two inches tall. Wayne's father was short, perhaps five feet six, and, like many short men, exceedingly tough. He had fought in both world wars. He was from Tennessee. He was a countrified doctor with a liking for blacks. In his youth they were his hunting partners. After he became a doctor, in his office during regular office hours, he extracted a clot of maggots from a black bum's ear without appointment or charge. The black man had been in severe pain. Wayne's father couldn't remember how many of his appointed, waiting white clients walked out. He often went out of his way to help blacks. On the other hand, he was what we call a racist; he thought most blacks were of relatively low intelligence.

Wayne's mother had been a nurse. She worked in the office of her husband. For entertainment Wayne's parents drank a lot of beer and fought. They invited over a couple from across the street to join in their arguments. The dictionary was often brought out. Wayne, when he was young used to hide in his room during these debates. He would hang upside down in the narrow space between his bed and his chest of drawers and hum. Wayne's mother did a lot of work for charities. She was very kind. Neither of his parents thought to notice the effect their recreational arguments were having on their son.

When his father died, Wayne went to live with his widowed mother in Chula Vista, California. He had given up heroin but still drank heavily. Sometimes when he was drunk he would scream at his mother, blaming her for his wasted life, shifting blame from himself. He was like Ed. Wayne died two or three years after moving into the house in Chula Vista. He was drunk. He fell over, cut his head and lay unconscious in his mother's backyard. Head wounds usually bleed profusely. The alcohol kept the blood from clotting. He bled to death.

After his funeral, I began calling his mother every week until she died about a year later. Beginning with his drug use and dishonorable discharge from the Navy, Wayne, with my help, had broken her heart again and again. His dying drunk in her backyard left her consummately bereaved. She had almost no family or friends left, certainly none close by. When I talked to his mother after Wayne died I felt that I was hearing a distant, shrill cry behind her voice. I don't think I've ever talked to anyone in such profound emotional pain. Today I asked God to shorten Wayne's and his mother's time in Purgatory, in which I no longer believe to the best of my knowledge.

Two days after she broke up with Wayne, I finally slept with Sissy. She said to me, "Let's take off our clothes and go in the bedroom. We don't have to do anything." When we had taken off most of our clothes, she was standing by the bed removing her bra. I was sitting on the bed. I should have dug my hands into her breasts and ass while she was standing and I could get to all of it. I didn't. I sat there looking forlorn. She asked what was wrong. I said, "Nothing." She sat on the bed. Then she cupped her hand over my testicles, which was quite thrilling. Then she lay down, and I lay on top of her and sucked her breast. She said "Oh, Bobby!" That made me pull back immediately. The element of romance in sex disturbed me. It seemed phony. After that we slept together for about two months. She wouldn't let me touch her breasts with my mouth. I asked her why. She said it was because nursing her baby had made her breasts differently sensitive. I have a theory that nursing her baby had made her nipples protrude too much when excited and that my withdrawing had made her think that I noticed this. Consider the finger long nipples of some of the more mature Indian women in Amazon jungle photos. Maybe she didn't want me to draw milk, but she could have said that. I have another theory that some women just don't like foreplay and I had been unlucky enough to have them as lovers the first two times I had sex.

About two months after Sissy and I first made love, Sissy told me I couldn't sleep with her anymore, because in my frustration over my own inhibitions in bed, I had described to her perversions I wanted to engage in. I was lying, and she didn't believe me, but she felt that my mentioning those perversions was unforgivable. I think she just used it as an excuse to avoid further frustrating sex with me. She could have told me she was too frustrated to continue, because I was frustrated, too, or perhaps I should say bored. The breakup was a relief.

The perverse acts I told Sissy I wanted to perform were borrowed from John Carletta, the student who had stabbed me with the tip of his knife at Salpointe. We met fairly regularly at a bar that was the hangout of Joe and company for a little while. John detailed his sexual adventures when there were no girls around. He had told us it was especially thrilling for a girl to have the man, at the moment of her climax, spit back into her the mucus that accumulated in his mouth during cunnilingus. I had seen pictures of open vaginas and saw nothing attractive about them, even apart from such disgusting behavior. John's stories were numerous, all involving the same girl, a Catholic high school student, who was so naïve she didn't know what they were doing was a sin. He described their moments of "oneness" while fornicating in sitting postures on the toilet. John described getting a blister on the tip of his penis while fornicating through her closed thighs on a rug. He said he liked to "give her pearl necklaces" and stick his tongue into her anus. He spoke of feigning surprise when the girl explained to him that she had confessed what they were doing and had asked her confessor at what point it became a sin. She knew, she told the priest, that it would be a sin if she got pregnant. The priest, of course, was aghast. He expressed disgust and told her it was *all* a sin. That was the end of John Carletta's stories. He taught me more about sex than anyone ever had before. He made me grateful for my vow. The next time I heard him talk he was describing his fantasy sex life sucking a balloon. None of John's stories was erotic. Sex is ugly. I've broken my vow of celibacy with four women and only very briefly each time. I'm not sexually active.

My relationship with Sissy served to lower my opinion of sex further. Sex is so obviously unclean that AIDS hardly needs an explanation. Authorities have people thinking promiscuous sex and sodomy are ok if you use a condom. Studies conducted by the Alan Guttmacher Institute (AGI) in 2007 show that condoms, in "actual, typical" use, come off or otherwise fail 17.4% percent of the time. AGI is Planned Parenthood's source for most of its research and statistics and defends abortion. Subsequent studies of condom failure, testing with calibrated machines rather than actual use, show a much lower failure rate, but these later studies are, by definition, contrived. How are the calibrations determined? We're encouraged to have "safe sex," that is, to use condoms, which entails having sex.

> [A] vigorous condom promotion policy could increase rather than decrease unprotected sexual exposure if it has the unintended effect of encouraging a greater overall level of sexual activity.

"Condoms and seat belts: the parallels and the lessons" *The Lancet*, 29 Jan 2000.

Sex is dangerous.as well as disgusting.

The Creator Makes But One Demand

During the latter part of my drinking in Tucson, I compulsively spoke to whatever company I was in about being damned. Willy, a heroin addict at that time, told me I gave him the creeps because he could see that I meant what I said. He told me to steer clear of all things Catholic. Willy, after sinking to the depths of his addiction, became a doctor. I was told he got through his internship on methamphetamine. I don't know if he's still using. He was the only person other than my parents who ever showed any concern about my religious hysteria.

In fact, I was making a strident attempt to quit the faith. I had long forgotten Pilgrim Temple. Catholic doctrine reverberated unopposed in my mind. I had fallen into a trap. If you are a Catholic, you "sin against faith" if you don't believe in Church doctrine. In other words, if you don't believe in Hell, you go to Hell. The more you try to escape fear, the more you'll feel afraid. If you are somehow able to cease believing in Church doctrine, you'll have nothing you believe in to return to, so you are afraid to let go. Ceasing to believe is a sin that takes you outside the fear and dogma that compel belief. No one can throw you a line as you drift away. You are gone. You are probably, with finality, damned.

I tried desperately to break free of my Catholicism, first, by stealing from churches. Mickey, a member of our Tucson circle, taught me everything I know about being a thief. He was a down and dirty long-time heroin addict from D.C. and Jess's oldest and best friend. Mickey once stole diamond rings from a jewelers' display window by standing with his back to the open display and blindly feeling for the rings, all the while discussing a potential purchase with the jeweler. He could steal hundreds of dollars' worth of well-chosen clothes (he was a clothes horse himself) in a swift run through a department store. Mickey called this "boosting." He found out there was a doctor's office isolated in the desert north of Tucson. Late one night he crashed through the door without a moment's hesitation. He didn't "case the joint." He brought to my apartment an enormous cache of drugs.

I stole for different reasons than Mickey. I stole unmarketable ecclesiastical items: chasubles, stoles, brass fittings for candles, bells, censers, candelabras, a chalice, a ciborium, a monstrance, hosts (consecrated and unconsecrated) and similar things. The only tabernacle I had a shot at was screwed down. I sent one of the chasubles and a stole to Sandy, who wore them about an almost deserted Haight-Ashbury. I stole these things in the hope that sins of such magnitude would somehow separate me from the doctrines and morality of the Church.

Mickey had a fine looking girlfriend who posed for pornographers. We found out when we saw her picture in a sex magazine. She prostituted herself to win Mickey's release from a gangster who held him captive. I never found out what Mickey had done to get himself into this fix. Mickey killed himself. He borrowed Chente's car and drove to Nogales, Sonora, where he sold the car for two grams of heroin, which he did in one fix. When he was dead I thought of asking Mickey's girlfriend to sleep with me, but that seemed worse than stealing from churches.

Mickey hated Ed and wanted him to know it. In a suicide letter Mickey asked Jess to tell Ed. Jess didn't, even though he hated Ed, too. Jess had been talking about his dead father's habit of scourging himself. Jess's father did this behind his wife's back. One day she caught him and became hysterical. She made him promise to quit and he did quit. Mexican Catholicism among the poor is only slightly to the right of believing in vampires. I can't criticize them. I often believed in Aworac and its companions. I resemble poor Mexican Catholics, except they're only delusional. I'm psychotic. When Jess told the story of the scourging to Ed, Ed said, "Well, Jess, among primitive people that kind of behavior is normal." Ed always was, and still is, that callous.

Theft from churches didn't work. To distance myself from Catholicism, I next tried blaspheming the Holy Ghost. Very deliberately, I said, "Fuck the Holy Ghost" many times. It was hard. I came near to choking every time I said it. Twice in the Gospels blasphemy against the Holy Ghost is declared to be forever unforgiveable. When I blasphemed the Holy Ghost, I was irredeemably damned. I figured that after my blasphemies I would not be able to afford a faith that only damned me, and would, therefore, be compelled to reject the faith. I wanted to stop thinking about religion entirely. Attempts to reject the faith are mortal sins, of course. My blasphemies only created more fear and guilt.

Remembering these things makes me suicidal. As I said, I have been suicidal off and on since the fourth grade and have made two attempts, both mortal sins, of course. Each was the result of the fear of Hell with the purpose of escaping Hell, which I feared might be my destiny if the attempts were successful. However, I finally escaped my fear for a long time as the eventual result of the following incident.

Like Jess, Joe was a connoisseur of avant-garde jazz, the kind in which musical instruments screech atonally like fingernails scraping a blackboard. I went to Joe's house weekly. As I entered the door he always handed me a lit marijuana cigarette. I would take a puff, get high, and then everything I saw and heard would tell me I was damned. An abstract painting on the wall with absolutely nothing identifiable in it would demonstrate irrefutably that I was damned. A comment from Joe or his wife would tell me I was damned. But most of all the screeching music would tell me I was damned. I always accepted the marijuana because I thought that if I could smoke marijuana just once with good effect, I would be saved. As I mentioned, marijuana addicts you by ideas. When the fear hit me, I would rush down to the nearby liquor store and buy two quarts of Colt 45 malt liquor, carry them back to Joe's and drink them to diminish the fear. All this happened many times. One day, as I entered Joe's apartment, he handed me a joint and went over to his stereo saying, "I have a new album; listen to this." After a moment's hesitation, I lifted the joint to my lips. This time, like President Clinton, I didn't inhale. For fear, I couldn't even draw the smoke into my mouth. As the fuzzy blank space on the record began to sound, I thought, "Now Hell is going to start." To my surprise, the music that I heard wasn't dissonant. It was mellifluous and effulgent, and a clear voice in the background began to sing:

> The Creator has a master plan
> For His own, and He owns every man.

> The Creator has a working plan,
> Peace and happiness for every man.
> The Creator makes but one demand,
> [I thought, "This is why I'll go to Hell,"
> but heard only:]
> Peace and happiness through all the land.

Freedom washed through me. I was in tears. I was no longer wholly trapped in my sealed self. Thereafter, fear that I was in Hell ceased to be the only air I breathed. The song said I *belonged* to my *Creator.* Therefore, He preceded me, was outside me and not me. If God existed my self-centeredness was false. After my first emotional response, I considered the words of the song cautiously and carefully, but the near certainty that I was alone forever was gone. I was given a fighting chance, the chance that I was wholly God's possession.

When I had discovered some years earlier that I believed in Hell, morality, judgment, free will, responsibility and my own culpability but didn't believe in any God, persons or things outside myself, my fear was overwhelming. Only my creature companions, a growing number, tore through the shell of my solitude and only when I believed in them, but they frightened me in their own right.

The Redemptorists, whom I have mentioned, taught us that God loved us so much he wouldn't destroy our free will and that was why we could elect to go to Hell. They said that God was the measure of all measures, the infinity of all infinities, so there was no standard by which to judge God's acts, whatever he might do. However, in Joe's apartment my desperation gave the "master plan" a significance it couldn't have had otherwise. The song said that I was God's responsibility. I was His work. He "owned" me in the sense that the hippy counselors at the halfway house gave the word. Of course, they would have considered my assertion that God, not I, was responsibile for my destiny an extravagant "cop out." But I told myself, "If it's true it isn't a cop out." I'd had a lifetime of being infinitely responsible for my behavior, any particle of which could put me in Hell forever. For the moment a yoke of limitless weight was taken from my shoulders. If the song was true, I couldn't, by any act of mine, deserve damnation. I had a new premise from which I could hypothesize against Hell. I could rationalize it away as I had

194

rationalized away political guilt. Just as I made up theories when I was a child, I could argue with my fear. Hell might not exist. I couldn't *decide* to go there. I wasn't *free* to go there. I began to reason, relying heavily on Lorus to guide me.

After my musical experience in Joe's apartment, I began to truly believe in "the Creator". I bet on His existence, but not like Pascal. Pascal didn't bet on the existence of God; he bet on the existence of Hell. My new God was the annihilator of Hell. If He existed, Hell didn't. God and Hell contradicted each other. And God guaranteed my final happiness. I could ignore judgment, free will, responsibility and my own culpability and put all my eggs in the God basket.

My fear of Hell became sporadic for about a year, although it reappeared with full force in D.C during my first residence there. In the intense atmosphere of violence and fear, I forgot about God and His plan. When I got back to Arizona and entered AA, I began again to argue against Hell. My episodes of spiritual fear became less frequent. I sang the above lyrics every morning. Before the song, if it seemed possible that I was in Hell nothing worked as evidence against it. After the song, for awhile I had the ability to fend off my terror.

Violence

Many years ago I bought a 32-caliber revolver and joined the NRA. I agreed with their argument that, if more people helped promote the private ownership of weapons by supporting the NRA, thieves and policemen would be more hesitant to enter people's homes. I was given an NRA decal. I pasted it on my front door. Someone broke in but couldn't find my gun. For a long time, I was hanging out with other heroin addicts and thieves. Having a gun was advisable but I was having second thoughts. A second, wilier thief broke in and relieved me of my doubts.

I don't worry about armed violence here in Ixtec, Jalisco or its surrounding villages. There are narcotics here but heavy traffickers have not made inroads, so there are no gun battles in the streets. That's not so in the North. Perhaps it has never been so. Juarez, Chihuahua, the city where the insanely murderous Mexican Revolution began in earnest, is now the principle location of gun battles between narcotics gangs. A friend of mine, Kale, who celebrated her hundred and seventh birthday last year, grew up in El Paso, the American city adjacent to Juarez. She and other American children used to climb a hill to watch the Mexicans fight. Here, in Jalisco far to the south, Ixtec and nearby villages were as peaceful during the revolution as they are now. Things don't seem to change.

"Everything is the same thing, and nothing changes," Parmenides said. He held that existence was a solid sphere of pure, uniform matter. The sphere was perfectly dense — stuffed. No part of it could move. There was no empty space in it for any part of it to move into. Parmenides called the sphere "Eōn," which is translated as "the Plenum," the extreme opposite of a vacuum. In the Plenum all Being was perfected. Changeless, the Plenum abode in nothingness forever, like a black hole that has sucked up and crunched the entire universe.

Zeno defended Parmenides. His paradoxes were supposed to show that motion wasn't possible. For example, a man approaching a goal first had to reach a point midway to the goal and a point midway to that point and a point midway to that, *ad infinitum.* So all finite distances were really infinite and could not be crossed. All motion was an illusion.

That was as close as Parmenides ever came to not seeming silly. It wasn't very close. Nevertheless, I have spent much of my life desperately trying to refute such ideas.

Since I wrote the paragraphs above, things have changed. The assistant police chief of Metla, five miles from here, was killed in a drive-by-shooting, apparently for having slapped a drug dealer, and three policemen in Tlaxco, fifteen minutes from Ixtec, were murdered, causing the rest of the members of the small Tlaxco police force to resign., A policeman was kidnapped and murdered in Juatepec, about twenty-five minutes from here. Ixtec, Metla, Tlaxco and Juatepec are all relatively small villages. Their total population is a negligible fraction of the population of Juarez. A week ago there was a gun battle in Metla. The passengers of two cars exchanged shots. It isn't known if anyone was wounded or killed. Two Ixtec drug dealers had their limbs and heads cut off four days ago. Their parts were found in open garbage bags at Five Corners within easy walking distance of here. Four people were murdered in Ixtec and Metla three days ago. A policeman, the brother of a friend of mine, has been missing for weeks. Yesterday, an American in Ixtec was found shot to death. The dogs had gotten to him. At first it was reported that dogs had killed him. Whatever else happens from here on out, I'm not amending this paragraph. It and my life will remind me that things change much and fast.

When I was saved by the lyrics I've mentioned I was living at the halfway house. Ed was living nearby in the collapsing, thirty-five dollar-a-month, single family dwelling he and I had rented some months before. I had moved out, but I still paid half the rent. I was his ghost roommate. I wanted to keep my options open as I had at Norwalk. Ed made his living by bringing heroin across the border from Nogales, Sonora. He smuggled the heroin in balloons or condoms in his stomach. Back on the American side of the line, Ed would take syrup of Ipecac to help him vomit. If the heroin didn't come up, he had to wait until the condom passed through his intestines. It was *very* good heroin usually, and I got too much of it too cheaply.

One day, I decided it was time for me to make a change, and this meant getting away from heroin and heroin addicts. I quit the halfway house and bought a ticket for D.C. I chose D.C. because I had two brothers there and places to stay. I mailed my 32-caliber pistol to one of my brothers so that I wouldn't have to carry it aboard the plane. As I've noted, the pistol was to shoot myself with when I found the courage. I had a gram of "Mexican brown" heroin, which would have been a far more comfortable means of suicide requiring no courage. Almost immediately upon my arrival in D.C., I found in the Post that Washingtonians were dying as a result of underestimating the strength of the "Mexican brown" heroin that had recently arrived in town. Still it didn't occur to me that I could use my gram to kill myself until after I used up the gram. That's miraculous stupidity, surely an act of Providence. Furthermore, I had forgotten to send ammunition with my pistol, and D.C. and neighboring cities had laws forbidding guns and everything appurtenant to them.

Here in Ixtec I know where to go to score heroin. I will always remember Wayne's pulseless, breathless, "What a rush!" overdose. I envied him, especially since he didn't wake up describing visions of eternity.

In D.C. I stayed with Sammy and his girlfriend, Eve. The first day I went without heroin was difficult. I drank all the whisky I had bought to ease withdrawal. It doesn't help that much. I went to the liquor store on the corner about 11:00 p.m. to get more and discovered that D.C. liquor stores were required to close early. Over the next several evenings, after learning this fact, I stood by the window watching the store and my supply of liquor to make sure I didn't run out again. I put some distance between myself and heroin sitting at that window. For a while, Ed sent me heroin about every two weeks. I couldn't resist using it when I got it, so there was no question of saving up enough to commit suicide. I was afraid to try to score in D.C. because violence in D.C, usually drug-related, was far worse than anything in my experience. Eventually Ed stopped sending the dime bags. I'd kicked.

D.C. violence was much worse than San Francisco violence, which was bad enough. In D.C. a kid, about eleven, with a baseball bat got on the elevator with me in our apartment building one winter night. I pretended he was going to play baseball. When I walked out of the building there was a fight on our street corner. A young man was lying on the ground; an older man kicked him in the face.

Sammy was robbed at gunpoint. While one kid held a pistol to his neck, the other tried to grab Eve's purse. She wouldn't give it up. A tug of war began. My brother felt the increased tension of the first kid through the unsteady barrel of the gun against his neck. My brother said, "Give him the purse, Eve." She did, and the kids ran off with it.

On another occasion, when I was out walking, I saw two teenagers beating up a man on a bus while the people who had been on the bus with him poured out of it and stood outside watching. When they were finished with the bloody man, the teenagers exited the bus and stood around menacing the crowd outside with no apparent fear of apprehension. I hadn't been on the bus, but I stepped inside and asked the seated, bleeding man if he needed an ambulance. He said he didn't. So I got off, left the hoodlums loud-mouthing the passengers and went to my apartment building half a block away where I could phone the police. The hoodlums ran away before the police arrived.

One afternoon, I was headed to St. Elizabeth's Psychiatric Hospital in Anacostia to visit a friend who had come to the conclusion that he was the Buddha (he was an LSD victim from the sixties). I heard a man on the sidewalk say in anguish to a commiserating woman that his son had just been murdered in Anacostia, which he bitterly described as the most violent section of D.C. I decided to take the bus from the subway stop near St. Elizabeth's rather than walk the rest of the way to the hospital, as I had planned. On the bus, going up the hill to the hospital we passed two large teenagers walking with grim purpose in the opposite direction and carrying elaborated clubs. I would have had to walk past them if I hadn't been on the bus. The friend I visited at St. Elizabeth's told me one of the other patients had stolen his shoes.

Anacostia wasn't unique. Outside our apartment, if I waited no more than a minute any time after dark, I could hear gunshots.

Sammy had carefully explained to me that if you were walking down the sidewalk, especially at night, you should trust to your instincts and avoid black teenagers. The black teenagers did, in fact, commit nearly all the street crime. If young blacks were approaching, change sidewalks, Sammy told me. If the blacks changed sidewalks, too, he told me to go into the street and walk down the middle. Around this time, I saw on the D.C. television news a report featuring a sociological experiment by black teenagers in one of the local high schools. Two large boys tried to approach whites on the sidewalk at night to ask the time. The whites avoided them. The filmed result was supposed, by the black anchorman as well as by the kids, to be racism. But there was, in fact, a far, far greater chance of being robbed or hurt by blacks than by any other group. Black cabbies, especially, refrained from picking up blacks.

The mall was full one Fourth of July. The great majority of those present were black. There was a smattering of whites including Jimmy, most of them alone and vulnerable. A group of black teenagers began approaching solitary whites from behind. They ripped their back pockets open and took their wallets. Jimmy noticed several ripped pockets and saw a young white man on a knoll crying and screaming with rage. Around the young man, the crowd had opened up in a circle with a radius of about twenty feet. The red-faced young man was missing a back pocket. He challenged some teenagers in the crowd to fight while they threw glass bottles at his head from all sides. He had been hit several times. Eventually he screamed "Niggers!" The black teenagers laughed and continued to look for soda bottles to throw at the young man. Jimmy could see some approaching black teenagers nearby moving through the crowd. Jimmy guessed he was the teenagers' next target. He started moving away through the crowd as quickly as he could. It took him about ten minutes to escape into the open. He had heard one of the teenagers behind him say, "Man, don't this guy ever slow down!" None of the black adults made a single move or said a single word to stop the robberies or the stoning. *That* was racism.

I was at a party with Jimmy and Dee. We were on the second floor. Held apart by my usual paralyzing shyness at parties, I was standing at a window staring down at the sidewalk. A well-dressed couple walked into view. Suddenly two young men stood in front of them. One was holding a gun. The couple raised their hands and the man without the gun removed things from their pockets and purse as they stood there.

I turned to Jimmy and said, "There are people being robbed on the sidewalk."

"Bullshit," he responded and turned away. I insisted. It took about five seconds for the partiers to take me seriously. My brother suddenly got up, looked out the window and ran down the stairs. When he got to the sidewalk, I saw the robbery victims point out to him the receding back lights of a car about twenty yards away. Jimmy disappeared with the car under the arching trees.

The police had been called and soon arrived. They interviewed the breathless couple, me, and one of the partygoers who had managed to catch a glimpse of the robbers before they sped off. Dee, Jimmy's girlfriend, and I were sitting in one of the police cars talking to a policeman when we heard over the police radio that a white male had been shot in Southeast Washington, our section. Despite the fact that several people were shot every night in that area, Dee was instantly convinced that the person shot was Jimmy. The policeman radioed the unit that had reported the shooting and asked for a description. The man described couldn't possibly have been Jimmy.

Another announcement came over the radio. Quite near us on Pennsylvania Avenue, two youths had been cornered by the police and identified as the probable perpetrators of the robbery we had witnessed. The policeman in whose car we were sitting took us to the scene. There were three police cars, with their front lights, spotlights and siren lights turned on, parked in the grassy median near The Hawk 'n' Dove, a bar/restaurant we frequented. There was a crowd. With their backs pressed against the outer wall of the bar, two black adolescents, a girl and boy, perhaps 13 years old, stood terrified. They were not the robbers I saw on the street. We found Jimmy. He was telling the police that he was mistaken and that he couldn't have identified the robbers anyway, not having seen anything other than the trunk of their car. Jimmy hadn't thought to look at and remember the license number. We all walked back to the party. Several nights later Jimmy was beaten up in a bar. One morning I saw a dead man, victim of a shooting, in front of a bus stop. We circled around him to board the bus.

D.C., like New York City, was also the site of a lot of verbal aggression. In 1976, at the only ostensibly peaceful party I attended in Washington, I was trying to dance with Dee. I kept spazzing out. I started dancing spastically on purpose as a rebellion against my own shyness, the way children caricature the behavior they are made to feel self-conscious about. The result was break dancing. A man at the party screamed at me "You fucking creep! You *asshole!*" I immediately stopped forever. I don't claim all the credit for inventing break dancing; I'll just say I came up with it independently, the way Leibnitz and Newton came up with calculus.

Jimmy lived with Dee. Dee was a topless dancer and lots of fun. She said to me, "If you're good I might give you a blow job," while Jimmy was standing next to her. He stared at her in amazement. I think Dee was serious, but she only giggled at the look on his face. I had written a poem for Sissy shortly before I left Tucson. Sissy's family was from Iran. I recited the poem to Dee, which is when she started to like me. The poem dealt with the dark-haired, dark-eyed beauty of very white Persian women. Dee, who had no relevant family background as far as I know, apparently thought the poem was for her. She was white with dark hair and eyes, like Sissy. Jimmy later told me I could fuck Dee as far as he was concerned. I wasn't interested. Dee got drunk when Jimmy wasn't around, came over to Sammy's new apartment (we lived near them on Capitol Hill), threw her arms around me and kissed me. I was the only one at home at the time. I softly pushed her away. She loudly, foully cursed me for about a minute, then went for my face with her long fingernails. I managed to push her out the door.

Jimmy took me to the bar where Dee danced. We watched her and her coworkers wiggle around awhile. When they had a break, all but one came over to our table. The one who didn't come was the only girl among them who had a remarkably beautiful body. She had a grievously sour face. She sat at a separate table by herself waiting for one of the clients to ask if he could join her. The other girls said she was mean. She glared at us hatefully. The girls at our table were all fun to be with, like Dee (usually). Dee apparently didn't have any memory of the incident at Sammy's

Dee visited a photography studio that had advertised a job for a receptionist. They gave her the job, but when she showed up for work they told her she had to fuck all the men that worked there. She came over to our apartment crying and told Eve what had happened. Eve, who was a third year law student, commiserated with her but did nothing; law school, as I later found out, doesn't teach you to do stuff. The better the law school's reputation, the less practical instruction it will offer.

Eve's life was a wreck like mine but for different reasons. She took a pro-minority/women stand on every issue. We didn't get along. She had scathing things to say about men, all men, not individuals or even types of men. Like all bigots, she couldn't shoot straight, but she thought she was proof against any charge of prejudice because she was "ideologically sound." Television-obedient people *never* look at their own prejudices.

When we were children, my brothers and I had our fights, but normally we were generous with each other. When we divided food, we would often take the smaller portion for ourselves. Eve expressed alarm and sharp skepticism when I told her this. Her comments showed that she and her siblings would never have behaved in like manner. I appealed to Sammy and he acknowledged that we brothers were generous with each other. I and Sammy and Eve ate out a lot, often accompanied by friends. During one dinner, Eve repeated what I had told her in front of Sammy and several of Sammy's friends in a loud mocking voice. Sammy hid his head. I knew then that she had nagged him into saying that what I had told her was untrue. She perfectly fit Isak Dinesen's description: "The barbarian loves his own pride but hates and disbelieves in the pride of others."

Of course, Eve was Pro-choice. After sitting quietly through one of her Neo- feminist tantrums, I said, "Both Susan B. Anthony and Elizabeth Cady Stanton considered abortion to be infanticide. They didn't shed their humanity to pursue feminism."

Eve was shocked and replied rhetorically in the way typical of many Neo-feminists, "If men had babies abortion would be a sacrament."

"If men had babies they would be women," I replied. She hated me after that, not just as a male, but as a person.

Screaming

During my first exile in D.C., as I explained, I was terrified of violence, and I had forgotten about the Creator's master plan. I went about in fear for my body and fear for my soul. After I arrived in D.C. and kicked heroin, I looked sporadically for any kind of job and found nothing. Jimmy found me a patronage position as an elevator operator in the Cannon House Office Building. In a patronage position I could get away with almost anything. Any day I didn't show up for work, I was docked, but that was all that happened. It was a pretty good job for an alcoholic and the pay was fine for non-union blue-collar. Every morning I went to my elevator and turned a toggle switch from "automatic" to "manual." Then the button for one floor or another would light up, and I would press the lit button. Then the elevator would proceed to the indicated floor; the people would get on and tell me what floor they wanted , and I would press the corresponding buttons. My shift lasted six hours with one fifteen-minute break. One or the other of two Danny-DeVito-sized men would relieve me for that break.

One of the little men, Sam, was completely inarticulate. Sam never spoke whole words, only notes. At first I tried to understand him. Then I dismissed his happy chatter as though it were birdsong. He was pleased if I simply nodded and smiled in response. Sam's speech expressed a mood at most. When he relieved me for my break, I raced to the near bathroom to pee then ran to one of the huge cafeterias and bought the largest coffee and raced back to the elevator with it. That got me through the next three hours.

I liked to imagine that the building was a huge engine with dozens of pistons spread throughout. The pistons were me and my elevator and the other operators and their elevators. Of course, none of the elevators was in any way coordinated with any other. The operators didn't know each other. We didn't wear uniforms, so if we crossed paths, no doubt a rarity, we couldn't guess that we had anything in common. The stones and windows of the building were placed so that sunlight, if the sky was clear, shone brilliantly through parts of the building onto the white pillars and walls. For four seconds, as I ran through the rotunda on my break, I was on Mount Olympus. When my elevator opened onto the gray, windowless, cavernous basement, and passengers exited, I felt like Charon.

I failed to communicate in other than demented fashion with the humans who crossed my threshold. I was one step above Sam. In an effort to improve, I determined that I would give a wide smile to everyone who walked through the doors. I didn't know how to smile sincerely and scared a few people.

Senator Ervin sometimes rode with me. Another occasional passenger, a bearded, always disheveled man, using both feet in unison, would take a two-foot leap over the one-inch crack between the floor and the elevator. I learned to get out of the way when I saw him through the opening doors.

Other than my brother Jimmy, Artemis and the children of animals, I had only three acquaintances in D.C., John, Steve and Phillip. Steve and Phillip were homosexuals. Neither seemed to be bothered the day they came upon me screaming alone outside my apartment. They told me they'd just been to John's house, a room on the second floor of a deserted building. John was an LSD victim. He wandered the halls of Congress looking for a job. He had a sort of Ivy League version of filthy clothes. He crashed parties in the Congressional office buildings, met political celebrities, asked them for jobs and ate the food provided. John had no working toilet in his house. He peed in a jar. I don't know where he defecated. He wasn't at home when Steve and Phillip dropped in, so they emptied the full jar of urine on his bed. I wondered if I would be the next victim of their cruel comedy.

Steve was a waiter in a classy Italian restaurant. He talked endlessly about the various people he served in his restaurant, whether they were rude and how he got vengeance when they were. Late one night, Phillip pounded on my door screaming. He told me Steve was chasing him to beat him up for having had sex with another man. Steve wanted to take care of Phillip, who was an adolescent. He said that when Phillip got older and stopped looking like a child, like "chicken," few older homosexuals would have an interest in him, and Phillip would have to fend for himself.

206

Once inside my apartment, Phillip went to the bathroom and came back with clownishly heavy makeup from a compact and lipstick he carried. He stared at me for a long time seductively. I was repelled. Suddenly Phillip burst out with an excellent rendition of "Anything Goes" and followed it up with an equally good "Stag in the Forest" from "Cabaret."

My screaming on the streets and in the elevator during my first stay in D.C. was in part a matter of remembering ancient insults, but I mostly responded to insults from characters I invented, insults that I knew had never taken place. I played both parts in elaborate arguments and screamed when I was myself and had been outdone by the superior wit of my opponent. I was always outdone. I was full of anger and fear. The fear of Hell again obsessed me. Up to the time of my last, horrendous drunk in D.C., I screamed on the streets in daylight, and I screamed on the elevator. If I was waiting in my empty, closed elevator, I might start thinking about someone, real or make-believe, who had hurt me, and I would start saying angry things to him, though, of course, no one was present. If I got a call to the top floor, I would get louder and louder as the slow, clunky elevator rose. By the time I got to my passengers, I would be screaming. The elevator would jar to a halt and I would return to reality and shut up. The doors would open and one or more people would be standing in front of the elevator staring in and peeking around the doorjamb looking for my adversary before entering. People started avoiding my elevator. The man who jumped over the crack that divided the elevator from the floor stuck with me.

The screaming on the street was worse. In the elevator, I had some rudimentary conversation. People would tell me where they wanted to go and I would announce the floor when we arrived. There was some comfort in this. It's remarkable to me when I consider it now. Around people I didn't know well, in common social situations, I was tongue-tied by an acute shyness.

Nevertheless, I worked up the courage to ask one passenger, a very precocious teenager who worked as a summer intern in the building, to have dinner with me. At dinner, she asked me when my birthday was. I told her July 4. With a look in her eyes and a modulation in her voice that showed she thought it was a remarkable coincidence and omen, she told me her birthday was July 3. I failed to join with her in her surprise. The next time I saw her she asked me how old I was. I told her, and she said I was almost as old as her mother. I said, "Yeah, but I'm real immature."

My inability to respond to insults and my shyness had always been tremendously disturbing to me. If I couldn't think of a quick response to an insult, I believed I was not allowed to respond at all. I eventually learned I could reply the next day or the next week. That knowledge was a breakthrough, as was the ability to act on it. I don't know when I developed the ability to say things back fast. It wasn't until after I learned to say things back late. For the first 36 years of my life, the only defense I had against insults was to buy off potential insulters by being meek. My meekness showed people they could insult me and get away with it.

On the street, I was alone for all the notice I took of those around me. No one talked to me. There was no elevator cabin jarring to a halt; there were no opening doors to bring me back to reality. I screamed with unrestrained rage, more and more indifferent to the passers-by. I have no idea how to reconcile my shyness with my screaming.

But I eventually stopped being embarrassed by my screaming, which scared me because I started to drift into solipsism. I remembered Lorus saying,

> In order to be embarrassed you have to believe in some external witness, the laughing children of animals, for example, or anonymous passers-bye. For as long as you are embarrassed you can't believe you are alone.

Trying to apply what Lorus had told me, I thought up outlandish stunts to humiliate myself. I painted my face with mud. I covered my head to my temples and the back of my skull with a tight transparent plastic bag. It puffed up absurdly and stood higher than Lincoln's stove pipe hat as I walked to work. If I'd been invited to a Halloween party I could have gone as a Portuguese-Man- o'- War. If I had a cold I let my nose run until it was dripping down my chin. I sang loudly, atonally and arhythmically in subway cars, making up the "tune" as I went, like the caterwauling children who once begged by singing about their poverty on the Mexican trains. I carried a naked doll, a baby, on a thread tied to a stick pressed between my pursed lips and

my nose so I that I made an absurd face as I walked and the doll swung below my chin. I

shouted long strings of meaningless syllables. Later such small embarrassments worked with

diminishing effectiveness until I was inured to them. But they served as training for far more

grotesque, serious and outlandish behavior to come.

One day, the second elevator relief man came to relieve me. I asked what had happened

to his partner. The second relief man told me that Sam, the mutterer of bird-like nonsense, had

burst into tears and collapsed in one of the dark underground passageways leading from one

government building to the next. Sam was a drunk, a fact I hadn't noticed, and had severe

mental problems, the second relief man said. I felt bad for Sam, but mostly I felt bad for myself;

I felt foreboding. I decided to clean up my act

I went to a doctor and got a prescription for Antabuse. I took the stuff as prescribed for a

few months. I didn't have too much faith in it because in Tucson I had learned to drink on top of

it, not much, but enough to get me high in conjunction with a little codeine. The combination of

the three drugs felt like an allergy. My face got puffy, and I found it difficult to breath. In D.C.,

however, I stayed off the booze for as long as I took the Antabuse. Then I decided that anyone

who could kick heroin and give up alcohol would certainly be able to stop talking to himself. I

gave it a try. I couldn't do it. I tried harder than I had ever tried to do anything in my life. My

anger and screaming grew worse with my efforts. I screamed blasphemies. Then screaming on

the streets of D.C. or on the elevator began to degenerate into nonsense. I ceased to think of

the arguments that justified my resentments and only roared out my pain in inarticulate tones

of triumphant refutation. I was crazy on two counts, I screamed in public at people who didn't

exist, and I screamed meaningless gibberish.

In my wanderings one day I found a 32-caliber bullet. It lay on top of some trash at the

curb. It was an ensouled, palpable, shiny piece of metal in my hand. I no longer had my gun. I

had been burgled again.

I was now alone in the apartment I'd shared with Sammy and Eve who had married and moved to Phoenix. The landlady lived in an apartment immediately above mine. Without the presence of Sammy and Eve, I started screaming at home. I think the landlady could hear me. She was afraid of me. I soon moved in with Jimmy. We fought because of my screaming. I moved into a cheap, decrepit apartment in the tenderloin. One day I got lost in the near neighborhood. I walked for two or three hours. I got a cramp in one of my legs and was hoarse from screaming. I was frightened. I guessed that I was occupied with my screaming every time I passed a landmark that would have reoriented me, but I couldn't stop screaming. I was in tears. I lay down on a park bench and fell asleep for a moment. When I awoke, naked Artemis was standing over me smiling, the cramp was gone, and I knew where I was just in time to get home before the prostitutes and accompanying dangers leaked into the streets. Artemis walked me through the park, down my alley and up three flights of stairs to my door. When I unlocked it, I thought to invite her in, but I choked.

The next day I began screaming again.

My inability to stop talking to myself and to stop screaming on the streets and in the elevator left me deeply depressed. One day, when I hadn't been able to get to work for a week, Dee offered me some of the Dexedrine she was taking for weight loss. I stopped taking the Antabuse and took the Dexedrine instead. As soon as I figured most of the Antabuse had worn off, I got wildly drunk. I had moved into a better apartment. It had a bottle of Red Worm Mescal on a shelf as a decoration. I hated mescal. When I woke up from the drunk, the mescal and worm were gone. I was more depressed than I had ever been before. I wasn't even suicidal. I had no hope in death. "Death" sounded like "Hell" or "more of the same." I was in that state of despair the doctors at the UA Medical Center had described. I couldn't kill myself. I had forgotten about the song that had broken my psychosis, and I had forgotten about God. Nevertheless, I prayed. I said "God help me." The idea instantly came to me to leave D.C., go to Phoenix, since I was unwelcome in Tucson, and attend AA meetings. It didn't occur to me that I should go back to Arizona and quit drinking. The thought was to attend AA meetings to be around other people who were drunks and drug addicts like me, people I wouldn't feel inferior to, so that I wouldn't be so lonely. Maybe then I would be able to stop screaming.

While still in D.C., I went to the office of Congressman Roy Stenton who had been one of our nearest neighbors in Tucson. We stole lumber from the building site of his house when we were children. I was on his patronage. Only he could fire me. I said that if I quit I would have difficulty getting timely unemployment compensation. He agreed to fire me.

The next day, the last day I showed up at the elevator to work, I said to each of my still diminishing number of passengers, just as the doors closed sealing off the interior, "This is really a microwave!" No one laughed. The only one to react at all was the disheveled man who always leaped over the crack between the floor and the cab. He sounded like a man trying to scream his way out of a nightmare. It scared the hell out of me. When he ran off he stepped on the crack he normally leaped over.

That night I felt desperately lonely. I began speaking in tongues to keep myself company. It didn't work. I called an ex-girlfriend of Sammy's who lived in the city. I hadn't seen her in years. I asked if I could come to her house. When I arrived, after two minutes of conversation, I asked her if I could sleep with her. She said I could. She had become a pharmacist, I'd been told she was haughty. When our clothes were off, she said, "Is there anything you would like me to do?" cooing and drawing out the last syllable as though she were talking soothingly to a cat while petting it. I lied. I said I wanted her to perform fellatio. She took my penis in her mouth. I immediately lost my erection. We had only the most conventional sex. As at Norwalk my copulation freed me of some of my egocentricity for a moment.

Before I went to sleep that night I found several worms in my bed. They were not like Coleridge's water snakes; there was nothing beautiful about them.

The next day the pharmacist phoned me and asked if I was the person who had called her shortly after I left her house and told her she was a whore. I was almost sure it hadn't been me. I swore it hadn't been me.

The Choose Religion

I applied for unemployment compensation to be sent to the Phoenix office and two weeks later, I went back to Arizona and tried AA. This was something of a miracle, not because I decided to do it but because I did it. Depressed, mentally imbalanced, emotionally confused people aren't good at carrying out plans.

In Phoenix, I called the AA number in the directory, and, a few hours later, I was picked up and driven to my first meeting. At the meeting I was told to buy and read the "Big Book," the book Alcoholics Anonymous. I was told that the Big Book was AA. I was told to read only the "black part."

I knew that meant, "Don't interpret." I bought the book and, when I got home, set about reading it, studiously not interpreting. It was clearly written. Nothing in it was cabalism or code. I was particularly encouraged by, "[t]here are those, too, who suffer from grave mental and emotional disorders, but many of them do recover if they have the capacity to be honest." The book was a revelation in other ways, not so much because of what it said about alcoholism, but because of what it said about God.

The exact wording of the first three steps of the program is as follows:

1. We admitted we were powerless over alcohol; that our lives had become unmanageable;
2. Came to believe that a power greater than ourselves could restore us to sanity;
3. Made a decision to turn our will and our lives over to the care of God, as we understood Him;

I was amazed. The third step said I could abdicate moral responsibility for myself and give my will and life to God! It was like selling my soul to the Devil; I was taught that nothing could undo such a contract. The memory of the song, "The Creator has a Master Plan" came back to me with greater force than the original experience. I saw that I might entirely escape my psychotic religious fears.

Gene, a staunch Baptist, the owner of a desert junk yard, guided me through the third step prayer. I repeated the words after him: "God, I offer myself to Thee to build with me and to do with me as Thou wilt..." We were praying in a Humpty Dumpty's. People at the other tables could hear us. This was embarrassing for me, but I continued. By the time I had finished, my conscience was dying. Indeed my will, whatever that is, and the rest of me did belong to God. I thought I might eventually be able to forget any fear of Hell that remained to me. With time there would no longer be any moral dimension to my life, only clashing instincts. I was almost free. Boy, would Gene have been upset if I'd told him what I was thinking! From that point on, without effort or intention, I stopped screaming and almost stopped talking to myself. I was falling into God's love.

The fourth and fifth steps in AA are:

> 4. [We] Made a searching and fearless moral inventory of ourselves;
> 5. Admitted to God, to ourselves and to another human being the exact nature of our wrongs;

My moral failures are mostly petty, not often shocking. My biggest failure is cowardice. When I did my fourth step, every day, after I said my morning prayers, I added an entry to my inventory, each entry describing something that I remembered that the sisters would have called "sinful." I never wrote more than a short paragraph, and I only stopped writing the paragraphs when I had covered 47 sheets of legal-sized paper with small, hide-from-myself handwriting. Most AAs, following the model in the "Big Book,' write no more than a half dozen pages. The signal for me to stop was that I found I wasn't able to avoid repeating myself every day for about a week.

At the end of my fourth step I described my draft dodging. It seemed so ugly in so many ways that I wasn't sure I would be able to go on to my fifth step. I don't think I'm a very good person. I'm a taker, not a giver. I may not be allowed to go to Heaven if "deserve" means anything. (I don't think it does.) Lou, the man I chose to read my forty-seven pages to for my fifth step, was disposed, at first, to consider me a mostly innocent young man with an overly sensitive conscience. He kept interrupting me to tell me so. I insisted he stop interrupting me and save his comments for the end. He was quiet for the three hours it took me to read my inventory, and then he said:

> Bob, you're going to have to live with that for the rest of your life!   No! I mean take it and burn it and forget all about it.!

Between the first and second sentences I knew with certainty that he'd heard the secret I'd only managed to choke out, perhaps, I thought, inaudibly, at the end of the inventory. I was finished with both the fourth and fifth steps.

Poor Lou. I'd picked him because he was a deeply moral man, a Canadian veteran of WWII, sincerely religious, and wouldn't be too morally jaded to hear what I had written. I'd had considerable experience unsuccessfully fighting guilt. In my draft evasion, especially, I was like King Claudius trying to repent while in possession of the fruits of his sin. Nevertheless, I felt a great burden lifted from me, even when I saw how much, eleven years after the war was lost and over, my act shocked and disgusted Lou.

The sixth and seventh steps of the program bore out my understanding of the first three steps.

> 6. [We] Were entirely ready to have God remove all our defects of character;
> 7. Humbly asked Him to remove our shortcomings;

Even our faults were God's responsibility. Steps six and seven, like step 3, are entirely irresponsible.

I was aware that there were serious problems with the idea of *moral* responsibility. Hume's analysis held as far as I could see. If every choice I make is the necessary result of a chain of determining causes, then I'm not free and, therefore, not morally responsible. But if somewhere in such a chain of determining causes something happens spontaneously, freely, for *no* determining cause, it's just that for which no one and nothing can be accountable. What can moral responsibility mean then?

Most AAs say that we each choose every feeling we have. AA's suffer a kind of emotional isolation. No one and nothing outside them can ever touch them *whether they will or not*. Every emotion exists entirely because it is chosen. It has nothing to do with an outside world. AAs often try to erase their pain by an effort of introspective will. When I speak of the "Choose Religion" in a meeting, AA members usually argue with my sarcasm by declaring that they have a free will. Swami Vivekananda says, 'Free will' is a contradiction in terms." I like the irreverence of his statement. When I introspect I find no muscle of the soul, no choosing organ of the psyche. I have decided that "free will" means the roiling, changing, moving conglomeration of my desires. I give God my desires and my life. God changes me by changing my desires, not by pulling on strings attached to my limbs. I suggest that other AAs call their will their "chooser." Some do, defiantly asserting their willingness to believe that there is such a thing.

It's obvious that the surprising euphoria one initially experiences with alcohol and drugs is release from frustration, shame, fear, hatred, guilt, *etc*. When AA's say, "We choose our emotions," they are after the same thing they were after when they drank, control over their feelings regardless of what's going on around them. Their belief that they have this control leads them to treat their own and others' pain as sin and happiness as virtue.

I remember a priest lecturing us at one of our in-house retreats at Salpointe. He told a story about a Catholic boy and girl being found in each other's arms in the back seat of a car, dead and naked. They had been making illicit love when exhaust leaked into the closed cab from the engine they had left on to run the heater during the cold night. They were in mortal sin and they died without a chance to go to Confession. The priest said, "They *chose* to go to Hell!" "You chose it" is the final premise of morality, "You asked for it!" Only they didn't ask for it. They may have caused it, but they didn't choose it.

I have limited popularity in AA. An ex-convict and murderer who was in Mexico "on the lam" and with whom I quarrel a lot told me I had upset him so much that he made plans to burn me alive by setting fire to my house while I was asleep.

The next steps say,

8. [We] Made a list of all persons we had harmed and became willing to make amends to them all;
9. Made direct amends to such people wherever possible, except when to do so would injure them or others;

My belated unemployment checks came all at one time about three months after Congressman Stenton fired me. They amounted to about a thousand dollars. They came to me in the mail care of the Phoenix unemployment office the first day I was to open the church where my AA home group met and make coffee. Since I had *asked* Congressman Stenton's legislative aid to fire me and since I was still something of a moralist at the time, I considered the checks a departure from the "rigorous" honesty AA asks of its members. I tore the checks up and flushed them down the toilet in the church men's room to make a ninth step amend to the government. My sponsor later told me I hadn't had to destroy the checks. My deeper motive in doing so was to be able to say to myself, "If I drink I will have wasted a thousand dollars." I'm so miserly that it worked.

When I got to AA I was first required to repay the churches from which I had stolen. Making amends involved getting prices from various church ladies' catalogues and sending the churches corresponding amounts of money in the form of postal money orders.

Personal amends were more problematic. Once, when I was in Tucson, an old friend of mine came to town. He and I went over to Jess's house. Jess didn't know him well and on the basis of something innocuous my friend said, started hinting with a sneer that my friend was a racist. As I said, Jess had told me several times that he hated white people. I lost my temper and told Jess that *he* was the racist and that he liked to browbeat white people for no other reason than that they were white. In defense of whites, I asked Jess if it wasn't true that

216

Mexicans discriminated against Indians. He told me that Indians were ignorant and filthy, which surprised me because Chente, his good friend, was an Indian. Then my friend and I left the apartment. I fell out of contact with Jess for a couple of years as a result of our argument. Jess had officially "cut me loose."

Step nine requires us to make amends to those we have harmed regardless of what they may have done to us. After I joined AA I tried to apologize to Jess. I memorized what I was going to say to him and went to his mother's house in Tucson. I knocked at the door and Jess answered in typically hip dress: mirror sunglasses, goatee, and beret. I bowed my head and humbly recited the remarks I had prepared. When I finished, Jess said, "I'm sorry to hear you and Jess had a quarrel. I'm Bert, his older brother. Jess isn't here. We don't know where he is. The last we heard, he and his wife were picking fruit somewhere in California."

I mumbled, "Well, if you see him, tell him what I said" and headed back to Phoenix.

Sometime after that Jess moved back to Tucson. I was in Tucson for a few days myself making other amends to old friends. Jess and I got together. Jess launched into some remarks he had obviously prepared. Among other things, he said that he wasn't a racist; he was a "culturist." He objected to white culture. He said that, though the Mexicans hated Indians, at least they hadn't "killed them all the way the colonists did in the United States." Rather than refuting his dubious points, I simply told him that I was "proud of the accomplishments of English speaking people" and asked if that was all right with him.

He said "I guess so" and a couple of weeks later sent me a letter in which he flatly stated that he never wanted to speak to me again.

Some of my subsequent amends ended relationships, too. I decided step nine also required me to apologize to Joe and his wife. During my last visit to their house I said some awful things after they made a sneering remark about my draft dodging. I went to the café, now jointly owned by Joe and his wife, to see them and make amends. The counter man told me that they were at home, so I called them and apologized. However, I never took up with them again. AA doesn't require that. Later, Joe and his wife were divorced. Joe's wife ended up with the café. Joe worked for her.

The tenth and eleventh steps say,

10. [We] Continued to take personal inventory and when we were wrong promptly admitted it;
11. Sought through prayer and meditation to improve our conscious contact with God *as we understood Him* praying only for knowledge of His will for us and the power to carry that out.

Facing the wrongs I have done becomes easier each day, since I have only a small and dwindling conscience. From time to time I ask someone to forgive me for hurting them. Most mornings I ask God to keep me clean and sober, and I sing the song I learned in Joe's apartment. Singing the song is my meditation. Sometimes my prayer is deliberate nonsense, because it really doesn't matter what you say to God.

The twelfth step says,

12. Having had a spiritual awakening as the result of these steps, we tried to carry this message to alcoholics, and to practice these principles in all our affairs.

This is often called a "maintenance step." It helps us "trudge the road of happy destiny" so that we will never again be "shivering denizens of King Alcohol's mad realm." I love Big Book prose, but I am terrible at carrying the "message" for AA, as I think the following incident shows.

When I had been in AA in Phoenix more than two years, I met two raw AA newcomers. They were both strong young men who were desperately preoccupied with finding girls. They were on the street until Gene offered them a place to stay and food. Their lodgings were a two-bed trailer in Gene's junkyard. This was in Phoenix during the summer. In exchange for food and lodging they were to sort pieces of metal for sale as scrap. Gene had two inviolable rules: no intoxicants and no women. The two young men would have had difficulty coaxing any young women that far out of town, onto Gene's junkyard and into the trailer in the middle of a desert where the temperature could remain above 110 degrees at midnight. Furthermore, it was a long walk into town, and neither of the two young men had money for prostitutes.

One of these young men I never saw again. The other endured his circumstances for about two weeks before he got drunk. I saw him when he was hung over sitting on the sidewalk outside a Denny's with his head in his hands. I invited him into the restaurant for coffee. He got up, his arms and face blazing red from sunburn. He remembered me from AA and looked at me with distrust. He drank his coffee while I began to instruct him about the program using the word "we" to describe what AAs did to stay sober. Over and over I said things like "We try to take things one day at a time" or "We learn to rely on a Higher Power than ourselves." The young man suddenly stopped me by asking, "Whadya mean 'we'? Ya got a turd in yer pocket?" My mouth was stopped. I could think of no reply. I realized that I had been pontificating. I must have been as red as he was for a moment. My embarrassment awakened me to the fact that he was real, in real pain and not a tool of my self-righteousness. His anger frightened me; he was much larger than I. I hope I offered to buy him something to eat. I hope he found a girl. I never saw him again. I hadn't even remembered, let alone applied, AA's counsel, "Never talk down to an alcoholic from any moral or spiritual hill top."

Until three months ago I used a variety of medicines. That was the most difficult part of living in Mexico. I had to go to the United States every year and bring a huge bundle of pills, a year's supply, back across the border. I didn't declare the drugs because the duty would have been prohibitive and the paperwork grueling. I could have gone to jail.

Every day I swallowed ten pills in various dosages. They didn't produce a high. Certain organs simply worked better and I didn't want to kill myself all the time. I was told two of the pills would diminish my schizophrenia and calm the murderous rages that used to terrify me once they were over. The drugs had undesirable side effects. One morning, for example, I was surprised by the following note to myself scrawled in felt-tip on the bathroom mirror: "If you get any dumber you'll probably fall over." I developed something akin to a Thorazine shuffle. I had several bloody falls. So far there hasn't been any sign of withdrawal or a return to the hallucinations and delusions I suffered prior to taking these medications. Many of my fellow AAs say you should use the steps to rid yourself of violent feelings and leave even prescription drugs alone. I don't want to have anyone challenge my claim of 36 years sobriety. So I've rarely told other AAs about the drugs. I spend a lot of time in AA meetings in Ixtec quarrelling already. Many of the other AAs here resent me.

Most quarrels in AA are simple. The most common is the keep-coming-back fight. AAs normally tell each other to "Keep coming back!" as a friendly kind of goodbye after a meeting has closed. Sometimes, however, it's used as a rebuke meaning, "If you keep coming back you will get better, and, boy, do you need to get better! I have better sobriety than you do." A keep-coming-back fight might go something like this:

"Keep coming back."

"I don't need to keep coming back. You're the one who needs to keep coming back. Keep coming back!"

"You keep coming back."

"Well, keep coming back."

The one who says "Keep coming back" last wins.

My quarrels are more involved.

Sponsors and Sponsees

My first sponsor in AA was a mild-mannered real estate salesman. He married the Tiger Lady. Every time I called him, he would listen to my complaint. Then he would say, "If you think you have problems, listen to this," and he would hold the phone out toward his always-screaming wife. She tried to get him to drink. She had a waiter slip vodka into a coke her husband ordered. She went to a large AA meeting with him and stood up during a pause to denounce AA. She told all the alcoholics there that she hated them and that she liked her husband better when he was drunk. He decided that he couldn't pay enough attention to me, considering his circumstances, and suggested that I find another sponsor.

My second sponsor was also a mild man, but he affected a constant jollity. His good spirits were a kind of boast. He, too, was one of the AA majority; he believed that we always choose our feelings. Believers in the doctrine cannot be dissuaded by argument. To emphasize the need the alcoholic has to accept responsibility, my second sponsor often told the story of his hope, when he was drinking, that he had a brain tumor. He wished he had a brain tumor to explain the way he acted and felt; a brain tumor would make him innocent.

My second sponsor's wife was kind until, about a year after I met her, she suddenly turned vicious. My sponsor kept talking in AA meetings about the cruel things she said to him. He would put on his sturdy grin and say, "Well, if that's how she wants to feel, it's her problem." Then she was found to have an inoperable brain tumor. She soon died. My sponsor found a way to preserve his philosophy. He decided that his wife chose to have a brain tumor.

My third sponsor was John Callahan. He had been lead guitar and banjo for Ted Weems, Bob Crosby and Duke Ellington. After joining AA, he was with one of these bands in Hawaii. One free evening, he made a 12th step call to a man in a sleazy motel. The man was unresponsive to everything John said. John left. The band finished its gig and returned to the continental United States. A few months later the band was in Honolulu again. John was able to go to an AA meeting. He was asked to speak. After the meeting, a man came up to him and said, "I want to thank you. I got my family and job back, and I haven't had a drink in nine months."

John said, "Why are you thanking me? I don't know you." The man reminded him of the dingy motel. John looked closely at him and said, "But that wasn't you in the room."

The man said, "No. I was in the next room and heard everything you had to say."

Sometime after this John had a bad stroke. He was no longer able to play. He became a real estate broker. He was almost always cheerful but didn't credit himself for it. Like AA, John was corny.

After John died, Tito happened into AA. I sponsored him. Much like Chente, he was a handsome, dark Indian who carried himself with great dignity. He had been a middle tier heroin dealer. He didn't use heroin and wanted to quit drinking. Everybody liked him. Tito's pose was damaged by an amazing vulgarity that revealed itself from time to time. As soon as his "ship came in," Tito planned on having a small diamond implanted in one of his front teeth.

He had a prosperous landscaping business. Every weekday he would drive his truck to the LARC, pick up a few of the Mexicans and Indians loitering in front of the building and drive them to one of his landscaping sites. At the end of the day he would give them each a large jug of cheap wine and a small amount of cash.

Every few weeks, Tito got drunk and marred himself. He picked up a small scar on his upper lip. Then he cut a muscle in his right eyelid, leaving him unable to fully open it. After other drunken mishaps, he ended up in the LARC himself, a cast on one broken ankle. Later, driving drunk, he killed a woman and was sent to the brutal Arizona State Prison where he was murdered.

Frank was another sponsee of mine, a 65 year old retiree. He had a stutter, not the usual mechanical repetition of the first or second syllables of words. His stutter was intellectual. It wasn't a speech defect. It was grounded in the blockage of his ideas, not his tongue. He would often begin saying something and then interrupt himself. Then he would interrupt his interruptions. If he was emotionally caught up, he could never get to the end of his first sentence. He would become extremely frustrated and sometimes utter angry nonsense to avoid staying stuck. Frank was far more intelligent than I. I could hear his intelligence behind his broken and twisted efforts to complete a sentence.

Frank had been a fireman and had had an accident. He got a partial pension. He had been the driver of the fire engine when it crashed. Riding with him in his car could be difficult. If there were cars ahead in the distance, he had to accelerate sharply to catch up with them. Then he would curse them for blocking his path and recklessly maneuver his way around them. The car would jerk forward, brake and jerk forward again repeatedly.

Frank's anguish was obviously not commensurate with the problems that caused the anguish. He thought that he chose his anguish, and that increased his frustration. Frank refused to take medication his psychiatrist begged him to take. So, did Frank choose his misery? I don't think that's true or fair. That Frank wasn't fair to himself didn't mean he could avoid being unfair or that he deserved his pain. And if he did ask for it, so what?

He told me you could approach God from the depths of depravity; you didn't have to make yourself clean beforehand. If AA is any guide, you can't make yourself clean anyway. Frank said, "God's not afraid to get his hands dirty."

One evening, Frank and I heard the speaker at an AA meeting say that while drunk five years earlier she had left her baby inside the wooden house she was renting, gone outside and set fire to the house, burning it down and killing her baby. She said she didn't know whether she killed her baby on purpose or not. After she finished telling her story, one of several tough-looking female AA members at the meeting said, "It took a lot of brass tits to tell that story, baby!"

AA's policy of confidentiality wouldn't have kept me from reporting the arson and the murder/manslaughter of the baby. I didn't report the matter to the police because the prospect of reporting it didn't occur to me until an hour after the meeting dispersed. I didn't know the speaker or her full name and probably couldn't have identified her. It seemed obvious that the police would have already investigated the five year old arson and death. Maybe the speaker had already served time in jail. Still, it bothers me that I did nothing. Murders of small children by their mothers are increasingly common.

Marty was my lover and friend. She was 56. I was 32. Our sex wasn't very satisfying; I was inhibited and that inhibited Marty. I called it off but we stayed close friends. She wouldn't sponsor me because we weren't the same sex. She was a Spinozan; the idea that we decide our destiny struck her as stupid. She was a real estate broker. Marty brokered for a single agent who concocted convoluted real estate deals of questionable legality and needed a broker to legitimize them. When Marty could no longer understand what the man was doing, she quit. This was during a depressed housing market. Nobody was hiring brokers. Marty called on me several times to help her move to new apartments when she was under threat of eviction. She had a huge plaster-of-Paris statue of God's white bearded head emerging from the wall. She thought it was funny. It must have weighed fifty pounds. She had a painting of devils roasting in Hell on the opposite wall. She thought that was funny, too. She reminded me of Brother Dixon.

I sold real estate where Marty finally got a position as broker and hired me. Another salesman was always fishing to discover whether Marty was an AA member. Once he said that he was developing a drinking problem and couldn't drink much anymore; the liquor went right to his head. "Well, *that's* your problem!" Marty said, "You're out of practice!"

Marty laughed with great openhearted joy, a lot like the whores in Nogales. She wouldn't tell anyone how many husbands she had had. She did say that sometimes she forgot to get divorced before remarrying.

One week, Marty repeatedly heard her numerous sponsees express their doubts that AA was working for them, even though they were staying sober, because they couldn't find the serenity that came with "true sobriety," and everybody else they heard speak in AA had found it. One of AA's texts says "Whenever I'm disturbed, there's something wrong with me."

"Well, yah, *I'm disturbed*!" Marty would add. Marty was asked to chair the plumbers meeting. It was the job of the chairman to pick a topic. Marty asked the members to speak about a recent time when they were disturbed. Half the members sat at one table, half at another. We started round my table. Everyone who spoke said he was serene and had been so since shortly after he came to AA. As the opportunity to speak worked around to me, I tried to think of a recent time when I had lost my serenity. I could think of nothing. I lied and described the fictional anguish I suffered earlier that day. As soon as I finished speaking, I remembered that I had gotten quite upset over a certain matter that morning. Sometimes I tell the truth by accident. There was only one more speaker after me. She, too, claimed serenity.

Marty was waiting for me at the hall entrance after my group was done. The girl who had spoken after me walked past us on her way out. She and Marty exchanged greetings. I said the girl had been in my group. Marty asked how she was doing. I said, "She's perfectly serene." Marty said, "That's good to hear; she told me yesterday she was thinking about suicide."

Sometimes AA is sick and there's no way to fix it. In one AA meeting, an AA newcomer explained that he was in the process of making amends. He said that there was a warrant for his arrest in New York where he had been charged with selling heroin. This was after Nelson Rockefeller signed draconian legislation requiring convicted drug dealers to serve a minimum of 15 years in prison. Someone listening, a woman with long-term sobriety, told the newcomer that step nine required him to go back to New York and turn himself in to the police. I argued with that, but I only had three months of sobriety, and so I had no authority. I never saw the newcomer again.

Sometimes AAs are simply mean. Another newcomer came into an AA meeting. He was five days sober. He was surprised he had gone five days without a drink. He felt a scintilla of hope. He was a little bit proud of his five days and a little bit surprised. When it was his turn to speak, he said, "I'm new. I've been sober five days." The room burst into cheering and loud applause. The newcomer was the kind of loser who had never been applauded for anything. When he realized that the cheering was for him, he beamed like the morning sun. After the meeting, a woman, sober for a year, approached the still amazed man and said, "You know, you're not really sober. You're just *dry*."

Most newcomers to AA feel some shame when they enter the program, but a few are truly broken and vulnerable. I remember a quiet little man who had worked on horse farms in Kentucky. When I talked to him after a meeting, he shyly boasted that the owner of one horse farm had named a horse after him. He had been told in the meeting to "take the cotton out of your ears and stick it in your mouth" when he raised his hand as though he were in school to say something.

Another humble man, Davy, decided to go to bartender school. Often AA members are bartenders. Davy was simple and unbelievably boring. At his school he was proud to have learned to use the gender neutral word "waitron" to describe both waiters and waitresses. He boasted to me that next semester he would be taking a class in "mixology." An AA old timer and bartender said to him scornfully *"Nobody* goes to *bartender* school. *Nobody!"*

Davy proposed to a Salvadoran woman, an illegal immigrant., with two young children. He believed she would seize the chance to become an American citizen and have a father for her sons. She rejected him. He worked in a McDonald's for several years. He was 47 years old. One Christmas he proudly presented me with a litany of good wishes for every culture that had an important celebration near December 25th. He reminded me of myself as a child reciting the distance of each planet from the sun.

Snobbishness and exclusivity aren't foreign to AA. (See my condescension described under the discussion of step 12, above.) A friend of mine was approached after a meeting and asked if she wanted to join the "spiritual center" of AA in Phoenix. The inviter was recruiting select, spiritually advanced AA members for some kind of higher level AA group. Many, perhaps most AAs pretend that they have transcended their problems with alcoholism. "Alcohol is no longer an issue for me," I heard one say, "I'm just trying to deepen my spiritual life." The Big Book, in its instructions on how to carry the AA message to newcomers, tells us not to patronize them. How are those who have placed themselves on a higher spiritual plane going to do this? It's the situation Father Damien faced in Molokai. Few of the lepers would listen to him until, one day, he announced that he, too, had become a leper.

Sometimes AA is harshly competitive. At one AA meeting the succession of speakers was determined by whoever was most persistent. After one speaker finished, a chorus of loud voices broke out. The speaker, presumably the most arrogant, left speaking after all the other speakers were silent had the floor. Sometimes the competition lasted a minute or more without anybody being able to understand what any of several competitive, simultaneous speakers was saying. At the meeting I attended, the first winning speaker talked about the sexual abuse she suffered as a child. Every speaker thereafter claimed to have been sexually abused as a child. Sometimes their only basis for the claim was that they had, apparently voluntarily, taken part in sex games with other children. I imagined myself claiming that four-year-old Kathy's invitations to play doctor or my mother's enemas constituted child abuse. Then I remembered my experience on the sand in the arroyo when I was a boy. Its ambiguity still disturbed me. Chuck, the heroin addict, when he was eleven and asleep in his room during his mother's parties would always wake to find his penis being sucked by the same homosexual guest. That's child abuse. It's usually unmistakable. Everyone who spoke at the meeting I just described was entirely superficial. In the large crowd there were those who truly needed to speak but couldn't.

The worst AA meetings in Phoenix are held in the Local Alcoholic Rehabilitation Center (LARC). The LARC was a filthy place. It had few beds, but street drunks were allowed to come in on winter nights and sleep on the floor in a large, warm room leading into the AA meeting room. The building had no back entrance. There was a receptionist at the front door. Outsiders who came to attend the meeting had to step over fifteen or twenty drunks who had passed out and were lying in each other's urine, vomit and feces. Many sponsors with new sponsees took them to LARC to show them where they would end up if they continued drinking. It was the last stop before dying. A tall fat man sitting in the filth in a fine suit pulled out a roll of bills one evening and waved it in the air while shouting at the receptionist that he should be given a bed because he was a person of importance. Someone sitting behind the man whispered, "I'm going to help that guy," stood up, grabbed the roll of bills and ran out the door.

Normally AA meetings are much more formal than the ones described above. As I mentioned, one of the things about AA that I like is that it's corny. I say, "I'm Bob and I'm an alcoholic," and everybody in unison answers, "Hi, Bob!" Often everybody speaks according to some pre-established order. No one interrupts. We pray before every meeting. There are standard readings that take place toward the beginning and sometimes toward the end of meetings. The meetings all close with a group prayer. The members nowadays join hands when they say it. When the prayer is finished, they pump their joined hands saying, "Keep coming back—It works—if you work it—So work it—You're worth it." The phrases separated by the dashes were added one at a time over decades without any group decision. One person added a phrase and pretty soon everybody was saying it. Sometimes there were competing versions. For a little while, "But not if you don't" gave "So work it. You're worth it" a run for its money.

When I came in, they didn't even hold hands let alone chant the formula we have now. I liked not holding hands. After AAs were doing it everywhere, I stood outside the circle of joined hands at the end of meetings with a friend who also objected to the handholding. Before the closing prayer started, I said "We would like to invite all of you to join us in the solidarity of not holding hands." That's the kind of thing I think is funny and other people don't. Eventually, I went along with all of it. AA ceremony gives socially inept people like me an opportunity to fit in.

Nonsense

In AA I replaced my D.C. screaming with a softer nonsense. Today my nonsense is like "heladotin" or the race to finish the Confiteor first or my brothers' inexplicable taunts or Pilgrim Temple's "henini" and language of the angels or pretending to speak Spanish or "mogololulu" or elevator Sam's chirping ." My nonsense syllables articulate nothing and, because of that, they give me the freedom of anarchy and a moment of perverse glee. They break the ubiquitous constraints that allow language to work and put me elsewhere for as long as I continue to jabber. When I stop, the insufferable seriousness of the world closes in again. My screaming sometimes had the same effect, but the new nonsense isn't usually violent. With most of my nonsense I strive for incoherence and a dissolving mind. My nonsense works like the shock treatments I've been given, but doesn't last as long. I wonder if my nonsense could become fully involuntary, in the way crossing your eyes too much was supposed to make you permanently cross-eyed. Lately I've taken to singing nonsense, to the tune of Christmas carols usually, but I often make up my own tunes. I occasionally shout nonsense at myself when I'm suddenly overwhelmed by some embarrassing memory. Shouting something embarrassing to overcome embarrassment works sometimes for a little while. Quoron told me that nonsense can also diminish guilt because nonsense diminishes me; I take myself less seriously. In this unique way we can sometimes *choose* to feel embarrassment and remorse less keenly. AAs aren't entirely wrong. We can also *choose* to take anti-depressants.

There are different kinds of nonsense. My present idiocy now divides into nonsense syllables, nonsense phrases, broken-backed assertions, meaningful language whose meaning isn't noted by the speaker, scientific nonsense and mixtures of these. Nonsense syllables, such as "Dizzim cratfretch lafalata scutch praconiam," contain not a single meaningful syllable. As a mutterer of this sort of nonsense, I have to admire the Zen folks' "kwatz!" which reminds me of the materialist's assertion that, in doing metaphysics we feel ourselves reduced to a series of grunts.

The nonsense phrases are made of real words combined in a manner that defies any realistic interpretation but makes grammatical sense. There is much pleasure to be gotten from saying, in the manner of Joe and Memo, "The farm's dots eat cabalistic animal mules." An increasingly common broken-backed assertion is, "What's true for you is true for you, and what's true for me is true for me." I'm a collector of assertions of this type. My favorite example is Samuel Johnson's, "Oh, Philosophy! I know all about that. 'Why was the world made? And, since it was *to be* made, why was it not made sooner?'"

I also like:

> ....Whatever is, is right.
> If the universe
> Didn't have pain in it, it might
> Have to have something that hurt worse.

There are three commonly spoken generalities that fit into this class: "Sensations aren't real," "We always choose what we feel," and "All truth is relative and subjective."

I have been told that there used to be a Moslem sect that believed that God was above all names and descriptions, because names and descriptions limited Him. God was the "Unnamable" and the "Indescribable," two names and two descriptions. Of course, the sect's members didn't have much to say about God after they concluded that God couldn't be named or described. Maybe the members grunted a little, or shouted "Kwatz," until their sect ceased to exist. As I said, sometimes my nonsense is prayer.

Meaningful nonsense includes any phrase that we recite purely for the sound of it without regard to meaning and any statement whose recitation produces glee rather than thought. Rhyming or alliterative phrases are instances. Meaningful statements aren't nonsense, technically speaking, but they can provoke the same perverse joy. In "One-eyed Jacks," Marlon Brando, who has just shot a man, is asked by Carl Mauldin, the sheriff, "Did you shoot this man?"

Brando answers, "He didn't gimme no selection."

Before my deliverance, I thought the pain of Hell was boundless, making the slightest chance that there was a Hell infinitely menacing. I ended by imagining that I had died and was already in Hell. There was no escape until I was permitted to argue against my own beliefs by the lyrics I heard in Joe's apartment and by AA's third step. Not long after that, I could refute, under Lorus' guidance, several assertions I sometimes credited that led to visions of damnation, for example, the nonsense I just mentioned: "Sensations aren't real," "We choose what we feel," and "All truth is relative and subjective." Among other such foolishness, these statements created Hells for me. They had little comic value and preoccupied me for years. They are refuted conclusively in the Appendix to this book.

In the meantime, here is a more laborious piece of gibberish, a Hell that Lorus was able to rebut immediately after hearing it.

Stephen Hawking had a hypothesis that the universe was slowing in its rate of expansion and would eventually contract along exactly the same lines that traced its earlier growth. Light would shrink into itself and the reverse of everything that happened since the big bang would occur. We would live our lives backwards. The universe would sink back into the pinpoint that initiated the big bang and explode again into a repetition of the same occurrences in exactly the same way, only forwards. In this endlessly repetitive world everything is predestined.

But if time can change direction, there is no cause and effect, only a succession of discrete, unconnected events. Nothing truly touches anything else. This is eternal solitude and Hell, the Hell of Hamlet, who, dreading damnation, was irresolute. I, too, in my Hell-driven pusillanimity, turned first one way then the other, never getting anywhere. Those who fear Hell are punished for it in Hawking's Hell. .

Lorus said that, if the whole universe is pulsing in time, we can't know in what direction time is presently taking us, Hawking's theory has no rigor. If you close your eyes tightly and concentrate you can think you're falling backwards in time. If you're a hippy, a little marijuana might help. But there are no criteria by which to determine directions of time. Assigning *temporal* direction to *time* is as silly as the current practice of describing the whole of space as curved. "Time is moving backwards" isn't coherent. The statement can have no meaning in experience. Our real criteria for chronological order can be illustrated with pictures like those cartoons psychologists use to test their patients: a woman with a pitcher on a tray; a cat in front of one of her legs; the woman tilted forward and the pitcher in the air; water in a pool with chards of a pitcher on the floor. The cartoons have only one true order. Time reduces to causes and effects.

Lorus' reasoning may be moot. Astronomers have recently discovered that the universe is expanding at an accelerating rate, and Hawking has abandoned his theory. Instead he proposes another theory. He says there can't be a Creator-God because, before the big bang, time didn't exist, and so there was never a time in which a God could exist to create the big bang. But God isn't temporal, according to the good Sisters.

Do I understand and believe my arguments? At least I don't believe in Hawking's Hell.

Desks Fly

You can't imagine how bad a classroom of kids can make you feel. The kids will say to the teacher or sub, "You don't mess with us and we won't mess with you." I reacted to bullying students with a terrible pride. I wouldn't accept the bargain. I was clean and sober now and determined that it wasn't going to be like Morenci six years before. After I joined AA I subbed in eight different high schools and two junior highs. I taught full time in four high schools. In the United States I taught for ten years. It was during that time that I learned courage

Fights at high schools are still commonplace but differ somewhat in character from those I described above. Once, at Union High School, a soft-spoken, studious black boy who spoke without a black accent was bullied and his lunch money was stolen daily. A decent fellow student explained to me that he had run to the teachers' lounge to report that several stronger black children had surrounded the accentless child and were beating him up. None of the teachers in the lounge went to break up the fight. Teachers claim they are responsible "for the whole child." They have to let the kids "lead their own lives," "be who they are" and "learn social skills." Of course, bullied children sometimes kill themselves.

Once, I took a knife away from a student who had *playfully* jabbed another student with it. The jabbed student cried out but later refused to admit she'd been jabbed. I took the guilty student and the knife to the Vice Principal who gave the knife back to the student and told him not to bring it to school anymore.

One student's reputedly tough father, a gold miner, came to school to beat me up for holding his son after class the day before as a punishment. I was teaching class when he came. The Principal pacified him before he could get to me.

Once, a teacher was forced from her classroom into the hall where she was beaten by three students with whom she had had difficulty the previous semester. When she finished describing what had happened and identified the students to the school's security officers, they stared at her. Finally one of them said, "What do you expect us to do about it?"

Once, I tore up the homework of a student who had Xeroxed the homework of a student who sat near him, crossed out the name of that student and written his own name just below the deletion. When I asked the subscribed student if he thought I was stupid, he said the student whose name was crossed out had been the cheater and copier.

Many times, students told me to fuck off and called me obscene names. Almost always I refused to ignore disrespect. Often desks flew.

Once, a student murdered another student, his romantic rival, with a shotgun in the school parking lot.

Once, a student broke another student's jaw.

Once, a student and his student girlfriend gave an illegal alien a ride from Nogales to the outskirts of Tucson then murdered the illegal alien when they discovered he didn't have the agreed upon payment. A student who had heard of the incident told her teacher. The teacher didn't report it. The police only found out about it because I heard about it in the teachers' lounge and wrote the police a letter. The police did nothing.

Once, between classes, a group of about thirty black students formed a gauntlet in a stairwell other students had to pass through to get to the classrooms from the schoolyard. There was punching and spitting. I stopped to try to break up the line and was hit in the back of the head. When I turned, every student had his eyes averted. I placed my back to the wall and remained there as a witness to intimidate the students until the Principal arrived and ordered the black students to their classrooms. The black kids went away without having hit anyone else. The Principal looked at me as though I were a moron white radical trying to cozy up to the black kids by taking their side in a racial conflict. There are many such teachers.

Once, students poured sulfuric acid from the chemistry lab in the curved seat of a teacher's chair just before she came to class. No one warned her, and she sat in it. She went to the hospital.

Once, returning home from an away game, a group of varsity baseball players cornered some members of the freshman team in the back of the bus, beat them and made them take

234

down their pants and try to masturbate. A varsity player took a photograph of one of the freshmen doing this under the eyes of a laughing cheerleader and posted the clear photo on the cafeteria door the next morning just before lunch. This so shamed the kid in the photograph that he refused to leave his parents' house for any reason for two years. Six teachers sat at the front of the bus while the abuse was going on. None ever got up to investigate the cries because "teachers are responsible for giving kids the room they need to learn to interact with their peers."

In one school, getting pregnant became fashionable. Female students, one by one, every couple of weeks for several months, announced in the schoolyard that they were pregnant. The announcement always provoked cheers from their fellow students who had been gathered round to hear. They were happy that that day's announcer would soon be able to quit school and receive Aid to Families with Dependent Children. Eleven students left school that year because they were pregnant.

I'm told that, of the usually listed demographic groups, teenagers now have the highest incidence of AIDS.

One day at the end of a class, a student on his way out the door threw a bundle of sharpened pencils at my head very hard. The bundle was wrapped with a rubber band in a mace-like cluster, sharpened ends extended outward, and could easily have damaged me. The student escaped down the crowded hall. I showed the mace-like ball of pencils to the administrator in charge of discipline. Turning and studying the ball of pencils, he said it showed creativity. He said I was responsible if I couldn't control my students. Seeing my astonishment, he added, "You weren't hurt."

Once, a white student was beaten up for dating a black student. Black girls beat her up. (Did your television-obedient heart just whisper, "Oh, that's all right then.")

Once, in a nearly all white school, a student wanted out of my class because he was black and the rest of the students in that class were violent racists, the result of their experiences at Jaine, a nearly all black school to which they had been bused before bussing was suspended.

235

The black student, who spoke without any trace of a black accent, was a refugee from the same school. If he could be isolated on the grounds of the white school, the black kid would be beaten by the other kids in my class. When he was absent, I told my students that the black kid was "not really black," but that was an obvious falsehood. So I tried a different approach, "He's not really a Nigger," I said, "Listen to him. He was driven out of Jaine just like you were driven out. He probably had it worse than you guys." Then I told them the story of the black kid at Union who had no black accent and who was beaten by other black kids until he was nearly blind in one eye. When I used the racist term "Nigger" it showed the students that I wasn't trying to be a civil rights hero. At Jaine, I knew, there were administrators who were "civil rights" poseurs, automatically siding with black kids in any conflict with a member of the white minority, denying the latter the right to defend themselves. The black kid wasn't touched that entire year by anyone, and no one ratted on me.

In one school three teachers, who didn't think their fellow teachers should be martinets, presented a seminar on how to teach students to "discipline themselves." When asked how classes could be made quiet and attentive enough to receive such a lesson, the three teachers had no answer.

Once, at the entrance to the students' parking lot, an entering and an exiting car met head-to-head. The drivers began screaming at each other to back up and make room. Then they crashed their cars into each other over and over until both cars were nearly totaled.

Once, at the beginning of an assembly on the first day of school, the five newly contracted teachers were asked to sit in a line of chairs on the gym floor facing the assembled students. A line of five students standing behind the teachers covered them with shaving cream, smashed peeled bananas into their faces, and poured a variety of viscous fluids over their heads while the entire student body watched from the bleachers, screaming with laughter. When I realized what was going to happen I grabbed the arms of the student standing behind me and avoided the mess. I was later warned that touching the student behind me was illegal.

Once, one student raped another.

When it became known that a teacher had had sex with several of her students, other students drove round and round her apartment building honking their horns and shouting lascivious epithets night after night. She continued having sex with her students.

On any given day you could walk by a classroom in any high school, open the door and see a whole class of students talking in full voice with an oblivious teacher inaudibly imparting a lesson.

Once, a school administrator said to me, after I had disciplined a black student for cursing me, "That's racist! It's part of their culture!" I replied that she was the racist if she thought blacks as a class approved of cursing teachers

Once, a teacher had fourteen student teaching assistants attending a remedial English class for twelve boys. The teacher thought that was the only way she could assure herself of protection.

Once, a class of students tormented a teacher by throwing pieces of gravel at her every five or ten minutes while she taught class weeping. This went on day after day for months. The teacher said that when she was hit it hurt like the sting of a hornet. The administration did nothing until the teacher consented to sleep with the vice principal.

Once, a 12-year-old girl was pinned to the floor, partially undressed and fondled by several of her junior high classmates who had decided they were lesbians. They were no such thing. They just knew that being a lesbian was stylish. When they finally left her, the sobbing girl pulled her torn clothes back on and went home for good. The girls who did this to her went unpunished. The administrators didn't want anyone to think they discriminated against lesbians.

Intolerance is sometimes hard to identify. A photography teacher at one school, an asthmatic who was known for getting jobs for his students upon graduation, became the target of angry protests because he was a Mormon and the kids found out that the Mormon Church at the time prevented its black members from advancing in the Mormon hierarchy. The teacher had been well liked by the kids. No more. For days they protested outside his classroom. The teacher told them that he opposed the policy of the Mormon Church and wanted to change it. The students were indifferent. The teacher couldn't calm himself enough to sleep. One night, the teacher had an asthma attack and suffocated. The kids thought of him as an intolerant Mormon opposed by righteous protestors. Some fun!

Once, a student tried to jab a needle into the eye of a teacher fortunate enough to have good reflexes. The student just laughed. He was schizophrenic, which was to say, in this case, "mean," so he couldn't be expelled said a judge who became involved.

Another judge ordered a large school district to create a special school for retarded children. Operation of the school took up over half of the district's budget, and most of the students were incapable of learning anything. The day I visited them I assumed the students would at least be able to speak. They weren't, except for one boy who only said over and over again, "Can I go home?" No response evoked any change. A teaching assistant who knew the kids' routine came into the room with them. Each student was led to his separate worktable. They each had a project they were working on. I decided to help a blind boy who was supposed to be stringing cranberries. He hovered above his chair with bent knees, perfectly still like Oliver Sack's encephalitis patient, while I strung his cranberries. Another boy sat motionless with an unchanging, exaggerated expression of deep anguish. Another boy became progressively more excited during the class. When he reached a certain pitch the teaching assistant pulled a large sleeping bag out of a closet and guided him into it. Then she zipped him up all the way around his body and head. The bag convulsed and, over a period of perhaps ten minutes, slowly quieted until there was no motion at all. The teaching assistant then let the boy out of the bag. The kids needed "assisted living," not a school.

One high school graduated an eighteen-year-old boy who was not retarded but who couldn't tell time.

I once saw "ungin" written in a student's essay while passing by his desk as he was writing and asked him what it meant. He could only repeat the word emphatically to define it, "You know, 'ungin!'" I asked the other students, "What does 'ungin' mean?" I assumed it was some novel teenage slang, but the other students didn't understand it either.

When I asked a student where her test paper was, she said, "I betoo it back there," holding up a flat palm like a policeman stopping traffic. She repeated "betoo" twice over, puzzled that I couldn't understand her.

In one grade school, the black female security officer would encourage black students to pick fights with white students. When she got a couple of kids to fight she would stand by and shout advice and encouragement to the black student. This came to the attention of administrators who did nothing.

There is more of this, but I'm tired of writing it down. I should add that a few times, classes were cooperative and polite. I should also add that, on one occasion, my own behavior with a student was illegal and wrong. Before Jess and I ever had a falling out, Sammy was living across the street from Jess in one of a set of apartments owned by Jess's family. I found myself alone one day with Jess's littlest sister, Magda. She was sixteen and attractive. I led her into my brother's apartment when no one was at home. I fell upon her on the bed, kissing her and grabbing her breast. This was during the time I was student teaching at THS, her school. On the bed I suddenly thought of my vow. I said, "No, I can't!" and left the room.

As I left I heard Aworac and Artemis quarrelling in the kitchen about my vow of celibacy. Artemis argued that I should feel continuous sexual frustration. Aworac insisted that alternatives, such as humiliation, might sometimes be found. After they noticed me they stared at each other as though there were something more to say that couldn't be said in front of me. I told them I didn't want to be humiliated. Artemis looked at Aworac triumphantly. Then she turned and walked towards me without any attempt to hide her breasts or pubis, bent down, kissed me on the lips and walked away. Aworac congratulated me for not fucking Magda. I imagined a dangerous deathly pale thing skittering into a wood to hide.

Believing What I Say

Working for Sammy in his election campaigns, I changed politics. I don't know when it happened, but I remember when I became aware of the change. Each day during his first campaign, he and I would go out canvassing the neighborhoods. This continued from June through October and included the hottest days of the Phoenix summer. The all-time high there is 122 degrees. One or the other of us knocked at every door in his election district twice. At high noon on one of those days, I knocked at a man's door. He answered. I gave my spiel, pointing out that Sammy was a Democrat. He listened politely and when I finished looked at me and said, in a soft voice: "I don't want to argue with you or be rude to you, but I don't understand how anyone in his right mind can be a Democrat."

Through my sweat and exhaustion, I responded with perfect candor, "Neither do I." I heard what I had said with surprise. It was a revelation to me. I could and did argue the Democratic line vigorously, even furiously. Sammy was probably the most left-leaning politician in Arizona at the time. But when I said, "Neither do I" I realized that I didn't believe what I had been saying to the people who opened their doors to me. I continued to campaign for Sammy.

Another time, I knocked at the door of a young woman who had gone to school with Sammy's wife, Eve. After my spiel, she said, "I wouldn't vote for anyone who would marry that vicious bitch." I explained that I thought Sammy regretted his marriage and that I didn't believe it was fair to punish Sammy just because his wife was awful, as indeed she was. The woman and I had a pleasant conversation after that. Sammy got divorced a couple of months later. Eve eventually went on to become a county supervisor.

I continued canvassing for my brother through the next two campaigns, one more for State Senator and one for Corporation Commissioner. All three campaigns were successful. There were serious, sometimes quite unusual, difficulties that he had to overcome. During his second race for the State Senate, for example, he came home after an afternoon of campaigning to find the police in his house. His campaign manager, a fellow nicknamed Broom because he played pool with a broomstick, had called the police and told them he was going to kill Sammy. The police were questioning Broom, who was suddenly full of psychotic delusions. I had recommended Broom, a fellow AA.

Just after his second election, Sammy took me to see the old senate chamber in the old capitol building. The chamber had been refurbished as a historical showpiece. It was impossibly small. The gallery couldn't have held more than twenty people. It sparked a piquant memory of our childhood and of Dad, who took us there when it was still in use. He had bragged to us about being able to throw a wadded up ball of paper into the wastebasket from ten feet away over his shoulder without looking while sitting at his desk. The refurbished chamber, which included the rewoven carpet, looked like something out of the Old West.

Other things had changed by the time Sammy was in the senate. Sammy received one gift, a two-foot tall statue of Santa Clause kneeling over a manger containing the baby Jesus. I guess that gift passed muster because it was so absurd. I don't know what happened to it. It could have been sold for a reasonable sum to a department store for a Christmas display. Despite its absurdity, it was beautifully made and obviously expensive.

Before the next election cycle, the legislature gerrymandered Sammy's district. He ran for Corporation Commissioner, a race in which all the money and all the utilities were on the other side. I had a bright idea. It was to put small notices under the windshield wipers of parked cars. The notices read in bold letters, "You were robbed!" and then explained in smaller type that Sammy would put a stop to exorbitant utility rate hikes if elected. Hundreds of people called to volunteer. I personally printed, using Charlie's machines, 250,000 of these pieces of paper. There were some strident complaints.

After I left Nogales to teach in Hermosillo, Sammy decided to resign from the Corporation Commission and run for the United States Senate. Senator Milcore resigned under threat of prosecution, so his seat was vacant. Sammy had no significant opposition in the Democratic primary. In the general election he ran against the ex-governor, John Procnow, and lost badly.

My teaching in Hermosillo prevented me from helping in the campaign. The campaign was apparently awful. Everything went wrong. Sammy had to fire his campaign manager again. The unusually conservative Arizona press hated him. His car broke down on two occasions when he was traveling between Phoenix and Tucson, forcing him to hitchhike. There were other problems.

ITESM

"What is truth? said jesting Pilate and would not stay for
an answer." Essays, Francis Bacon

As a regular teacher, I often had immigrant Mexican students. They were always surprisingly well-behaved. I determined to find out what it was like to teach in Latin America. I ended up in Mexico in Hermosillo, which is about 300 miles below Nogales, Arizona, where I had last taught. In Hermosillo, I taught at the Instituto Tecnologico y de Estudios Superiores de Monterrey, Campus Sonora Norte, or ITESM, as it was widely known. I taught in two divisions. In the Preparatoria, I taught an elementary class in Philosophy and other, more conventional high school subjects. I also taught a variety of subjects in the Bicultural, where students improved their English by taking their classes in English. The students were wonderful. There was never a discipline problem.

When we studied Socrates and the Sophists, I asked the students in my freshman Philosophy class in the Preparatory what was wrong with the sophists' statement, "There is no truth." Almost immediately, a girl, 13 years old, raised her hand and asked, rhetorically, "How can it be *true* that there is no *truth*?" The girl was pretty and was modestly but prettily dressed. She had the personality of a Natasha Rostova. I later found out that she had a devotion to the Blessed Virgin. She had graduated from Regis, the local, illegal Catholic grade school. On her own, Maria had conclusively refuted not only the Sophists, but the many contemporary philosophers who try to destroy the idea of truth. She did this concisely and with the tiniest fraction of the effort those philosophers dedicate to composing their pseudo-intellectual trash.

Five years after the incident with the 13-year-old Regis graduate, outside a law class at UVA, I told the self-styled Deconstructionist professor that something he had said simply wasn't true. He responded, triumphantly, "There is no truth!"

I asked, "How can it be true that there is no truth?"

He said, "All truth is subjective."

I replied, "Really?"

He said, "That's very clever!" He was the perfect Sophist: rhetorician, lawyer and casuist. He was articulate, but dumb as a toad. Like many present-day academics, he had been hired to publish lots of verbiage. Within the past 30 years, the publish-or-perish universities have produced many professors who are both glib and stupid.

The other night on TV I watched a panel discussion. The panel included a Moslem, a minister, a Catholic priest, a rabbi, a Buddhist and Deepak Chopra in all his unctuous niceness. There may have been one or two others. At one point in the show, Chopra said sweetly to the minister: "What *you* believe is true *for you* and what *I* believe is true *for me*."

The minister calmly replied: "No. What I believe is true, and what you believe is false." For a moment, cool, smooth Deepak Chopra lost his temper, angrily appealing to the moderator, apparently for some kind of ruling. That someone would be unique enough to believe things could be objectively true shocked Deepak.

I remember puzzling some philosophical issue in the cafeteria with some students at the UA. We'd pretty much exhausted the theme's possibilities. Then one of us, an Oriental Studies major, said, with an air of great profundity "Well those are all the logical answers, but what about the *illogical* answers?" The laughter was fulsome, but, among my generation, Eastern mysticism and kindred Western philosophies went on to triumph, in part because of a false paradox. It goes something like this, "Using reason to prove that reason is reasonable is question-begging; therefore, reason isn't reasonable."

Reason is reasonable by definition. Saying that x is x isn't question begging. Reason isn't a method or system. "To reason" means, "to find *reasons* that justify a belief." If a person grants that a persuasive reason has been given for a belief but disputes the reason because it *is* a reason, he is very foolish.

Later, Oriental Studies majors, Deconstructionists and Postmodernists, confronted with a reasoned opinion, learned to say, "That's very symmetrical."

During summer vacations, ITESM sent me to its campus in Monterrey for "capacitacion" courses that enabled me to teach Logic, Problem Solving and a variety of other preparatory subjects unique to ITESM. Monterrey was full of cowboys, confident Texas types. As often as not, I liked them. In Monterrey I watched a world cup soccer match. Some of the British in the stands pulled down their pants to protest the fact that they were losing. The Mexicans laughed heartily. I left quickly because it looked like the British, who were beaten by the Moroccans, were getting ready to fight with the Mexicans, who had cheered for Morocco. Mexicans tend to cheer for the team that's ahead. Very sensible and it breaks no rules, Quoron assured me.

I took courses one summer at one of the ITESM campuses in Mexico City, which is unlike the rest of Mexico. At the time, Mexico City's Greater Metropolitan Area (GMA) was generally considered the largest in the world. A very large portion of the 23,000,000 inhabitants of Mexico City's GMA live in very substandard housing, if it can be called housing at all. Near the apartment I had there was a bridge over railroad tracks. On either side of those tracks were tiny tarpaper and cardboard hovels built side by side, with no space between. They stood in parallel lines so near the rails that it seemed impossible that a train could pass between the rows of shacks without dashing them to pieces. The motley shacks were visible until they reached the horizon.

A French woman I met in Mexico City, an actress and an AA member, told me she had just been to a fine restaurant with some friends. The actress said she slapped their waiter. The waiter wasn't moving fast enough to suit her. She took it as insolence. He couldn't hit her back; he would have lost his job, a terrible thing to lose in Mexico City, and the restaurant management did nothing. I asked her what the waiter did in response. "What *could* he do?" she said.

"He could have traded tables with another waiter, for one thing." She found my curiosity offensive.

Introduced by Ricardo Montalban on a stage in front of a huge auditorium-full of noisy Mexicans, an American actor attempted to coax the Mexico City audience into respectful silence. It was just after the earthquake. Thousands of Mexicans had died and wreckage was abundant everywhere. The Montalban-hosted event was an internationally televised fund-raiser. The actor asked the typically noisy Mexican crowd to "think of the children." When the crowd continued its boisterous enjoyment of the occasion, the actor tried to cry. The Mexicans thought this was hilarious, and Ricardo Montalban had to take back the mike.

Mexico City contains another city, long since engulfed by Mexico City's GMA. The other city is called Nezahualcoyotle. As late as 1986 it was so poor that it had no domestic plumbing. The population was 3,000,000. On a day when I had no class, I asked a taxi driver to drive me through it. I offered fare and a generous bonus. He refused. Nezahualcoyotle was extremely dangerous. I was reminded of the D.C. taxi drivers who refused to pick up blacks.

Nezahualcoyotle was an Indian poet, king and philosopher some of whose poems are said to survive. But how would you translate, even into spoken Nahuatl, poems Nezahualcoyotle composed orally and later rendered in pictographs that were essentially rebuses. Nevertheless:

> I love the song of the mockingbird
> Bird of four hundred voices,
> I love the color of the jadestone
> And the invigorating perfume of flowers,
> But more than all I love my brother man.

In Nezahualcoyotle's kingdom human sacrifice was rife. Early in his reign he had bravely tried to put a stop to it.

Outside of Mexico City the Mexicans are anything but hard-hearted. I saw a mentally disturbed, deaf-mute boy perform with frantic energy on an air guitar in front of a large crowd of Mexicans during carnival in Guaymas. He went on for quite some time. The Mexicans, who had formed a thick circle around him, applauded the ecstatic boy for a couple of minutes as he bowed over and over again from the concrete basketball court he used as a stage. Many of the Mexicans were "applauding" without touching their palms.

I traveled with Dr. Navarro, the Principal of the Preparatoria at ITESM, to Tucson to hire a math teacher. While we drove to Tucson to conduct the interviews, Dr. Navarro talked to me about himself. He was a member of the Knights of Columbus, a square, conforming Catholic in every way. He had gotten his doctorate at Purdue, which at the time had the best mathematics department in the U.S. and probably in the world. Dr. Navarro excelled in math in ITESM as a student. In ITESM top-flight math students are almost the norm. He wanted passionately to study math in the graduate school at Purdue but determined he could better serve his country by studying agriculture. So that's what he did. The Americans who are capable of such self-sacrifice are stay-at-home moms and some nuns.

After we hired the new teacher, we headed home. On the road back to Hermosillo, on the stretch between Green Valley and Tumacacori, Dr. Navarro's car broke down. We hitchhiked. The wife of a man who had stopped to pick us up asked, "What language do they speak in Mexico?" We told her, and she asked, "Do you live in caves." Apparently she had heard on some television documentary that there were excavations in the sides of hills outside Mexico City in which a community of the very poor lived. The driver who had given us a lift let us off in the next town where we found someone to tow and fix Dr. Navarro's car.

Angry Parents

ITESM had been contracted to teach the children of the American engineers who were setting up the Ford maquiladora on the outskirts of Hermosillo. Most of the children had been in Japan while their parents studied automation techniques for the six months prior to coming to Mexico. So the students had some confidence in a foreign setting. They gave the Mexican teachers a hard time. The Mexican teachers were not used to that. Their authority in class was absolute. The American parents began complaining about the Mexican teachers defensively. Then they got the first semester's grades and exploded. They had never dealt with teachers like those. Their children had never been in a real school, not even in Japan. In ITESM teachers expect students to *master* the material.

The parents asked for a group conference with the administration. I was to attend, along with the Director of the school and the Principal of the Preparatoria. I sat among the parents. The Principal and Director entered the crowded room after conferring outside. The first thing they did was announce that I was to be named the Director of the Bicultural Division of the Preparatoria. I knew nothing about it. The American children were in the Bicultural. The parents felt betrayed and I felt like a traitor. I was furious, but I didn't want to embarrass my Mexican employers. I was invited to the front of the room to chair the rest of the meeting. With a red face, I got up and sat between the Principal and the Director. I asked the parents to state their complaints. They talked about the grades some of their children got. One at a time, I discussed the behavior of the children they mentioned. Most of them were, at best, goof-off American teenagers who didn't take school at all seriously. At least one Mexican teacher had come to fear them and was talking about leaving. The parents started to become embarrassed. Then one of them said to me: "The students must not respect you much if they misbehave." There had been earlier troubles that I didn't mention. One day, a Mexican student had spotted one of the American students smoking marijuana while driving to school. Marijuana smoking was seen as the contemptible habit of very low class people. If the school administration had

248

found out that the student smoked marijuana, the student would have been immediately expelled. That the student smoked it off campus would have meant nothing. I didn't mention this incident at the conference because both the Principal and the Director would have insisted that I tell them the marijuana smoker's name.

The school wasn't by any means undeserving of the parents' anger. There had been a month when none of the toilets was working. A backhoe for a construction project adding a new wing to the college kept cutting the pipes. The toilets were full, and the parents screamed bloody murder. Eventually the problem was solved but not until the kids began walking out into the desert to go to the bathroom.

The conference ended in sullen quiet. The next day, some of the parents began discussing the withdrawal of their children from ITESM and the creation of their own school. The Mexican students began shunning the American students. Most of the Ford engineers eventually withdrew their children from ITESM.

Apart from some of the older American kids who continued in their classes in the college division, only three American children remained in the school. The first was a fourteen-year-old Mexican-American girl who had spent her school time in bilingual primary and secondary schools in the United States. The girl spoke no more than a few hundred words of Spanish and no more than a few hundred words of English. She couldn't understand what was said in any of her classes. She ended up spending her day outside her classes "talking" to the secretary of the Preparatoria who had marvelous patience and tried to teach her some Spanish.

The second remaining American student was a bright, decent, high school senior. She stayed at ITESM to learn Spanish and because her mother realized that she would receive a better education there than at the American School the angry parents were setting up. One day I was sitting in the patio talking to the blond girl. She had had an outbreak of pimples, as she did from time to time. One of the American college students, ostensibly a friend of hers, called her a "zit garden." I exploded. I narrowly avoided profanity, resorting to flavorless epithets like "jerk" and "ass." The blond girl thanked me and walked away. In public in Japan, the Japanese had approached her wherever she was to feel her extremely blond hair. They wouldn't even ask permission; they just walked up and started picking at it. She was only thirteen at the time and learned to be submissive.

The third remaining American student was an outspoken Appalachian girl who hadn't been liked by the other American kids. Her father was an independent contractor for the Ford plant. She didn't like her Mexican classmates using the word "Gringo." She finally objected aloud in the middle of class: "That's like me calling you guys 'beaners!'" Her classmates, most of whom spoke good English, roared with laughter. I especially liked this girl and those Mexican kids.

The southern Sonoran desert is different from the Northern part. There are almost no Saguaros in the southern part. Instead of the stately cacti that resemble candelabras, they have Pitaya, a smaller cactus whose thinner more numerous arms bend outward almost as much as they bend up. On the highway leading south from Nogales, Arizona to Hermosillo, there is abundant road kill, everything from skunks and burros to deer and red-tailed hawks. The hawks descend to feed on the earlier road kill. The insects are larger on the Mexican side of the border. Centipedes can be as long as a child's forearm and thicker than many snakes. The scorpions are huge, too, and can kill the centipedes, as I found out when one of my students brought me a live sample of each and I put them in the same jar. When I looked in on them later that day, the bottom half of the centipede was paralyzed. I assume the scorpion, whole and well, was storing up more poison to finish the job.

On two sides, Hermosillo is bordered by huge makeshift neighborhoods of squatter's tarpaper, cardboard and scrap lumber shacks, like the shacks I described in Mexico City. I don't know where the occupants get their water. Many of the shacks are used by people waiting to get enough money to venture into the United States to find work. Nogales, Sonora, is swollen with many more who wait to sneak in.

One of my sisters-in-law has abused and exhausted her visa privileges forever and about every two years, after visiting her family, buses up from Lazaro Cardenas in Michoacan, where her parents and siblings live, to Nogales, Sonora, or Nuevo Laredo, Tamaulipas. She waits for an opportunity to cross into the desert and find transportation in the nearest large American city. She flies or buses to Miami.

Twenty years ago it wasn't at all difficult to cross the border itself. Mexicans regularly crossed over from Nogales, Sonora, to Nogales, Arizona, just to attend American AA meetings. The Mexicans had their own AA meetings but liked a little variety. They could enter through a drainage ditch or through a break in a chain link fence. For the latter, they were charged a dollar by whatever thug was the first to commandeer the opening that evening.

However, leaving the immediate area of the border and going into the desert is very dangerous. The immigrants have to cross the desert on foot because Immigration regularly stops and searches buses leaving the border towns and traveling northwards. I have seen them arrest one or two illegals every time I have taken the Nogales to Tucson bus. I offered to marry my sister-in-law so she could be legalized, but she refused. I insisted that the marriage would not be consummated. She had romantic notions about marriage. She wanted a real marriage and later started brightening her appearance when she was around me.

My sisters-in-law in Miami are all Tarasco Indians. They are neither proud nor ashamed of their Indian blood. They're lucky. At ITESM, I asked one of the darker skinned janitors if the term "Indio" was an insult. He was immediately, visibly and deeply hurt. He defended himself against the "aspersion" by claiming Spanish blood on his father's side. For a moment, I thought he was going to cry. I felt terrible. I had just wanted to know the connotation of the word. I never made the mistake again. The courteous word would have been "Indígena." "Indio," the slur, gets its power from being politely suppressed. In a few years "Indian" in the U.S. will suffer the same fate if Americans continue to browbeat each other for using it. We will only be allowed to say "Native American," and racists will have been given a new tool.

In Mexico City, a few years ago, many light skinned women refrained from shaving their legs because the hair was proof that they had little or no Indian blood.

Before I left Hermosillo, a nine-year-old boy in one of the local public schools was beaten to death by his third grade classmates for being a "Guacho." "Guacho" is Sonoran slang for a straight-haired, black-haired, dark-skinned southerner or "Indio." It is derogatory in the extreme.

In Mexico City a man was introducing an American visitor to his family. He introduced his wife and son, who were white. Two other children were standing off to one side. The father didn't bother to introduce them. When the American asked who they were, the father said, simply, "They're brown." They were his other sons.

George Bush the elder, when asked at a family reunion which of his many grandchildren there were Mexican, replied, "The brown ones over there." John Chancellor, reporting this event, drew from it the lesson that Bush was racist. But the children really were brown. Claiming that it is racist to mention this fact is racist. (Reporters are stupid.) Non-racist Mexican mothers will call their browner children endearingly "morenitos" (little brown ones). Non-racists don't think there is anything wrong with being brown or mentioning the fact. Those of my acquaintance who display "sensitivity" in matters of race relations think like John Chancellor. They want to protect minorities from the "knowledge" that minorities are inferior.

Similar bigotry can be found among those people who consider themselves sensitive when they refer to Mexicans as "Spanish" instead of "Mexican." That piece of vulgarity has been around for a long time. Being Mexican isn't a disgusting thing.

I was struck by the contrast between my Mexican ITESM students and the American students I had taught in Nogales. It came as a revelation one day in one of my ITESM classes that the students were happy. Just *happy.* Another revelation followed on the heels of the first. The kids I had taught in the United States were miserable. In ten years of teaching Americans I had never noticed that their neurotic, erratic, vicious energy was unhappiness. The reasons for the contrast were evident. The Mexican kids came from whole families: mom, dad, brothers, sisters, grandparents, uncles, aunts, cousins, godfathers, godmothers and in-laws. Most had a religion that represented the worldview of most of the people they knew, and among the family members, irreligious exceptions were always near at hand to counsel them if fear became a problem. They had clear moral standards, and none of them seemed to suffer the spiritual difficulties that had obsessed me.

When I summarized Oedipus for an American class and told them Oedipus unknowingly married his mother and had four children by her, the class burst into laughter. One of my Mexican classes actually read the play and reacted with horror, as had the ancient Greeks presumably. In my English classes at ITESM the students' elected to read "Lear." They were familiar with the plot. My American high school students, even when they were bright enough to read Shakespeare, would never have made such a choice. They wouldn't have understood the pathos of a father being betrayed by his daughters or a daughter being betrayed by her father.

Brotherly Differences

Charlie was uncharacteristically humble about his work. He owned and ran his own printingl shops, five of them, I think. A parole officer he knew would call Charlie and ask him to hire a parolee from time to time. He always did, but he was very tough on them. He was tough on all his employees, including me when I worked for him. The parolees were afraid of him. I kept waiting for one of them to explode and attack Charlie. None of them ever had the courage.

Charlie, as a young man, was grotesquely heterosexual. He had a bad girlfriend and a good girlfriend. He fucked the bad girlfriend. His bad girlfriend told him she wanted to have his penis laminated so she could carry it around in her purse. To the chagrin of the social climbing mother of his bad girlfriend, he later married his good girlfriend, who didn't much like sex.

When Charlie and his wife were invited to dinner by another couple, the couple spoke of their French maid, who was in the kitchen. The host explained that she seemed shy but sunbathed in the nude each day by the pool. Charlie drank his fifth or sixth drink, got up from the table without finishing his food and found the maid. In a suggestive tone of voice, somewhere between drunkenness and lust, he said to her, "I understand you sunbathe in the nude." When the host came into the kitchen a few minutes later to see what had happened to him, Charlie was still talking to the maid, oblivious of her sobbing. Charlie cheated on his wife readily. He has two legitimate children and three grandchildren.

Sammy runs a non-profit, bi-partisan organization that gathers information about senatorial, gubernatorial and congressional candidates and makes it available over the Internet. It's a very successful enterprise.

As a young man, Sammy was handsome. He asked girls out and had his way with them. Before his first date, Charlie counseled him, "Remember, no matter what happens, you're better than she is!" Sammy told me that, on that date, while he was driving the girl home after they'd had sex, the girl sank into the dark space beneath the dashboard and told him, as he tried to coax her up, that she didn't want to come out because she was so ashamed. Sammy decided shame was categorically wrong. (Shame reduces the spread of venereal disease.) Sammy doesn't cheat on his wife. He has no children, but wishes he did.

Like Charlie, Jimmy became a small businessman. His business was located in Miami. It was an alternative energy store selling mostly photovoltaic panels. He sold to Latin America. In Columbia, a hall he had hired in a hotel for a solar energy display was bombed. Smaller mishaps became commonplace. His competition was ferocious. Twice, employees swindled him big time. He was in anguish and called me up for solace more times than I can count. One of his employees, mentally retarded or close to it, painted the shop's bathroom sink black. He thought Jimmy would be pleased with his initiative. Jimmy's business survived and prospered. Now he sells, at one time, multiple container loads of panels.

As a young man Jimmy was promiscuous before he married. After twice cheating on his wife and confessing, Jimmy is faithful. He appears to have given up sex. He has two children.

Between my brothers and myself, I was the shyest about sexual matters and probably the most obsessed. As I said, I thought that sex was repugnant. The disgust I felt was probably a way of keeping my vow. In burgeoning desire, when that disgust broke down, I found other ways.

When I was an adult I took out a girl who laughed when she saw the way I was dressed. I had on dressy slacks pulled up and cinched at the level of my navel in a style we ridiculed by calling it, "Boston pachuco." I think my manner of dress was a way of avoiding sex. In Tucson, I always wore a butch. This was at a time when long hair was still the ubiquitous fashion. I looked absurd and knew it. I have no children and am glad.

One of the writers I most admire is Swift. We share the same attitude toward literature and sex. In "The Battle of the Books," Swift describes the difference between ancient and modern literature as being like the difference between the bee, which collects from nature and produces sweetness and light, Homer, for example, and the spider, which weaves tangled webs "out of its own filth," an anonymous Cavalier poet, for example. The Cavaliers' patroness in "The Battle of the Books" is Venus, probably because prominent Cavalier poets contracted syphilis. The Cavalier poet in The Battle of the Books is described as "degenerate." His degeneracy dooms him.

Swift weaves his own filth in the chapters of Gulliver's Travels dealing with Brobdingnag and the Yahoos, where he gives a much more grotesque portrayal of sensuality. Much of the book I am writing here is woven out of my own filth.

Other modern writers' descriptions of sex are similarly disgusting but are supposed to be the products of liberated sexual attitudes. In the last Rabbit novel, the revolutionary staying in Rabbit's house invites him to sodomize a mentally disturbed girl while the revolutionary is receiving fellatio from her. "She gots lots a holes," the revolutionary says.

I hate open-mouthed kissing on television, and I don't care for it in person. I'm told most Japanese and Chinese don't see any attraction in it. If that's true, what do they do? Are they like the Eskimos? I've never tried cunnilingus and never will. I wish I had no testicles; although it would be wrong to have them removed. I'd like to keep my penis, since it helps me aim when I urinate. I wish Artemis would remove my sexual desires instead of inspiring them.

Charlottesville

After I left teaching, at the age of 45, I moved to Charlottesville to attend the University of Virginia School of Law. Classes were very boring. My life centered around AA. However, some of the students at UVA law school and I ventured into the lush Virginia countryside to help illegal Mexican apple pickers apply retroactively for their work permits. I was the bumbling translator. I and the other students spent the afternoon among the migrants. When we were ready to leave it was dark. Looking up, I saw the Milky Way. The stars were so thick in it that it looked like a rent bridal veil. I was amazed and pointed it out to the other students. One of them said, "What is it?" I told them it was our galaxy seen edge on and partially obscured by huge opaque dust clouds, and that, without the clouds, it would be, at every point, brighter than the full Moon. They looked briefly but showed no reaction. Their only interests were bound up with their self-righteousness, their "ideals," as I was beginning to discover. "When the stars threw down their spears/ and watered heaven with their tears," they were indifferent.

The students' naïveté with regard to politics was just as profound. I remember a conversation in the car as we drove to the camps. I cautioned a young radical not to assume that rightwing forces committed every vicious act in the Latin American mess. He replied that he hadn't ever heard of "*leftwing* death squads." I told him that was because the American press called leftwing terrorists "revolutionaries" and dismissed accusations of revolutionary terrorism as rightwing propaganda. The press usually doesn't investigate or report accusations of terrorism committed by the left. At the time no American journalist that I know of was writing of the unspeakable depredations of the Shining Path. Reporters are worse than stupid.

Albemarle County, where Charlottesville and the UVA law school are situated, is supposed to be the second richest county in the United States. Rich people go in for pop psychology. At an AA meeting there, a young woman was quietly weeping. She said her grandmother, with whom she was very close, had just died. The second person to speak, a young man, said, "I had to spend two years in AA before I learned that grief was a process." You would have thought by the way he spoke the word "process" that he was talking about holiness. A third speaker disagreed with the second, insisting that grief was a "journey."

I once attended a very large AA meeting in Charlottesville in which there was an unofficial guiding clique. Grace, a woman in the clique, had, that day, lost her teenage son in a traffic accident. She was present at the meeting. The leader of the clique stood behind the podium and said,

> I think we can all allow Grace a few days to grieve. Losing her son isn't the real cause of her grief, of course, but she may need a little extra time to come to grips with that fact.

This meant that she was *choosing* to hurt. The speaker was a locally famous reporter, a member of the Choose Religion, the religion of the guiding clique.

The second time I lived in D.C., Charlie called to tell me our mother had died. I went to an AA meeting because that seemed the appropriate thing to do. I didn't need solace. In fact, as I explained at the meeting, I only felt relief. I wouldn't be burdened with my mother in her old age and she was out of her misery. After the meeting a short, fat, middle-aged woman waddled across the room and said to me, "Grief is a process," like the young man described above. She continued, "You're in the first stage, denial," and then she proceeded to list all the other stages I had to go through. My initial thought was that this pompous fool should be stepped on. Instead, I kept quiet and listened to her. When she was finished, I thanked her. I did this because it had occurred to me that suffering her was something I could "offer up" for my mother. "Offering up" is a Catholic concept meant to make suffering count for something and, therefore, more endurable. If the Church is right, my mother got a little time lopped off her sentence in Purgatory. I flew back to Tucson to attend the funeral.

Believing What I See

Toward the end of law school, I was given a position with the Federal Government that I could only keep if I passed the bar. Most of the summer after I graduated, I studied for the bar with great intensity. At one point my remaining roommate started playing loud music in his room. I shouted to him to turn off the music. He shouted back that he had a right to listen to music in his own room. I ran over and tried the handle of his door. It was locked. I kicked the door in and broke my toe. My roommate was standing there shaking with a kitchen knife in his hand. He said, "Please don't kill me! Please don't kill me!" Then he dropped the knife and went over and turned off the music. It didn't bother me in the least that I had done this, but, when I realized that I felt no remorse it frightened me. This was a pitfall that I had never expected. I became afraid for myself. As I've indicated, I had only a remnant of conscience left from decades of guilt and hate, and that was slipping away. I felt empty. For a moment I feared the return of my nothingness Hell dream and panicked. I didn't want that and I certainly didn't want to resume my guilt and hate or my scrupulosity. By the time I graduated from UV School of Law, I had decided to adopt political causes to fill the hole left by my retreating conscience. Political causes inspire self-righteousness in the partisan in vast quantities but normally not guilt. I remembered Solzhenitzyn's observation that gulags come into existence when the natural criteria for truth are replaced by adherence to an ideology. But I didn't want an ideology, just a heartfelt cause. Before I even started looking, I found one.

I rode to Roanoke to take the bar exam with a friend of mine. He was very bright but not at all vain about it. He was a devote Catholic and one of those who was trying to lead me back to the Church. He didn't study at all for the Virginia law section of the exam and was worried. We shared a motel room. I went to bed early the evening before the exam. While I slept, he sat outside on the stairs all night saying the rosary. Three years after accepting a prestigious position in the Federal Government he became a priest.

They draft private lawyers to grade the part of the exam that deals solely with Virginia law. Grading is a horrible job. Handwriting is likely to be nearly eligible most of the time. People are writing desperately, which tends to make their answers windy. I hoped the person who graded my paper would be a lawyer in his fifties wasted by too much drinking, mentally exhausted by the essays he had already graded, and kind.

After we had finished with the two-day exam, preparatory to heading back to Charlottesville, my Catholic friend and I decided to take our gear out of the back seat of his car and put it into the trunk. He handed me some of the things that were already in the trunk. One of the things he handed me was a large comic poster of an outraged baby that had had a bowl of spaghetti overturned on his head. I had seen it before, so I barely glanced at it. Something was wrong. I looked again. It was a picture of a baby's bloody, severed head being held up by forceps over what appeared to be a petri dish. I was horrified and gasped, "What is this?" My friend explained that it was part of an aborted fetus. But I had recognized and still did recognize a baby. The dehumanizing word "fetus" did not change that. I was more interested in my own perception than I was in the picture, at which I continued to stare. Copies of the picture were distributed at the March for Life, in which my friend and his family participated. He was squeamish about publicly displaying the photograph. I told him it was information people needed and the television stations sure weren't going to give it to them, though they would, as they should, continue to show horribly emaciated bodies and piles of naked, decaying corpses to illustrate the ghastliness of the Holocaust. Neither will the television networks be showing any dead "neonates" when killing them becomes acceptable. My spontaneous recognition of a baby in the abortion poster taught me what my opinion was in the same way my statement "Neither do I" taught me my opinion of Democrats during my brother's door-to-door election campaign. The photograph of the baby had been real enough. I'd happened upon a cause; I became an abortion opponent on the spot and without making any decision. I was advancing in "the art of discovering what [I]… believed." That's when I began researching abortion.

Kings of Judah

Kings of Judah, Ahaz and Manasseh, burned their children before Moloch, a Canaanite god, in Hinnom, that is, "Gehenna" which became a name for Hell. II Chronicles 28:3, 33:6; II Kings 23:10; Mark 9:47. Later Jeremiah and Ezekiel raged there while commoners of Judah joined with the Canaanites in rituals of sexual wantonness and the sacrifice of their offspring. Jeremiah 19:4-5; Ezekiel 16: 20-21. Ezekiel remonstrated with the Judeans for having "caused to pass through the fire all that openeth the womb." Ezekiel 20:26, 23:37-39 The sacrifice of infants was idolatry's sacrament, the worship of the strange gods "in the high places." It was prohibited by Yahweh and mentioned repeatedly in the Old Testament. "They have built the high places of Tophet, which is in the valley of the son of Hinnom, to burn their sons and their daughters in the fire, which I commanded them not, neither came it into my heart!" Jeremiah 7:31 (speaking God's anguish).

Carthage was a colony of the Phoenicians, who were Canaanites. In the ruins of Carthage archaeologists uncovered a graveyard filled with tens of thousands of urns containing the charred bones of infants, many of them fetuses apparently aborted to fill a quota. As it turned out, there was more than one such graveyard. In some, the urns of the children were disposed in layers. Often there were two or more children to an urn. The Carthaginians sometimes sacrificed hundreds of infants at a time. While these sacrifices were occurring, the area before the statue of the god was filled with a loud noise of flutes and drums so that the people wouldn't hear the screams of the infants. Plutarch, Lives, Life of Pyrrhus. The god's statue was formed so that its hands inclined downward over a brazier towards the offering parents. The worshipers could see, though they could not hear, the dying children. The flames engulfed the statue's hands and wrapped themselves around the infant placed in them. The infant's limbs would begin to contract as they burned. Its mouth would open and seem "almost to be laughing." The grin widened until the contracted body slipped between the hands of the god into the brazier. Cleitarchus, as paraphrased by Diodorus Siculus, Library of World History,

261

Book 17 The name of the god had changed but not the manner of sacrifice. Five hundred years after Jeremiah, in Carthage the descendents of the Canaanites burned their children alive in sacrifice to Ba'al Hammon.

The American devaluation of children probably began when we made abortion so common as to be banal. The arguments that have made abortion acceptable will make infanticide ok, too. In the meantime, the evidence that even the human embryo is a living being is piling up. In 2006, a team of researchers from Yale and Oxford discovered cortical neurons, the type that constitute the cerebral cortex, in embryos 31 days after fertilization. There were "vast networks" of these neurons. The announcement upset the abortion rights lobby. They have long disputed the claim that brainwaves have been detected in embryos 40 days after fertilization.

In Casey the Supreme Court upheld abortion rights on the grounds that, "for two decades, [Americans have]...defined their views of themselves and their place in society in reliance on the availability of abortion in the event that contraception should fail." In other words, Americans have grown used to fucking without having to accept the predictable consequences of fucking, and that's "who we are." Even if there are medical reasons that could justify occasional abortions, occasional, justified abortions aren't what's going on. There have been over 50,000,000, American abortions since Roe v. Wade. Approximately 6,000,000 or 12% have been second and third trimester abortions.

The Center for Disease Control (CDC) which has tallied maternal abortion-related deaths each year for decades, says that the number of such deaths steadily declined from just over 300 in 1950 to a little under 200 in1965, two years before some states began to rescind parts of their anti-abortion laws. Even before penicillin was discovered, the number of abortion-related maternal deaths never approached the number suggested in Roe.

I have found, in one hour-long session on the Internet, eight professors at prominent colleges, including Princeton, The University of Colorado and King's College London, who advocate allowing women to have their doctors kill their babies regardless of the reason. This killing should be allowed up to 28 days after the child is born, according to one professor, and up to four months, according to another. The professors seem to share a common argument: the infant is not yet a conscious being because he can't "conceptualize" things. (I'll bet a day-old, retarded baby can smell creosote.) To dehumanize newborns, the professors refer to them as "neonates," a Latin term that means "newborns." Popularizing the once obscure Latin term "fetus" has been very effective for the abortion lobby. It's easier to kill a fetus or a neonate than it is to kill a baby. If legal infanticide comes to pass, Jonathan Swift's cutting sarcasm will have lost its edge. Some will be eating neonates the way some Chinese are now eating fetuses. Those who disapprove will be told to be more tolerant.

After Aworac showed me these things and for several weeks, I no longer believed in God. Therefore, for those same weeks, I believed in Hell.

The research above was not the basis of my new ideology. Its results could not have filled the place of my lost conscience. They were peripheral to my belief and cause, which were of the heart. I was no longer just a vacant conscience. In my friend's poster I had *seen* a photograph of evil. "Abortion" is a euphemism. Now I stood for something. And another terrible cause was looming. Was I motivated by the self-righteousness I abhorred in others? No. In the course of this autobiography I argue that blame, praise, guilt, vindication and moral responsibility are all incoherent ideas. I'm not amoral, however. Aworac agrees; actions can still be right or wrong absent culpability.

After the bar exam, when my rosary praying friend and I got back to Charlottesville, I discussed my revelation with my other Catholic friend, an Italian whose Catholicism was intense, albeit with an admixture of Italian chauvinism. He held that the city of Rome really was eternal and could never be destroyed, thermonuclear bombs notwithstanding, because it was the Episcopal seat of the Pope. My Italian friend now has a doctorate in Physics. He'd seen the beheaded baby poster. Some weeks later, when I was beginning to believe in God again, he took me to Mass and I went to Confession. I told the priest I wanted to reenter the Church but couldn't believe in Hell. I said it was too terrifying. He said, "That's what it's for!" But he absolved me of my sins. My abortion revelation was the whole substance of my reconversion to Catholic sexual morality which was the whole substance of my reconversion to the Church. I was back, sort of.

If You Pay for Them You Can Play with Them

An English woman I met in London at a theater where I was contemplating buying a ticket recommended the play that was current. I told her I didn't want to see anything Neo-feminist. She suddenly lost her composure, denouncing feminism in America. She attributed its success to the fact that "American men have no balls." I told her she was right, in general, but added that some American men fought back and declared myself one of them. To back up my claim, I related a much abridged version of the stories that follow.

I started a men's AA meeting in Charlottesville, where political intolerance was becoming oppressive. The first meeting in which I announced my intention broke into a chaos of hooted objections. Charlottesville is a university town. The university was Neo-feminist and the town followed suit. There were three women's AA meetings in Charlottesville at the time. I set about going to every integrated meeting in town stating the time and place of the men's meeting and saying it was for "men only" in a voice that invited challenge. There never was a further challenge.

The men's meeting was sparsely attended. I knew it would dissolve if there were no leader and no residual membership. Many men were afraid to attend. When I left to take up my job in D.C. Brad, a sponsee of mine, offered to take my place as leader of the meeting. Brad liked to do favors for people and then call in the favor. He had a prison mentality. His manner of calling in the favor was to dominate the person receiving the favor by speaking to him in a rude, loud manner. He did that to me. I told him I wouldn't have it. He walked away. The men's meeting dissolved. But I had fought back against feminist bigotry for the first time. Here in Mexico, such quarrels were unnecessary.

Brad was very rich, a sharer in the Vanderbilt fortune. His family home was in Newport where his mother still lived. He had an extraordinary fantasy life. He bought two black Mercedes so that he and an equally peculiar friend could dress in black suits and sit together in one of the two cars, parked one behind the other, in front of an extremely expensive Georgetown restaurant. Brad liked "that motorcade effect." He told me he was contemplating buying a black helicopter to park on the front lawn of his glass house in Charlottesville. Of course, he didn't know how to fly a helicopter and had no intention of learning.

Brad had been married and had two children. When he sought a divorce from his wife on the grounds of incompatibility, his lawyer insisted that he and the children undergo medical tests to see if he was truly their father. It had never occurred to Brad that he might not be the father. He had never had any reason to suspect his wife of adultery. It turned out he wasn't the father of either child. Brad's mother in Newport unofficially adopted the wife and children, who would otherwise have had to resort to welfare.

I fired Brad as a sponsee because he, too, made one of those "What was so wrong with Hitler?" comments. It turned out that he hated Jews. He started wearing a black and white checkered Palestinian scarf. He liked to imagine he was a terrorist murdering Americans for their support of Israel. That he would tell me of his fantasies struck me as remarkable. He was a crazier version of Brian Steen (the batboy) and Salvatore (the "Indian" Actor). It took a while to fire Brad. After all he was my sponsee. I was not supposed to judge him, and I felt sorry for him for the severe cuckolding he still suffered.

In a meeting in D.C. the second time I lived there, a woman said that her co-workers, were "dumb white boys," accentuating the words "white boys" with hard scorn. She was one of those dumpy middle-aged white women who discover the Neo-feminists' opportunity for self-aggrandizement, victim status and counterfeit love just as they are losing their looks and the attention of men. She was not yet altogether unattractive. There was an older man sitting next to her who was interested.

I spoke. I told her I was tired of derogatory Neo-feminist remarks, repeated her phrase "dumb white boys," and told her she was a bigot. I spoke with great unsteadiness. I was afraid that I would be laughed at for being upset by three small, common words, "dumb white boys." The word "bigot" shocked her. At the end of the meeting she asked for another chance to speak. The man next to her seconded this request. I said, "If you get a second chance to speak, so do I." She and I traded a few hard words.

Finally, she said, "Well, there's nothing left I can say except, you're an asshole."

I said, "No. *You're* an asshole and a *bigot*."

The man piped up. "You're a jerk," he said. One of the women AAs attending the meeting had already managed to maneuver the group into the handholding prayer ring preparatory to saying the final prayer.

I replied to the man "Fuck you, fuck face!" just as we started the Our Father. The other white males in the room said nothing. Most of us have to be willing to be grotesque to start fighting back, and we have to be willing to fight back alone. Rather than fighting back, we keep our hearts hidden.

Finally, when I was fifty-two, after an AA meeting in D.C., a woman who had made advances towards me was talking about the, then recent, discovery that certain kinds of breast implants caused cancer. She described this as an example of the cruel exploitation of women by men. Men liked big breasts, and so they, not women, should be blamed for the implants. Absurd Neo-feminist denial of women's accountability in any matter and their relentless, condemnation of men as a class had been angering me, obviously, for some time. I left the room and went home stewing.

Several months later, the same girl, whom I had continued to spurn, came into a different AA meeting, one I attended regularly. The group's senior in sobriety, a beloved, white-haired old man, was my sponsor. The Neo-feminist, who blamed men for women getting breast implants, received a warm hug from my sponsor when she entered the room. After he hugged her, she said loudly to another woman. "Doesn't he give great hugs?" Then, at me, in a louder voice, she said, "Most men can't do anything well."

She had been asked to chair the meeting. There was a man sitting alone in a back row a little bit behind me whom I couldn't see. We were speaking in turns around the table. When it was my turn, just as I began to speak, the chairwoman interrupted me and indicated that the man behind me was to speak first. I said, "No, I'll speak," taking control of the meeting. Then I related the following events:

Jimmy had a prospective girlfriend, Jamaican, from a very poor background. She had small breasts. She wouldn't let him touch her. When he tried too hard she smashed him in the face with a nearby picture frame. He had to get stitches. A few weeks later, she proposed that he pay for breast implants for her. She told him, "If you pay for them, you can play with them."

After describing this incident, I reminded the girl chairing the meeting that she held men responsible for women getting breast implants, and I quoted her comment about men being unable to "do anything well." I told her I was sick of Neo-feminist browbeating. I said I didn't like her. Finally I told her she was a bigot.

"Fighting back is the best cause, but it's selfish and vindictive, and we don't want to look selfish and vindictive. So we allow abuse even as we resent it. That's cowardice," Aworac said.

Apart from Aworac, everybody who talked after me at the meeting refrained from commenting about what I had said. My sponsor said nothing about it. He was craven as a matter of policy. He would sometimes joke in meetings, "I agree with everything everybody has said so far; what's more, I agree with everything everybody's going to say."

After the meeting my craven sponsor, told me he was a Feminist and a Communist and sought to dismiss the atrocities of Stalin and Mao. I immediately felt towards him the way one feels towards those rare beings, like Brad, who suddenly pop off with a comment like "Hitler wasn't all bad!" Their Gestalt immediately changes. You no longer know them. I fired my sponsor. It was easier than firing Brad. I was supposed to judge the fitness of my sponsor.

About a year later, the Neo-feminist died of AIDS. I had had no idea she had AIDS. She was attractive. I thought how lucky I was to have spurned her. My vow of celibacy helped and so did her bigotry.

The malice of Neo-feminists is extreme. I was in another D.C. AA meeting where one of the women discussed a television show she'd seen the night before. In the show a young man had set off into the Canadian wilderness with a camera and tripod to do a one-man documentary on grizzly bears. The woman smiled and said she was glad the bears had killed and eaten him. She was glad, she said, because he was a "white macho male." I'd seen the program myself. The narrator said only a section of the man's spine and his head remained after the bears had finished with him. The mention of this fact reminded me of road kill on the thoroughfares nearest our old house in Tucson and the strange, bright green nacre of the attendant death flies that so fascinated us when my brothers and I were little.

One of the other female members in attendance at the AA meeting said that she also was glad that the young man had died. Four decades of pervasive bigotry directed against males as a class desensitize us to even the most obvious examples of prejudice. I asked, "what would happen if I said I was happy that a "white bitch female had died."

The browbeaten men all sat with their heads bowed, saying nothing.

A Wounded Child

When Sissy and I had broken up, we remained friends. She told me that she wanted another child, but her then current boyfriend, Roger, refused to cooperate. Sissy asked me if I thought it would be all right for her to secretly suspend birth control and let Roger unknowingly impregnate her. I was aghast. I saw a chance to prevent a possibly immortal life. I insisted that she not do it. She did it.

As a baby, Sissy's second child, Teresa, was amazingly affectionate. She would thrust her face into yours for a snuggle. It could hurt. Her father, Roger, was a crack addict who liked to fuck Sissy but would not pay attention to Teresa. When she could walk, Teresa would sit on the sidewalk in front of Sissy's house waiting for a promised date with her daddy. He would rarely make an appearance. After a couple of hours she would begin crying, and Sissy would bring her into the house. Sissy brought a paternity suit against Roger. It seemed unfair to me. Sissy had tricked Roger into fathering their baby and Sissy had plenty of money. Men, unlike women, are held accountable for the results of sex. Paternity suits force men to support their children even though the decision to have a child is finally entirely the choice of the mother. This is called an "intervening cause." Because the mother, by herself, makes the decision to have an abortion or give birth, the father's sexual act is only a *sine qua non,* a necessary but not a sufficient cause. The presence of an intervening cause under the control of the plaintiff used to be enough to defeat a lawsuit. Despite the injustice, I support paternity suits. They discourage abortion.

When Teresa was three, she took a pot of cooked lentils off the kitchen table and emptied it into the garbage. She said to her astounded mother, "That's ugly food!" Sissy says that was when she knew something was wrong with Teresa. Teresa began indulging in screaming tirades without rational pretext and could not be calmed down. Sissy took her to a psychiatrist. He didn't know what was wrong with her but began prescribing medications. Teresa wouldn't take them. The tirades continued. She was desperately depressed. She started talking about suicide when she was nine, reminding me of my prayers at that age. When she was in fifth grade, Teresa refused to go to school anymore. She had gained a lot of weight and the other children teased her. When I heard how difficult she was I tried to think how I could help. I crassly started buying presents and sending them to her. Sissy said it helped quite a bit. I kept it up for over a year. I was working for the FCC by then and was well paid, so the cost wasn't a problem. Often I would send Teresa four or five presents a week in separate mailings. Teresa started taking her medication. The psychiatrist tried giving her Zyprexa. Teresa took the pills and they did some good. I took Zyprexa, too, until recently, and I'm much improved.

When I began work at the Federal Communications Commission, I found out I had passed the bar, thus securing my job. I broke into tears in my apartment over the announcement letter. I decided to celebrate. That was when I invited Ed to visit me in D.C., an imprudent decision, as I have indicated. He stayed with me and, while I was at work, decided to visit the Martin Luther King Junior Library. He assumed from the name that the library was a tourist site. That evening he told me that he had entered a restroom in the library and found a homeless man with his shirt off bathing at one of the sinks while another bum, his pants at his ankles and a gun sliding out of his back pocket, stood in front of one of the stalls masturbating. Neither seemed at all self-conscious. In fact, one asked Ed for a cigarette. I was reminded of myself screaming on the elevator and in the streets of D.C. fifteen years earlier. I did feel self-conscious. Maybe that's what saved me.

The Opposite of a Zombie

Posing me a riddle, Aworac asked, "Who is the opposite of a zombie?" I accepted the challenge. I decided that a zombie was a moving corpse; it could act mechanically, but it couldn't think or feel. It was an empty body, as purely physical as a rock. So the opposite of a zombie had to be pure spirit. Jesus was God *incarnate* and so not pure spirit. That meant that God was not pure spirit either, and the Holy Ghost was God. Saints had human bodies and so they weren't pure spirits. But, according to the Church, Angels were pure spirits. I told Aworac. It said Angels could see. So they weren't the opposite of a zombie. With this hint, I set out again to find the riddle's answer.

I remembered the story of a woman who had escaped Communist East Germany. The woman's name was Uta. I made fun of it. She looked at me icily and told me to shut up. I could suddenly see how mentally and physically strong she was. She had been stuffed deep into the trunk of a French friend's car and covered with a blanket, tires and lots of other paraphernalia. She rode in still darkness through East Germany, Czechoslovakia, Hungary, Romania and Bulgaria without stopping except to register the French friend's passport as they entered each successive Communist country. At the last border crossing, leading into Greece, where inspections were said to be more casual than at other crossings into the West, the guards opened the trunk and shifted a few of the items that covered her. She had been in her cramped, fetal position for more than fifteen hours. She was numb. She couldn't move at all. She couldn't whisper. She couldn't connect the desire to move with any of her muscles; she didn't know where her muscles were. Uta told me she was in such pain that she might have cried out if she could have, just to get the guards to pull off her coverings and pull her out of the trunk where she lay paralyzed and suffering. Then she felt one of the guards grab her ankle through the blanket. The guard didn't realize he had touched a living thing. But she knew she'd been touched . She wasn't entirely numb. So she wasn't an example of the opposite of a zombie.

I had a friend, Moe, who escaped Poland at the age of sixteen with his younger brother just after World War II. They reached West Germany on foot by way of Czechoslovakia and East Germany through the most closely guarded borders in the world. Moe's story is like Uta's, but over a period of months, on foot, crouching in ditches, stealing from farmers and almost being caught on several occasions. Once, he ate a frog. He said it had no taste. He claimed that when you have been hungry for a long time your sense of taste is inactive. He described a condition he entered into when it was winter that must have involved starvation and hypothermia. For a few moments he couldn't tell whether he was walking. He couldn't feel his body and wasn't sure he had one, but he knew he was with his brother; he could hear when his brother spoke. So he wasn't the opposite of a zombie.

In D.C., after an AA meeting, a few of us went to a coffee shop. We took along a newcomer. He was a short, sad man who resembled Buster Keaton. He had the look of many AA newcomers who hope for sympathy. They often lie to get it. In the course of the conversation Buster told us about an operation he had had that involved taking some veins in his thighs and transplanting them to an area near his heart. He said that when the anesthesiologist put him under, all the anesthetic did was paralyze him. He felt everything but couldn't move or cry out. After the surgery he told his doctor. The doctor was skeptical but investigated. Buster's pulse rate hadn't changed significantly during the surgery. (Is this possible? Could a person be entirely unable to show pain and still be in excruciating pain? "Buster" stories are increasingly common and likely to become fashionable.Buster, if he spoke the truth, was a motionless, thinking hive of pain but not the opposite of a zombie. He felt and believed the surgeon's knife. He was touched by something outside himself. So he wasn't an example of the opposite of a zombie.

I gave up. I asked for the solution to the riddle. Aworac said, "When I believe there aren't reasons outside me for the things inside me I'm the opposite of a zombie." Studying me, Aworac paused and added, "It's what you thought; the opposite of a zombie is pure spirit. You're the example – sometimes."

"Are you a demon?" I asked it, suddenly realizing my solipsistic fears and wanting to confirm Aworac's existence to escape them. Bowing its head, seeming to admonish itself; it said, "I'm just reckless."

A Near and Rising Planet

Among my few hiking experiences were two attempts to climb Mica Mountain, the highest of the Rincon range overlooking Tucson on the east. The first time, I tried to climb it by myself. I got a trail map. Ed gave me a ride to a place where a paved road ran through Reddington Pass, the pass between the Rincon and the Catalina ranges, the pass that eventually inclined upward to Mica Mountain.

The mountain interested me because it appeared to be the source of the water that flowed through the arroyo and flooded the desert near our old house during summer storms. I also wanted to suffer among the old growth pines at the cold top of the mountain to convince myself there was something other than me; I imagined an enormous pinch waking me up. But I was mostly fascinated by the mountain's beauty. From the city, it stood over the horizon in a long smooth blue and white arc. It looked like

> A near and rising planet,
> A clouded sister world
> So close that if its bulk of fog and granite
> Could have slowly whirled above us,
> We might have bridged the distance
> Without the crude mechanical assistance
> Of groaning engines and fiery rocketry.

When I was let off, I had to climb a great distance through horny toads, cactus, snakes and gophers. I couldn't find any of the trails. I found myself in a large, dry streambed. Ed had warned me to stay out of low places at night because the cold air came down from the mountains and could be very uncomfortable. The only way out of the streambed was up a steep dirt cliff. I started up it and, just as the sun set, made the top. There was Tucson spread below me. I lit a fire and ate something, but couldn't get to sleep. In the morning, as I started off, I heard a terrible squawk and turned to find a golden eagle staring at me from its nest. I walked on and ran into some cows. I still couldn't find any of the trails. So I set off, smoking, with no sleep and with aching muscles from the day before. I stared up at the mountain. When I could see individual pines at its top, I gave up. I felt as though I were prohibited from the summit and punished for not reaching it. "God doesn't like …those who draw back," I remembered.

When I got back to the Reddington Pass Road, I hitched a ride with a cowboy who said he had seen my fire during the night, expressed surprise that I hadn't made it to the top, and braked violently to a stop to gather stones to kill a rattlesnake in the road. When it was dead, he cut off its rattle for a trophy. There were other rattles strung on a thread hanging down from the mirror.

Years later I tried again to climb Mica Mountain. I was on semester break from UVA. Jimmy, who was taking a break from his business in Miami was climbing with me. He found a dirt road that led much further in towards the mountain. We parked the car and walked through largely flat terrain until we entered into the succession of folds that hide and reveal and hide, again and again, the approaching mountain. After much hard climbing, we began to think we were on the final ascent every time we started up a new incline. Again there was no visible trail. We were covered with small scratches from climbing through tightly packed denuded bushes. In twilight, well above the first pines we finally achieved what we were sure was the base of the final ascent, a relatively flat plateau covered with dry, bleached, dead tree branches that resembled huge pieces of driftwood. Since the ground was spread everywhere with these branches and the danger of starting an uncontrollable fire was great, we might have gone without, but the air was becoming quite cold. It being the height of summer, Jimmy only had shorts on and a t-shirt. I was dressed lightly, too. It got so cold that we built the fire between us and dug into the ground, covering ourselves with small litter and dirt. The fire was almost on top of us. We had to repeatedly dig ourselves out to go get more firewood and burrow back in again. We could feel insects crawling over us under the dirt. It was so cold we didn't care. We got no sleep that night. When we got up in the morning, Jimmy pointed to the mountaintop. We couldn't tell how far away it was but we still thought we could see a clear line, unbroken by any possible folds, connecting the crest and ourselves. I voted to go back. He agreed. God spit me out again. By the time we got to the desert, we were more than exhausted. When we got into our car, Jimmy pulled two fat oranges out from under the front seat. Pure gold.

Fathers

Charlie's wife always gave him credit for being a good provider, but little else. In Phoenix, I accompanied Charlie on a delivery. He was on his way out the door of one of his shops with some brochures he had printed when I bumped into him. The brochures were advertisements covered with arcane symbols for a fortune-telling business run by a huge family of gypsies. Charlie placed the box of brochures in the back of his Porsche, a "delivery vehicle" for tax purposes, and off we went to the fortune-tellers. What must have been the entire family of gypsies, fifteen or twenty swarthy people, was seated on benches lining the walls of a kind of hall decorated with more arcane symbols. There were large statues of Jesus and the Virgin Mary placed in opposite corners, as though they didn't like each other. At a third corner there was a crude two-foot tall statue of the Devil. Charlie handed the box of printing to one of the gypsies, who took a quick look and refused delivery. He said the telephone number was wrong. Charlie looked at a brochure and then at the invoice. He pointed to the telephone number written on the invoice and declared in a loud voice that that was the telephone number he had been given. Standing in the center of the hall surrounded by the gypsies, he raised his arms in a way reminiscent of Al Gore's attempts to be an "alpha male" during the first G. W. Bush campaign. Charlie really was an alpha male. He spoke in a voice one degree lower than a bellow. Among other things, he threatened the gypsies. "What'er you, a bunch of queers? Maybe I'll smash yer statues." I feared they would pull out knives, but they were visibly intimidated and paid him. In the car on the way back to the shop he said with a smile, "It was the shop's fault. I forged the invoice." I didn't reprove him; his performance in the hall had scared me, too, and he was providing for his family. Besides, the gypsies were con artists. Still, I wondered if AAs would insist that I rat on my brother.

I invited Charlie to an AA meeting. We went to an unusually old-fashioned meeting where the subjects were alcoholism as a disease, powerlessness, and giving one's will to God. When we left he said, "Oh, I get it. You're all pitiful!" and never went to another meeting.

One day, Charlie's wife told Charlie they needed to talk. She had to announce the occasion because Charlie never did talk to her spontaneously. He just drank and worked. He said to her, as was his habit when she announced the need to talk, "Is there someone else?" This time, to his great surprise, the answer was "Yes." She explained that the man spoke to her; they had long discussions. That had been the thrust of his seduction of her.

Charlie had two daughters. The older one decided to stay with him. It saved his life. He stopped drinking and went around making amends to people he had hurt. He knew nothing of AA's ninth step. During his drinking, he had been quite mean. For example, he used his printing skills to create a perfect facsimile of the County Health Department's letterhead and envelope and sent a letter to an enemy announcing that the enemy had tested positive for syphilis. Charlie knew that the man's wife opened all his mail. This dirty trick destroyed the man's marriage. When the amends were made, the man said that the trick had been a favor because his ex-wife was an "asshole."

When I imagine Charlie making amends I remember an AA friend of mine, a used car salesman, standing up and confessing to the group that he had sold a defective car to a man he couldn't locate. He asked the group how he should make amends. He said he sold the man a car that could only turn right and couldn't be repaired. The salesman refused to take the car back when the buyer drove it around the block to return it. The salesman had destroyed the sales records. He had no way to make amends and so didn't have to.

Charlie became a sober, attentive and communicative father.

So far, Jimmy and his wife have one happy child. Jimmy has a much older daughter by another marriage. He was always an outstanding father which is the best thing a man can be if he's going to risk creating immortal lives. His two children are lively and well-behaved.

Sammy and I have no children. Sammy wishes he did.

Father Paul, the donut champion, became a priest after Nick coaxed him into taking the seminary exam. Nick truly wanted to be a priest. Nick failed the exam. Now Father Paul, like Monsignor Hughes, buys magic tricks and performs for the kids in his parish.

Nick later married and fathered seven children. He was a steelworker. Then he owned a grocery store, which failed. Then he got diabetes and started rotting away. He went blind. He had no toes on his only foot. I went to visit him where he lived near Chicago. We had a good visit. His oldest daughter, while still a minor, had run away with and married a hippy idiot. She had been partially reconciled with her family, largely because Nick doted on her. She and her husband came to visit while I was there. There was great tension between her and her mother. The daughter had large breasts and a clinging, low-cut sweater. She addressed me while bending over the table where we were seated. I could tell that she was showing me her breasts, but I didn't look down. I addressed her comments sternly, staring steadily into her eyes. After a little while she sat up, looking hurt and ashamed. Her mother treated me like Jesus after that. A few months later Nick died. His wife has my deepest admiration. Like my mother, she was a country girl; only she lasted longer than my mother. I've noticed that if some women see a man glancing at their partially exposed breasts, they say, "I'm up here," or its equivalent, apparently to shame the man for giving them the attention they wanted.

Barney, a longtime friend and junk sculptor, with a group of fellow artists, rented a huge deserted warehouse by a defunct railroad spur near downtown Tucson. Barney also designed playgrounds. The yard of the warehouse was embedded with thousands of interesting, untraceable pieces of metal, old parts of no one knew what. The parts were of different ages, judging from their stages of rust. Barney took many of the parts from that yard for his smaller junk sculptures, all birds with long legs. It was mesmerizing to walk over and sift through the dirt. Barney and I had a bond because we both liked to do that. So did Barney's children. For me, looking for strange objects in the company of those three kids was like being on Mt. Lemon again, looking for mica and horseshoe ingots, or in the desert looking for interesting stones or sparkplugs. In the company of those kids, gathering those pieces of metal at the warehouse, I ceased to be a fifty-four year old lawyer. I imagined I was four years old again. My speech almost became baby talk. Barney's children looked at me peculiarly. Quoron quietly argued me out of my embarrassing delusion.

Lawyering

As a new lawyer at the FCC I was surprised and dazed by the militancy of the Neo-feminists. One announced that the women were going to "take over the Commission." Promotions were regularly based on sex rather than merit. Women who truly didn't understand telecommunications issues were promoted over men who did. If there has ever been an ideology as adept as Communism at replacing the "natural criteria for truth" with conformity to an ideology, it is Neo-feminism. Most Neo-feminists are radically indifferent to truth. They create biased studies and quote jimmied statistics to promote their views, often using entirely unfounded accusations of biased "male research" as an excuse for their own dishonesty. They often attack the idea of objectivity. One said, "Reason is a tool of male oppression." Another tried to dominate her male colleagues by ordering them to do something whenever they were already in the process of doing that thing. For example, if she saw a man headed to the sink to wash his coffee cup, she would say, entirely seriously, "Wash that cup!" If a male colleague was on the point of stepping into her office, she would say, "Come here!" A new engineer in our division had taken a women's assertiveness training course. She had been taught that, in order to gain preeminence, instead of trying to slip orders in between people and what they were about to do, she should simply assume authority over them. One day, she called a meeting of four of her peers, including me, to start a project she had thought up. She stated that she was in charge and, by turns, started to tell each of us what to do. By that time I had gotten my bearings. I interrupted her, telling her I wasn't going to follow orders she was in no position to give. She started to cry and left. Earlier, entering her office, before I knew her math was incompetent, I had recited the following Jack Handy parody to her

Instead of having "answers" on a math test, they should just call them "impressions," and if you got a different "impression," So what? Can't we all be brothers?

The woman didn't laugh and didn't seem at all offended. She said, "That's the way they did it where I went to school."

During Lent, there was a party on my floor in the satellite branch of the Division. There was a lot of wine. I didn't attend. As I walked down the hall to get an "FCC Record" for a reference I needed, I walked by one of the women lawyers. She was an attractive, tall attorney, a graduate of Harvard Law School. She grabbed my ass as I walked by her office. I stopped. When I turned around, she ran inside and shut and locked the door. I saw her walking towards me in the hall with a girlfriend later in the day. As I passed her, without, at first, looking at her, I turned and grabbed the nearest of her buns and squeezed with full force. I worked out every day and was very strong at the time. I no doubt caused considerable pain and bruising. The woman's response, however, was to hike up her skirt and ass and walk quickly backwards towards me yelling, "I like it! I like it!"

I stared at her and shouted, so that everyone in the suite of offices could hear, "You're drunk!" It was true and caught her by surprise but she managed to sputter a denial. "You're drunk!" I shouted again, with conviction.

The best consequence of my work at the FCC was that I could afford to go to Europe. I spent altogether about three months there. My most delightful experience came when I turned a corner in Rome and found myself staring up at two neighborhood temples, first century, according to a crude tin plaque. They were hexagonal and about three stories tall but no more than twenty feet in diameter. They were so well preserved and so delicate they seemed haunted. They reminded me of Victorian lace. I wondered how they could have survived so long. They were not mentioned in my guidebook.

My itinerary while in Italy was mostly a matter of locating and looking at the Caravaggios. The quest took me to museums in several different cities. There was a Caravaggio in Florence that was located on a private estate. I waited outside the locked gates trying to figure a way to get in. Soon a black limousine drove up. The gates swung open. I slipped in just before they closed behind the car. There was a painter's studio in front of a huge residence. I went to the studio and asked the two women painting inside if I could see the Caravaggio. They told me it was in the mansion but there was nobody in the mansion at that time, so there was no one there to let me in. Even though I doubted their word, having seen the limousine enter, I called it quits and headed back. Then I remembered the locked gates. I went back to the studio. The girls now had a huge Rottweiler on a leash. I asked them to let me out. One of them did, bringing the Rottweiler with her. She freed the dog onto the grounds as soon as the gate closed behind me. After I left I was shaking. The Caravaggio inside the mansion was one of two depicting the conversion of St. Paul on the road to Damascus. It was the better of the two and the most operatic of all Caravaggio's paintings. It was my favorite.

Leaving, I spied Lorus, Artemis, Quoron and Aworac standing under a huge, overarching Aleppo pine discussing something. It was an idyllic scene until Artemis started hitting the others. They withdrew from her a few feet. I tried to sneak away, being already so agitated, but they called to me. I joined them angrily: "Where the *hell* do you come from and what the *hell* do *you want?*

After a remonstrative pause, Artemis quoted:

> "Who doesn't know that the Ephesians are the temple keepers of Artemis, whose sacred image fell from heaven?" Acts19:35. But fanatics destroyed my temple and carried away my stone. I'm once again a hunter in the meadows and the woods. I have no home from which I come and no home to return to.

Artemis continued:

> You want, by your vow, to rise above everything material and I want to drag you down. I want to fill you with lust and timidity, to make your life a story of missed chances, to seduce you from your willful chastity, leaving your desire constant and unsatisfied. I stir your conscience and see to it that the few women who will sleep with you can't defeat your inhibitions. In this way I nail you to your body again and again. I keep you from remaining the opposite of a zombie.

Lorus, speaking for the children of animals, recited:

> When the sons of God see the daughters of men that they are fair, they choose the women they want. They take them as wives to themselves, and the women bear children unto them.... "I will let the children live no more than120 years, for they are flesh" saith the Lord. Genesis 6:1-4

Lorus explained:

The children of animals are the children of angels, who can't sin, and people, who die. We're hybrids like mules, and can't have offspring. You prayed to be mortal and an angel and to have no children. We who have these attributes reason with you so that you'll leave your self-centeredness and see your mortality. We don't want you to have sex. We want you to humiliate yourself in other ways so you'll know you're not alone. We show you how to stop believing in Hell.

I walked away, once again questioning the existence of Artemis and the creatures but certain that I needed them to learn "how to stop believing in Hell," how to escape being "the opposite of a zombie."

Life

One Saturday, while our Pro-life group was saying the rosary in front of a clinic, a woman came down the sidewalk and wrestled her resistant, weeping daughter through the door. We stopped praying and shouted our objections. The police were called. The three that showed up didn't like us. After hearing our description of what happened, they went into the clinic to question the girl. When they came out they said she wanted an abortion. I didn't believe them. The last policeman, an insecure man, came out of the clinic and started walking towards me rather than towards his car. He came to a halt in front of me and asked, "Are you blocking my way?" If I had been it would have been a severely penalized criminal act.

I said, "No" and didn't move. He was embarrassed. After a pause he turned and walked to his car.

Once, another Pro-choice policeman threatened to arrest me because the fetus in my poster was naked.

Another Saturday, when a woman crossed our rosary line to enter the same clinic, someone asked her, "What would Jesus say?"

She stopped and responded, "He wouldn't be intolerant. He wouldn't judge me." with an air of triumph.

The questioner responded "You mean the way you judge your unborn child to be subhuman and rip him apart in your womb. What could possibly be more intolerant or judgmental than doing that tens of millions of times?"

One Sunday, there was a camera crew interviewing a young woman on the steps of the Cathedral, which was my parish church. I stopped to listen. The interviewer was asking the young woman if the partial birth abortion issue would cause her to oppose Clinton's re-election. "Not at all," she said and proceeded to explain that, although she was a Catholic, she did not necessarily accept Church doctrine.

I interrupted, walking up to her and shouting, "Why do you come to Church if you disagree with Church doctrine and accept partial birth abortion and that monster in the White House? In what sense are you a Catholic?" The statement about Clinton being a monster for his veto of the partial birth abortion ban was broadcast by CNN repeatedly that day. I was amazed.

Many D.C. policemen are Pro-life. There were two Pro-life Metro policemen who found me in the principal Metro subway station at rush hour holding up a five foot by four foot sign showing on both sides a picture of a quartered and loosely reassembled baby. I had half the boarding platform to myself. The passengers squeezed together at the other end. The policemen coaxed me into lowering my sign and going with them to the office of the Metro Police. After asking me a few questions like, "You're kind of a Jesus. Don't you think?" to see if I was crazy, they explained that my two opponents in the fistfight I had had the day before in the subway were pressing charges against me. They said that, to ignore the charges, they needed my version of events. I described the four sided brawl. The police told me I could carry my sign into the Metro as long as I was carrying it to some other site and did not loiter with it while in the Metro. The statement inspired me with a new scheme for protesting, one that would increase my audience many fold. I was encouraged. No charges were brought.

I never said rosaries more frantically than when I was alone with one of my signs on the highways during rush hour. Charles Manson theorized that fear was the most important emotion because it made people more awake and aware, but fear is hard to endure. The rosaries blunted my fear and the terrible pain of my embarrassment. I used my prayers to stuff my mind and leave my fear with less room to work. Still, I was vividly aware that other people existed at those times. And they seemed to be vividly aware of me. I usually said three rosaries before my heart resumed its normal pace and two thereafter. I had mapped out the eighteen principal routes taken by commuters into D.C. Monday through Friday. The overwhelming majority of those who spend their days in D.C. are commuters. Rush hour lasted from 6:30 a.m. to 9:30 a.m. I took the Metro to the day's protest site, loitering each time at the Metro boarding platform for as long as I could without entirely ignoring the warning of the Metro

Police not to loiter. When I emerged from the train, I walked the rest of the way to the day's selected commuter route and planted myself with my sign on the sidewalk or meridian where that route led into the city. I stood with my sign almost within touching distance of the passing cars. I believe I only caused one accident. I changed the route each day until I had picketed all eighteen sites. Then I went back to the beginning. When I was out protesting, people looked amazed as they drove past me. Others parked their cars on sidewalks and came after me on foot. Sometimes pedestrians tried to pick a fight or simply attacked me. I got in seven fights protesting in various fora and then stopped counting. Nobody ever managed to destroy any of my signs. Twice I was in court after being attacked, but the embarrassment was the most difficult part of protesting alone.

On Saturdays and Sundays when there were few commuters, I paced the sidewalk about fifteen feet from the front wall of the Holocaust Museum along which all who would enter the museum had to pass. I walked back and forth with my sign repeatedly shouting,

> If we can deny the evident humanity of these poor children, wouldn't we have denied the humanity of the Jews when that was the politically correct way to think?

The line moved slowly for perhaps half-an-hour before all the people were inside the museum.

I heard one man in the line say to his wife, "He's like John the Baptist." Others cursed me or called me a ghoul or the like. They had a right to be shocked and angry. The sign was worse than anything in the museum.

I carried out these activities every day for more than two years. One day, when I finished my protest without incident, I found myself and my sign on the longest, newest Metro exit in the city, six stories high, with as yet unstained white walls, shining silver escalators and blue sky at the top. It was the stairway to Heaven. As I started up, an old bum, who looked like Uncle Remus, held his hand out to me, I gave him what was in my pocket. He looked at it with surprise for a long time then called to me up the bright, echoing tunnel, "If you see any of the boys, tell them I'm ready to be picked up now." I guessed that in his psychosis I was one of the angels, the hope of my childhood.

I always draped my signs in several large black plastic bags and stowed it in the basement at work when I arrived. Almost all of my fellow employees at the FCC had seen me in the Metro or on the street with my signs. They were afraid of me. They whispered to each other. They made a wide arc when they passed me in the hall. One Commissioner was on the point of entering an elevator I was on. When she saw me she did a military about face, thought a moment and backed into the elevator without having to look at me again. If I hadn't been extremely proud of what I was doing I wouldn't have been able to show up for work without blushing. Everybody stared at me.

During the years of my protests Artemis tormented me constantly with lustful thoughts. At the same time, by means of my protests, she gave me the strength to maintain absolute celibacy.

Justice Brennan

Meanwhile, Justice Brennan died. He was widely known to have masterminded the <u>Roe</u> <u>v.</u> <u>Wade</u> decision, nominally written by Justice Blackmun. Brennan had attended Mass in his own parish regularly. Bishop Gavel granted the Brennan family's request to hold the funeral in the Cathedral so that it would have the prominence and dignity the family thought Justice Brennan deserved. The believing Catholics in the diocese, those who accepted the Church's teaching on abortion, were in anguish..

I was asked by another pro-lifer to show up outside the Cathedral to join in a demonstration against <u>Roe</u> <u>v.</u> <u>Wade</u> during Brennan's funeral. I showed up an hour early outside the church. I was standing with the press corps holding my second largest sign (four feet by five feet) showing a picture of a second trimester baby's severed head. The President was expected to show up and the Secret Service detail was running about in preparation. The detail was under the command of a young woman who was busily barking orders at her comrades. She was trying to act tough. I decided I was standing too close to the press and started to move away. She barked at me unnecessarily in passing, "Get that sign and your tush outta here!" The reporters laughed. I was reminded of the Neo-feminist at the FCC who ordered people to do whatever they were already doing. I stopped. I ignored her as she told me to get out a few more times. Then a D.C. policeman came up to me and told me they would arrest me if I didn't move. He grabbed me by the elbow and started leading me across the street. I turned my head while he was pulling me, pointed up at my sign and shouted with great volume, "This is just a part of the price that's paid so that women like you can pretend to be policemen." The policeman escorting me laughed. The reporters were silent. After a pause, with the people around her looking at her to see what she would say, she shouted lamely, "That's 'agent' to you, sir," which was followed by the supportive, artificial laughter of her associates and the press. The officer who was leading me away deposited me at the nearest corner about twenty yards from the Cathedral. I began walking my sign back and forth across the street with the changing light. The Secret Service had closed one end of the street in front of the Cathedral. Those hoping to attend the funeral had to park and walk past the corner where I was parading if they wanted to enter the church. The President's parked motorcade and my sign slowly attracted a large crowd of curious people, seemingly magnifying a "demonstration" that was otherwise minimal. This was during lunch at the very center of D.C.'s business district. By the time the funeral Mass began there were probably 2,000 people milling around on the street in front of the Cathedral. The Secret Service couldn't control the crowd and withdrew into the church. I was reminded of the "demonstration" I had witnessed in Haight-Ashbury thirty-three years before. The day after the Brennan funeral, too, newspaper articles called the people in the street "demonstrators."

There were only two other true demonstrators outside the church. One held up a sign that read, "Abortion stops a beating heart." The other had a very good bullhorn. He called out, "What about funerals for the babies?"

I grabbed the bullhorn and shouted, "Their only funeral is to be flushed down the toilets of abortion clinics like so much shit." The owner of the bullhorn was shocked and snatched it away from me as soon as he regained his presence of mind. A man came out of the church, slowly walked over to us and told us quietly but reprovingly that the bullhorn could be heard clearly inside the Cathedral. He didn't return to the Cathedral, but walked away.

During the years I protested in D.C, the House and Senate twice passed a partial-birth abortion ban. Clinton twice vetoed it, but Bush signed the ban into law and it was approved by the Supreme Court in 2007.

The New Rector

During my attempted reentry into the Church, I took up various church activities, including a stint as a "catcher" at a charismatic service in which a renowned priest touched the foreheads of people lined up standing at the altar rail. As soon as they were touched the people at the altar rail got the Holy Spirit and fell stiffly backwards onto the long double-layered row of carpets spread out behind them. They didn't convulse. I and two or three others stood behind them and caught them, softening their landing. When all those who wished to had received the Holy Spirit, the catchers caught each other. I was the last. A man who had recovered from his state of blessedness caught for me. The priest touched my forehead as he had with all the others and nothing happened. The priest looked shocked. I was the only one who didn't receive the Holy Spirit. The whole affair reminded me of my experience with the Holy Ghost in Pilgrim Temple. It struck me as consummately innocent.

Some things that happened at the Cathedral were crazy and not innocent. There was a short, slightly hunchbacked old man who walked stiff-legged into church, tottering like a mechanical toy. If you spoke to him after Mass he would loudly shout something like "Eat my shit, you faggot" calling attention to you and embarrassing you. Then he would try to spit on you, but he couldn't spit well and almost always fell short, sometimes dribbling on the front of his shirt. His ways were typical of many bums on the street, but he wasn't a bum; he was reasonably well dressed and lived in my apartment building. Sometime after he started attending Mass, He was caught in the church men's room with a host he'd pulled out of his mouth and hidden during communion. He was beginning a ritual of his own devising when someone walked in on him. He reminded me of my oaths and sack of churches and my blasphemies against the Holy Ghost many years before. I wondered if we had the same motive: to blaspheme and thereby separate ourselves from God.

When the old Rector retired, his replacement took the Cathedral in a new direction that was neither crazy nor innocent. The new Rector insisted that the other priests and deacons avoid all mention in their sermons of the fact that the Church considered homosexual acts sinful. The new Rector held services designed to attract homosexuals and made sure his homosexual associates at the Cathedral, of which there were several, communicated the time and nature of these services to the homosexual community. Soon a very large number of homosexual couples were attending Mass regularly, some showing their mutual affection by open mouthed kissing during "the sign of peace."

When these things started to happen, I encountered the name of the Rector through Westlaw in an old edition of the Washington Post. It turned out that at his previous parish, he had allowed a homosexual to have authority over a group of boys who regularly met in one of the parish activity rooms. Five boys were sodomized. I remembered my ambiguous experience in the arroyo when I was a boy and Emiles' statements about the men who hung out there. I became very angry. Here was another heartfelt cause with which I could fill the hole left by my dead conscience.

The Red Mass

It is the cause. It is the cause, my soul.
Let me not name it to you, you chaste stars!
It is the cause.

In America any adult/child relationship is potentially corrupt. Priests, among whom there are so many pederasts, provide the clearest example. We won't look honestly at the character of child abuse because it often implicates homosexuals, a protected class. Without an honest look we will have no way to diminish child abuse while we still want to.

There are those who think it's unfair to note any relationship between homosexuals and pedophiles. Tim Russet reported that in 85% of the sexual abuse cases perpetrated by American priests the victims were boys, the kind the homosexual community labels "chicken," a term referring to the sexual desirability of boys. Using the range of figures from the AGI and Battelle Institutes to calculate the ratio of homosexuals to heterosexuals in the United States and using the finding of the Journal of Sex Research that approximately one-third of child abuse cases are homosexual, male-to-male liaisons, one arrives at the conclusion that any given homosexual is, at a minimum, five times more likely to abuse a child than any given heterosexual, and the disparity may be much greater. Those in the press who cite Justice Department figures to claim that homosexuals abuse children less frequently than heterosexuals are not factoring in the proportion of homosexuals to heterosexuals in the general population, or, like Leslie Stahl, they are surreptitiously classifying male abusers of male children as heterosexual if those abusers have wives. For decades it has been reported that a man's marital state is no indication of his sexual preference. Before, that claim was useful for those who argued for tolerance of homosexual behavior; now, the denial of that claim is useful. Some assert that if a man sodomizes a boy, he is a pederast and, *therefore, not* a homosexual. It has *never* been a criterion for use of the word "homosexual" that sexual acts so described only take place between adults. Using one or another of these inconsistent standards to deny the homosexuality of so many child abusers, the press becomes ever more deceitful. The press is as guilty as the bishops who hide child-abusing priests among unwitting families in a neighboring diocese.

I don't approve of the word, "faggot," but neither do I approve of the homosexual word "breeder." It says heterosexuals and their children are like cattle. It diminishes the humanity and dignity of heterosexuals, which makes their children more vulnerable.

Within the next ten years pederasts in America will probably be seen by most as victims persecuted for their sexual orientation and the states will begin lowering the age of consent. At the Catholic Conference of Bishops in D.C., shortly before this movie was released, I was with a group protesting a recent Conference edict called "Always Our Children," in which the bishops declared that Catholic parents should try to understand, not criticize, the behavior of their homosexual children. I carried a large sign. It read, "The bishops say they want us to accept our 'homosexual' children. We fear they want us to accept the continuing abuse of our perfectly healthy children by homosexual clergy."

The Catholic Cathedral in D.C. is the location of The Red Mass, a Mass said annually in celebration of the legal profession. The John Carroll Society, a prestigious association of Catholic lawyers offering a variety of charitable services to the community, sponsors the Mass. The Red Mass is red because that is the color of the vestments worn by the numerous bishops, priests and deacons officiating at the service. The Mass is always attended by at least a couple of Supreme Court Justices who join with the clergy and the leaders of the John Carroll Society in the slow procession from the rectory down a hundred feet of sidewalk to the steps leading up to the church. One year, on the day of The Red Mass, I walked to the Cathedral and stood among 15 reporters on the opposite sidewalk about twenty feet from where the procession was forming. When the procession reached the steps, I called out in my loudest, stentorian, schoolyard bellow, "The red of your vestments signifies the blood and semen leaking from the torn anuses of little boys weeping in the toilets of your rectories." All conversations among the processors instantly stopped. I had no idea I was going to shout that.

Later, at Union Station, where I went for lunch, I met three Protestants, one a minister, who had been walking by the cathedral and stopped to see what all the cameras were there for. They came up and congratulated me for what I had done. They asked me to pray with them. I did. We stood there in the middle of the crowded Union Station food court, our arms wreathed over each other's shoulders with the minister leading us in a loud, freewheeling Protestant prayer, asking God to protect children and scaring people. It was like Jess leading me in the third step prayer in Humpty Dumpty's. The minister concluded:

> It would be better for him that a millstone were tied about his neck and that he be cast into the sea than that he should hurt one of these little ones. Luke 17:2

Jesus said that placing a little child in his lap. The Catholic Church says "little ones" refers to Christians, not children, a wildly self-serving and unlikely interpretation.

In Tucson where I was vacationing that summer the rains never came. By the end of August the heat and low humidity levels were setting all-time records. The mesquites were entirely leafless and black. Much of the cactus was baked wafer thin, crisp and yellow. If you went out without salve, your lips cracked so deeply they bled. I was on vacation and in Tucson visiting old friends. I visited Emile at his parents' house. We each noted the other's gray hair. Emile's parents were dead. So were mine, but my house had been given over to new owners long before. Emile still lived in his.

Despite the heat I wanted to see the arroyo. There were light, teasing clouds overhead, and it seemed like a good opportunity to walk down the arroyo's bank in the frail shade. We had reached the section of arroyo near my old house. The sun came out as we were walking. Dust devils sprang up on both sides of the arroyo. Emile stopped and was staring at a clump of prickly pear. Leaning against them was a crumpled piece of cardboard. It looked like the wreckage of one of the boxes sometimes carried up by the erratic winds until they rose out of sight. "What are you looking at?" I asked.

"There's a dead animal over there," he said, pointing, "a big one." We cautiously crossed the arroyo and walked toward the cardboard on the other side. The cardboard turned into a white-haired, mummified human corpse. It must have taken late spring and all three of the unnaturally hot, dry summer months to reduce the corpse to its present shrunken, leathery condition. There were three animal excavations in its abdomen. Some of its other skin was eaten away. Its eyes were gone. The face was in tatters. It couldn't have been recognized. Nevertheless Emile said, "He was the bum that tried to fuck kids in the ass."

"How do you know?" I asked, doubtfully.

Emile pointed to two curved series of small white scars in the darker skin of the mummy's right shoulder. "That's where I bit him," Emile said. Emile then pointed to two deep, semicircular folds of leather below the mummy's purplish, recessed nipples. "He worked himself up a pretty good pair of tits, too."

I proposed we call the police. Emile said not to, brought out a disposable lighter and set fire to the mummy, which, with its shreds of clothes as tinder, caught quickly and burned well. "Fucking pervert!" Emile said as we watched the flames and smoke.

Unlike guilt, shame often doesn't need to be justified, so it often can't be defeated by reason. Something else is needed. I'd never told anyone of the possibility that I had been violated as a child. At the time, I wouldn't have known what to call it and couldn't have described it. I didn't even know that it had happened. As the mummy continued to burn, I told Emile the story. He said, "Well, if you think you took it up the ass that young from this one, he must have had a pretty small dick even before he died." He was looking at the mummy's shriveled penis. I looked, too. Emile started laughing. Then I started laughing. As when I peed in church in second grade, the laughter made it all right. I still don't know if I was raped, and I don't care to know.

When we left, the mummy was still burning.

The Scapular

That year I also went to Miami to visit Jimmy. I had a t-shirt made up at one of the tourist shops in the nearest mall. I gave the printer a photo for the front of the t-shirt. A crowd gathered around the television that showed how the t-shirt was going to look. The photo showed a mutilated baby under the legend "Abortion is Murder." I thought of Teresa. The printer of the t-shirt became quite nervous. A man in the crowd turned to me and said, "How can any doctor do that?" The crowd saw from the photo that abortion was wrong. It was the same photo I had seen after the bar exam. The picture alone convinced the onlookers, as it had me. The printer relaxed. I wore the t-shirt on the plane for my return flight to D.C. When I got on the plane, there were gasps as I walked down the aisle. A stewardess followed me and, when I sat down, leaned over me and spoke to the lady sitting in the seat next to mine. The stewardess asked her if she and her child would like different seats. The lady said yes, but she agreed with the point of the t-shirt and told me so. I guess she was just afraid that a person who would wear such a thing might be dangerous. Maybe I'm dangerous.

When I went to the bathroom, I passed Quoron sitting in the back of the plane staring down at the clouds. The mild yellow sun setting over them shown in half his burnished face. When I came out of the bathroom Quoron was lying in a fetal position asleep in the two interior seats next to mine, the seats vacated by the woman and her child. I sat and raised the nearest armrest, turning Quoron's golden face slightly to do so. It awoke and sat up smiling. Pointing at the picture on my shirt, it said, "Innocents don't need scapulars." It reached into the neck of my shirt, grabbed my ancient, filthy scapular, tore it loose and ate it. I had never washed it or taken it off, even when I was blaspheming. The children of animals have no digestive systems, as I said. Quoron chewed for a long time, swallowed then immediately vomited the wet shreds of the scapular into an air-sickness bag. When we got off the plane at Dulles, two airport security personnel escorted me to the D.C. bus. Nothing was said about my shirt until the bus driver refused to let me board. My escorts negotiated a compromise. I was to reverse my shirt, putting the picture behind me. I did, but twisted my torso in my seat to face the back of the bus as other passengers got on.

I had a special refuge in D.C. I had volunteered to teach English to some Mexican nuns stationed there. They were the Oblatas de la Sanctisima Eucharista, a contemplative order with white habits and sweet dispositions. When I was no longer sure that my protests were justified, their arguments fortified me. I continued my protests until I retired to Mexico, but I didn't get a new scapular.

When I revealed my solipsism to the sisters, they argued with me three classes running. Their methods of persuasion were peculiar. They said such thoughts came from the Devil, so I should abandon them. I asked Lorus. It said there was no Devil. The nuns next told me to go to the chapel and put holy water on my tongue. The tongue, they said, was the root of the mind. At least that's what I thought they said: "la raíz de la mente."

Lorus insisted that that was true, despite my protestation that it had to be the other way around. "Jesus said we speak from the abundance of our hearts, not our minds. The mind is made of words," Lorus declared. The water in the font was filthy and tasted awful.

The Plenum

In the Plenum, my body is tightly enclosed. In the perfectly black, perfectly dense, perfectly hard quintessence of all matter, I can't move. The substance is molded to every prominence and concavity of my body. Nothing touches me because I'm touched everywhere. Neither is there light nor sound nor taste nor smell. The substance is inside me. It's inside my cells. It fills the space inside my atoms and between them. I'm enclosed and filled completely. Nothing changes. My lungs and heart are frozen. I have no breath. I have no pulse. Bodiless now, I'm without dimension or position. I am entirely without coordinates. I have lost contact with all matter and, because of it, with all other souls – unimaginable souls.

Nothing outside me reaches me. There isn't any outside of me. I'm inside of myself. Nauseous and insipid, the last, seized frame of my imagination and the horror of my eternal solitude are my whole wakeful being. The Plenum, the prodigious sphere, is a mighty wall. The Plenum is perfect emptiness. In the Plenum, I'm all there is forever. I'm the opposite of a zombie.

I believe I hear a trembling, siren voice. I'm aroused. The terrible hallucination is over. Artemis is standing over me. She smiles and leaves.

After imagining this Hell, I frantically sought reasons to deny it. It seemed to me that my disembodied self couldn't be reduced to a still thought in dead matter. Thoughts not attached to an expressive, live body can arbitrarily be attributed to anything from a man to the statue of a man. Therefore, they belong to no one. Even if a disembodied thought could exist, thoughts by nature are dynamic. Thought continues to change or it ceases to be. These arguments diminished my fear of the Plenum.

When this Hell first came to me I was in my fourth mental ward. This last hospitalization was in D.C. Though I could fight off my religious fears with considerable success, I was still crazy. I contemplated suicide fearlessly as a matter of habit. It was interesting. I thought it would be fun to talk to someone about it. After calling the number for psychological emergencies on the back of my health insurance card, I told the answering nurse I felt bad because I was facing $1,000 in dental bills. I had no reason that she would have understood. The nurse asked me if I was suicidal. I said I was. She asked what suicidal ideation I had. I told her I was thinking of tying a piece of razor wire around my neck and tying the other end to the back of a parked car. Then I would crouch and wait for the driver to return to his vehicle and drive away. I didn't tell the nurse, but I had already tried this. The owner found me squatting behind his car and freaked out when I explained what I was doing. When he helped me out of the razor wire his hands were shaking and he cut both of us. It was very embarrassing. The suicide attempt was probably the result of the Zoloft I was taking, not the result of misery. In fact, I was pretty content before the car owner found me. The psych nurse located the nearest hospital and told me to go there to be examined. She said that if she didn't hear from the hospital in 15 minutes she was going to have the police come to my apartment and take me there. I went. In the emergency room I told the emergency room physician that I was very strong and could beat up the male muscle-nurse who had tried to seize my clothes. The doctor was from Iceland. She said, "I haf new doot you cout bit him up." They put me in a hospital gown but I still didn't want to surrender my street clothes. There was a scuffle. They won. I entered the George Washington University Hospital (GWH) psych ward.

The doctor heading the ward had me take the MMPI again. I had to press the psychologist there to tell me the results. He finally read them off to me, and they said nothing about my sexuality. I told him I had taken the test before in San Francisco, and the psychologist there had said that the test results showed I was a homosexual. The D.C. psychologist was taken aback and mumbled something about sensitive men no longer being automatically classified as inverts. However, the results he had given me said nothing about my being sensitive. If I am an invert, it has presumably helped me to keep my vow of celibacy and childlessness and is, therefore, worth it.

I had a long series of shock treatments, which have short-term value. A girl I knew in GWH reacted to shock treatments like a clogged up nose reacts to nose drops. The girl felt better for

301

a little while after her treatments. The electroshock had the same temporary effect on me. The girl occasionally cut herself on the neck to cause herself pain, which also made her feel better for a little while. Maybe shock treatments are punishments. If you're punished for hurting will you stop hurting? If shock treatments are punishments a person would have to feel the pain of the shocks while under the influence of the anesthetic. I feared that I was awake but motionless during the treatments, like Buster, but, unlike Buster, I "repressed" the memory of the pain when my treatment was over.

One day, in the middle of a therapy session, one of the patients said she had had an abortion and broke into tears. I told her "The forgiveness of sins is perpetual, and righteousness first is not required" falsely attributing the quote to Jesus, instead of Saul Bellow. I stood up and started to cross the circle of chairs to hug her. Before I could reach her, I blacked out. I was conscious but entirely in silent darkness. I could feel nothing with any part of my body. That was when the Plenum revealed itself. It was a Hell for those whose lives are entirely circumscribed by fear. When I regained my sight, I was in restraints on a gurney in front of the nurses' station. A nurse noticed that I was awake and looking about. She called the doctor who scheduled me for some tests, asked me some questions, scheduled me for other tests and set me free.

LSD

The summer of 1982 there were seven large, independent fires on the south face of the Santa Catalinas. You could see the fires at night and the smoke by day from the red slab in front of our house. The fires were spectacular, and no serious harm was done. Ten years ago, a fire at the top of Mt. Lemon burnt out the entire community of Summerhaven and the surrounding cabins. I had thought of retiring there.

I came to Ixtec instead. You can't beat the weather in Ixtec. The drawback, judging by the comments on the Internet, is that there are too many Americans here. But I knew that meant good AA. Besides, I like my fellow Americans, usually. I'm offended by anti-American Americans. So are many Mexicans who see their condescension. I especially have no liking for Americans who denigrate their country because they want to feel superior to their countrymen. In Ixtec, some of the Americans who don't like Americans still take LSD. The image of a man in his late sixties sporting long gray hair in a gray ponytail and dropping acid is sordid. LSD, like marijuana, is a false religion. When I was doing my student teaching in 1970, a longhaired, red-haired kid who boasted of the transcendentality of his LSD experiences decided to record some of them when I asked the students to write an essay on any subject they liked. His essay, which he read aloud, described his experience of seeing tiny elves leap from a Beatles album as it played. He read the essay at first as though he were describing an astonishing revelation, but realized midway that his experience had been a cartoon. LSD makes one mischaracterize one's experiences and remember mostly the mischaracterization and one's misplaced awe. Some people on LSD describe seeing "a color that isn't in the visible spectrum." When they are lucky enough to remember the experience, and not just their false characterization of it, the magic color always turns out to be ordinary, the faded yellow paint on the living room wall, for example, a color that they had simply forgotten under the influence of LSD. Of course, there is something to be said for seeing a color again for the first time.

LSD victims are sometimes more deeply confused in other ways. I knew one, Whistle, who lost the power of articulate speech; he only whistled in various peculiar ways. He made hand signs, too, that were equally meaningless. At a party he found a loaded gun in one of the host's bedrooms and shot himself in the head. He died, unlike one of the clients at the halfway house who did the same thing. She walked around dressed in a knitted wool cap to hide the part of her skull that was caved in. But she never took LSD. She was perfectly articulate.

Almost every tripper I know who took LSD several times wonders if he is God. They are like me, but my delusion is terrifying. They embrace theirs and try to justify it long after the drug wears off. Among those who have taken LSD several times, I believe I've seen six exceptions to the LSD/God rule. Sammy didn't end up thinking he was God. Jimmy gave Sammy and his closest friend doses of LSD then disappeared. Sammy and his friend walked the meandering streets of our old neighborhood while waiting for the drug to take effect. Jimmy hid from them and, when he was sure the LSD had kicked in, hurled numerous oranges at them from a neighbor's orange tree behind a hedge. Having oranges smash into you while you are high on LSD permanently refutes the belief that you are God.

Another exception to the rule was a high school student who saw every move she made as the effect of an external will that worked her like a puppet. She enjoyed the sensation. I think of her when I remember that I have given my will to God. As I said I will always do what I want, and God leads me to want things.

The third exception was the girl I slept with at Norwalk. She said she had a set of real-world problems and an entirely different set of LSD-world problems. The two sets of problems were mutually exclusive. She took LSD from time to time to change the set of problems that confronted her.

The fourth person who took LSD but didn't conclude that he was God was Shelley when he hallucinated the end of the world by atomic destruction twice. As a death worshiper I'm not disturbed by the fact, scope or persistence of Shelley's vision. In fact, at one time I wished for death by thermonuclear war. That way, I wouldn't be missing anything when I was gone.

The fifth exception was Jimmy. He took LSD at a friend's ranch in Mexico. He had gone off by himself when the LSD kicked in. He found himself barefoot in a field of glass, huge sharp crystals of it, everywhere. He came to the realization that he had to be punished. So he went about jamming his bare feet into one crystal clump after another. His friends found him and took him back to the house. After great efforts to overcome his infinite embarrassment, he confessed that he needed to go to the bathroom but had forgotten how. His companions tried to instruct him but they weren't successful. He had to wait until the LSD wore off. Jimmy told me about these events when he was back in the United States. The chess playing medical student who tried to get me to go into the room where the student nurse was waiting was the son of the owner of the ranch in Mexico where Jimmy had his LSD trip. The student told me that he and his other companions had found Jimmy barefoot wandering in a field among countless chards of glass. They were amazed that he wasn't cut. Laughing, the student described trying to tell Jimmy how to go to the bathroom.

The sixth exception, was a girl who had taken LSD at a party. She thought she had become the wall she was facing. She told us of her delusion as though it were a commonplace truth. "I'm the wall," she said matter-of-factly. She repeated it over and over again. "I'm the wall. I'm the wall," she intoned, until you could hear fear enter into her voice. Then she began to cry. Suddenly she started screaming so loudly and shrilly that she shocked and scared the rest of us. We tried calming her by telling her she wasn't the wall. We embraced her and pointed her away from the wall. Nothing diminished her horror. She started vomiting and continued to do so long after she had emptied her stomach. Then she had a long, violent seizure. Blood ascended to her mouth. We took her to the nearest emergency room. The very large amount of drugs the doctor gave her had no effect whatsoever. He said he was afraid to increase the dosage. The hospital kept her. I saw her later on the street. I can only describe her as empty.

I think that in the wakeful prelude to my nothingness Hell dream, immersed in matter, on the cusp of sleep, then shot into the void, I was the girl who thought she was a wall. I quickly woke up, whereas she was trapped for the duration of the drug. She, too, may have been the opposite of a zombie.

LSD is tacky and meaningless. LSD-inspired illusions have no depth, truth or wisdom. For those trippers not looking for holiness or something akin to it, the hallucinations can be comic when one looks back on them. Because of their superficiality, their falsehood is discoverable, and, for some psychotics, discovery ends belief in delusions and hallucinations altogether.

When I was at GWH, a week after my blackout, I took LSD. I learned that it was more mechanical and less convincing than my "straight" delusions. An acquaintance, a freshly admitted patient, because he "thought it would be cool to take LSD on a mental ward," had managed to smuggle in the LSD despite the inspection of his clothes and a body search. He gave me one of two tablets he'd held in his fist throughout the admission process. I thought to reject it but figured my mental state could hardly get any worse. This was just after my experience in the Plenum and I was still shaken. At this extreme of my insanity I believed that LSD would diminish my fear, and, happy accident, I was right. My acquaintance assured me that it would and told me it wouldn't get me high, that it was only an "experience" and wouldn't affect my AA sobriety date. I took it and managed to slip away from a group of patients being taken on a walk outside by a single escorting nurse for a cigarette break. I wandered about George Washington University's large complex. Hearing what I thought was construction work, I stepped into a gymnasium.

Thirteen golden-faced creatures were linked hand-in-hand in a slowly revolving circle, stomping together on the gym-resonant boards of the basketball court. Without breaking step or formation, they moved up and down and left and right like a floor waxing machine, lazily covering the whole court while maintaining their constant clockwise rotation. Tangent to this circle was another smaller circle rapidly spinning counterclockwise. The smaller circle was made up of five Artemises. At much higher rpm, they also wheeled hand-in-hand but leaned centrifugally backwards away from each other. The head of each Artemis by turns served as the tooth of a gear, inserting itself over the outstretched joined hands of the two proximate creatures in the other circle. The creatures and Artemises wore scintillating uniforms of a color not found in the visible spectrum.

Suddenly I realized that they weren't marching; they were methodically crushing writhing worms strewn all over the court, which was already filthy with small, squashed corpses. As loudly as I could I called out to the revolving creatures and Artemises that they were staining the wood of the basketball court, but they paid no attention to me. No one would ever pay any attention to me again I realized with absolute conviction. "Half of solipsism is coming true," I thought, until I remembered how I both commanded the attention of people and feared them during my protests and realized that solipsism was an 'atom' that had no halves, that Artemis was not manufactured in sets of five, that the children of animals could not abide looking alike so each constantly mugged to distinguish itself from the others, and that the worm-stains on the court were identical, small, three-fingered hand prints, palms up as though asking for change. I laughed. "This is my universe and I'm the God of it," I shouted, still laughing, as I ran three steps at a time down to the court and smacked my hallucinations into each other like bowling pins. I felt nothing. My "trip" came to an abrupt end and with it my psychosis.

Full of hope, I went back to the hospital, found our escorting nurse in tears, pretended I had gotten lost accidently and lay down in my room. When I woke up, I was afraid to open my eyes for fear of discovering that nothing had changed, that Artemis or Lorus would be standing over me. When I finally looked, the drab, close room was all I saw. I still knew that solipsism was impossible. The song in Joe's apartment, AA's third step, Las Oblatas de la Sanctisima Eucharista, the reasoning of the children of animals, my lust for Artemis, my campaigns against abortion and pederasty, Emile, and my LSD experience had freed me entirely from my delusions and hallucinations, even the ones that helped me.

Big Sky Country

The clouds above Tucson, when they're there, are always of the most dramatic kind. "Huge cloudy symbols of a high romance," they pull at the imagination. They have a hundred different and striking aspects. In the summer the sky is a theatre with camel, weasel and whale parading together or by turns until a curtain of rain falls over them. Not just mounting thunderheads but clouds of various kinds are sharply defined and substantial seen from the desert. I think this is because of the desert's low elevation. Smudged edges don't show; there is less to suggest the gaseous, insubstantial nature of clouds. Even the cirrus clouds often seem to have a shape. Sometimes the clouds descend. The larger mountains are occasionally capped or girdled with flowing clouds drawn down from a blue sky. Once only, I walked out the front door of our old house directly into a thick cloud. I couldn't see the door from six feet away. There were no sounds. I was enveloped. The cloud welcomed me. It kissed my face. It was a wet kiss. That doesn't happen in the desert. Such a thing is much rarer than the rare snows.

On the other hand, few things can make you feel more unwelcome than the desert's nearly cloudless, metallic winter sky at twilight. It's like the transmissions Voyager 2 sent back to earth showing Neptune and the pieces of its frail, broken ring. The fact that we can see the fragmented ring is attributed to the passage of a small, illuminating moon near the ring area at the time the image was transmitted. The grainy, silver pictures of Neptune and its ring remind me of the black and white woodcuts used to illustrate the most nightmarish of children's stories in the forties and fifties. Emptiness has to be framed to be seen. Neptune is one such frame. Its blue surface could swallow many earths. Neptune may have a water-ocean. That's *water*, not ice. The temperature at Neptune's core is about 7,000 degrees Kelvin. The Voyager images of Neptune show a huge evanescent dark spot rising into view, then falling back out of sight, then rising into view again somewhere else. Scientists don't know what it is. There are a few long wisps of silver cirrus-like cloud drawn out over half the planet's surface and smaller, torn cirri circling the dark spot. Winds on Neptune reach 1,200 mph. Neptune is the farthest planet from the sun. It's almost 3,000,000,000 miles away, at the very edge of the interstellar void. Seen from Neptune, the sun is a brilliant period.

Like Neptune, distant and immense, the nearly empty winter sky over the desert at dusk is a pale cold blue leaking into silver and broken streaks of cloud bordering darkness. Neptune and the desert's winter sky are vaster than the ocean that made Pip mad.

I've seen more dramatic skies four times. Twice during late summer, in Tucson, I saw red and black sunsets. There were no other colors, just deep, pure red and deep, pure black. When Keats came, finally and convincingly, to equate beauty and death, he might have been responding to such a sunset. The last and only other time I saw a red and black sunset was here in Ixtec, which specializes in appalling sunsets. And of course, I saw Xiuhtecuhtli's terrifying sunset in San Francisco.

In Hermosillo, the clouds are frail. During the day, the sky holds no clouds at all. It is a fiercer desert than Tucson's. When it rains, it rains at night. There are mostly small, worn mountains in uninteresting shapes. The narrow highway leading north out of Hermosillo splits. Part of it ascends into a long range of more substantial, lightly forested mountains. On that highway, there are many small villages built in the early 1600s and nearly unchanged.

In one of the villages, there is a church with a pointed Moorish dome entirely blackened by centuries of dead moss. There is an elaborate Mexican confessional inside. In American confessionals the confessing party and priest are separated by a screen and enclosed. The confessional is built into a wall. One confesses anonymously, unheard by anyone other than the priest and entirely unseen. Ancient Mexican confessionals are huge integrated pieces of dark furniture that five or six men can move as a unit. The priest sits under an elaborately carved hood in an elevated throne-like chair and the confessing party kneels on a platform at his feet facing him without any intervening screen. The confessional is open; the priest and the penitent are entirely visible. Unless they speak in very subdued whispers, there is nothing to prevent worshippers in the near pews from hearing the penitent's sins. *Other people exist!* Such is the power of shame.

The people who live in the villages are usually shy of visitors. If you are invited into their houses, they might serve you bacanora, Sonora's primitive, unofficial state liquor, and pit-barbequed goat. The first time I visited the area, I drove slowly by the plazas. Looking through the occasional open doorway, through the narrow hall, I saw the shadowy interior or green garden reminiscent of Graciela's dark house and bright patio.

I stopped in Baviacora, the largest of the mountain towns. The languor of the afternoon there frightened me. If you're an alcoholic, when you're sober, there is often a sense of eons of lost time impossible to redeem. The feeling is akin to nostalgia, but stronger. It's chilling. It makes you want to drink. That's how it felt to be in those ancient villages among the black-green foliage in the orange light of late afternoon. Everything beautiful told me how much I had lost.

I knew then why one might forswear drugs as a means of suicide: "For shade to shade will come too drowsily/And drown the wakeful anguish of the soul." Maybe I won't use heroin to kill myself after all. On the other hand, the "wakeful anguish" of losing beauty irredeemably sounds like some of my Hells and very like the "worm [of remorse that] dieth not" in St. Thomas Aquinas' depiction of Hell.

Returning to Mexico I always feel as though I have removed a starched shirt after a long hour in church. One afternoon, I took the bus from Oaxaca City to the sea. The descent through dramatic, jungle-covered mountains was slow. The declining sun silhouetted the foliage at some turns and changed it to DayGlo green at others. I sat with my forehead against the cool window and spotted a jaguar by the side of the road. We arrived in Puerto Escondido near 9:00 p.m. I walked about trying to find a hotel room. At the time there were only three small hotels in Puerto Escondido. All rooms were occupied. I ended up sleeping on the beach.

Suddenly, I awoke. Children were scurrying in different directions all around me. I felt for my pack, on which I had been sleeping. It was intact. The children, with some supervising parents, were chasing small crabs across the sand. There were hundreds of crabs and dozens of children. One of the crabs skittered over me. A child jumped over me after it. I watched until the children and adults left with their catch. I stared up at the stars. I had never seen such stars, not even in the Virginia countryside or as a child in Tucson or in Sabino Canyon. Saturn, Mars, Venus and Jupiter shone brightly as they rose and descended, but so did the stars that normally dimmed in the company of the planets. Arcturus, Rigel, Aldebaran, Deneb, Vega, Altair and others blazed in the wheeling sky by twos and threes. They were as ridiculous as the stars in Van Gogh's "Café Terrace at Night." Hours later, I remembered that, as a child, I had been astonished by a star in my out-of-focus telescope. I put my glasses on. The sky was only differently resplendent.

Do lions see stars? They don't seem to. Do they see them indifferently? What quirk of evolution enables us or any animal to see stars light-years away? Presumably the indigo bunting saw stars long before it learned to navigate by them. Why did it see stars when that ability alone provided no natural advantage? Was it just a peripheral and strangely persistent accident of vision until it became useful? Or are stars visible to remind us that there are things outside ourselves and that we belong to our Creator.

In the evening, one can walk through many neighborhoods in larger American cities and not see any stars or any children. The absence of children is in large part the result of massive abortion. I no longer believe in Hell. There is no such thing as an immortal life. But I see stars and children here in abundance and that's enough.

Now, decades after my last hospitalization, whenever an image of Hell comes to me, I pray and, like a dud skyrocket, streaking then falling into the dark invisibly without an explosion, the image fails to complete itself.

In mirrors at dawn and twilight my golden face becomes a circumambient halo like the soft focus in 1930s movies. I think it's much more becoming than the gilded dinner plates resting on the heads of angels and saints in Renaissance paintings. I'm happy. Nevertheless, I often have the desire to commit suicide, an old habit, as I said. I have hope in death and am at peace. Now's my chance. I'm a man sitting on a ledge enjoying the fresh air. I'm not afraid to die; I'm just afraid I'll miss something.

Appendix

St. Thomas Aquinas determined that the Saints in Heaven look down upon the sufferings of the damned and rejoice in those sufferings.

<u>Summa Theologica, Supplement to the Third Part</u>, Question 94, The relations of the Saints towards the damned <u>Article 3, The Saints rejoice in the sufferings of the damned</u>. **Objection 3 and Reply to Objection 3**

From his arguments we see that Aquinas was aware of the ugliness of his conclusion. He presented the losing positions, the "objections," first and forcefully. I have framed the following arguments in accordance with Aquinas' method of discourse, which requires careful consideration of all sides of an issue. The premise in all these arguments is that Hell is eternal and complete solitude where even the idea of an outside world can have no meaning.

<u>How to Stop Believing in Hell, Supplement to the Last Chapter</u>, Question 1, Whether Hell Exists, .<u>Article 1: Hell Doesn't Exist.</u> **Objections 1-5 and Replies to Objections 1-5**.

Objection 1:

It seems there is a Hell. All our sensations are nothing more than the sparking of neurons in our brains. Between an object and a corresponding mental image there are many intermediate mechanisms: sound waves, eardrums, auditory nerves, light, eyes, optical nerves, *etc.*; these or other mechanisms stand between us and everything we think we sense. If we were to see light, we'd still never see the objects that reflect light. Instead of opening a path, the mechanisms of the senses block the path to consciousness.

Nothing outside us ever touches our thoughts or is ever included among them. We only see representations on a mental screen. We have no way to judge their accuracy or location. In this Hell, wherever we turn we're all that we see.

Reply to Objection 1:

If our sensations are only the sparking of neurons, we have no access to the objective world in which neurons presumably exist and were discovered. The claim that we only experience the mechanisms of our senses, that we only see light, for example, never the objects that reflect or emit light, is silly. Usually, we don't see cornea, retinae, neurons, *etc*. We don't see the things that enable us to see; we *see*.

Thoughts are insubstantial. It's nonsense to speak of touching them. We can't be trapped in them either. They can't be entered. Being awake, even in dreams, isn't a container or medium. Being awake isn't a thing.

So we're not sitting in a cinema inside our skulls watching representations of the world as they pass over a screen. There is no screen. There are no representations. We see the world. We see other people in it. We're not in Hell.

Objection 2:

We choose all our emotions. If we decide to love a woman, nothing about her causes us to love her. Then how is it her that we love? We can't feel the world, even if we ornament it like a dead Christmas tree with all our entirely detached sentiments. Nothing outside us ever moves us. Our feelings feel only themselves. We're all we can ever love. In this Hell, we're perfectly selfish.

Reply to Objection 2

Normally, we choose what we want because we want it. We don't want what we choose because we choose it. Emotions determine choices. If I didn't have any emotions I wouldn't move. I wouldn't choose. Our emotions are usually caused by the world and connect us to the world. People and things outside us are able to move us, to reveal themselves to us, to cause us joy or pain, whether we will or not. We're not imprisoned in perfect selfishness. We're not in Hell.

Objection 3:

At Mass, God's essence is hidden behind the false appearances of bread and wine. All things have essences and appearances. All appearances are present, subjective and false. All essences are hidden, objective and true. Reality never appears. If it did it would be an appearance. In this Hell, everything we think we know is false.

Reply to Objection 3:

The appearance of a thing must be *de rigueur* to be the appearance of that thing and not something else. There can be no other criteria for deciding what the *true* appearance of a thing *really* is. If something is apparent, it is exposed, though it includes things hidden. We discover more of a thing by revealing its hidden aspects. Those once hidden aspects are all "essence" can signify. If we define "essence" as something we can never see, the word will have no more meaning than the word "green" has to the congenitally blind. Appearances are reality most of the time. We're not in Hell.

Objection 4:

Modern scientific theories prove that what we call truth is a matter of perspective. Therefore, there is no objective truth. The absence of truth means that everything is illusory. In this Hell, we can't even know ourselves.

Reply to Objection 4:

Modern scientific theories can't *prove* anything unless the theories are true. "There is no truth," *an assertion*, is self-contradictory. There's the whole real world around us. It's usually heard, felt, seen, *etc.*, as it is. We're not in Hell.

Objection 5:

By the time their light finally reaches us, the stars are no longer where they were when that light began. We can't see the stars themselves. We can't see anything as it is. The smallest moment is an impenetrable wall between our senses and the world. We never see anything "live." In this and all Hells, we're alone forever.

Reply to Objection 5:

A star *is* its light. There's no time or distance separating a star from its appearance. Objects nearer at hand are also their appearances. (See Reply to Objection 3.)

Likewise, we see the past, not just an image of the past. We see the past as it *is*, as it is indelibly established and hardened in truth. Time isn't a wall. We're not in Hell.

www.ingramcontent.com/pod-product-compliance
Lightning Source LLC
Chambersburg PA
CBHW080016280326
41934CB00015B/3364